Animal Use
by the Cozumel Maya

Animal Use
by the Cozumel Maya

NANCY L. HAMBLIN

The University of Arizona Press

Tucson, Arizona

About the Author

NANCY L. HAMBLIN, a zooarchaeologist, has been involved since 1975 in the Cozumel Archaeological Project, directed by William L. Rathje and Jeremy Sabloff. Hamblin received her doctorate in anthropology from the University of Arizona in 1980. She has published several articles on various topics in zooarchaeology.

THE UNIVERSITY OF ARIZONA PRESS

Copyright © 1984
The Arizona Board of Regents
All Rights Reserved

This book was set in 10/11 Linotron 202 Baskerville
Manufactured in the U.S.A.

Library of Congress Cataloging-in-Publication Data

Hamblin, Nancy L.
Animal use by the Cozumel Maya.

Bibliography: p.
Includes index.
1. Mayas— Ethnozoology. 2. Mayas—Food. 3. Ethno-
zoology—Mexico—Cozumel Island. 4. Animal remains
(Archaeology)—Mexico—Cozumel Island. 5. Indians of
Mexico—Cozumel Island—Ethnozoology. 6. Indians of
Mexico—Cozumel Island—Food. 7. Mayas—Antiquities.
8. Indians of Mexico—Cozumel Island—Antiquities.
9. Cozumel Island (Mexico)—Antiquities. 10. Mexico—
Antiquities. I. Title.
F1435.3.E76H36   1984   972.81'01   84-213
ISBN 0-8165-0824-0

Table of Contents

Illustrations

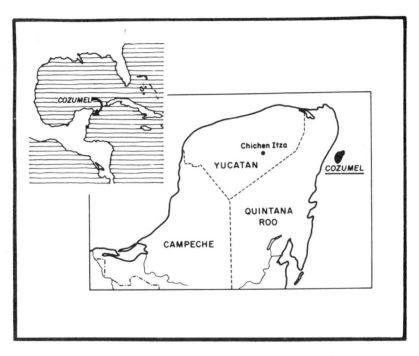

Figure 1.1. Cozumel relative to the Yucatán Peninsula.

1. Cozumel and the Cozumel Maya

LOCATED ABOUT ELEVEN MILES off the northeastern coast of the Yucatán Peninsula in Mexico and covering 151 square miles of land, Cozumel is the largest island to have been occupied by people of the Maya cultural tradition. Geologically, it is a block of coralline limestone containing caves and sinkholes and rising only about fifty feet above sea level. The warm Caribbean and the easterly trade winds combine to produce a generally moderate climate for island residents. Beginning in the Late Formative period, which ended about A.D. 300 (see Fig. 1.2), settlers on the island hunted, fished, and lived in thatched-roof huts. The Maya, as these people came to be called, developed a civilization in the Yucatán and Central America which manifested itself in impressive art and architecture, a writing system that was as of the early 1980s still poorly understood, a complex religion, long-distance trade networks, and large cities.

This study is concerned with examining the many ways in which the Cozumel Maya used animals in their everyday lives. An unusually large and complete faunal sample excavated from ten different sites on the island and spanning time periods from the Late Formative (A.D. 100–300) through the Late Postclassic (A.D. 1250–1500) has made possible deductions concerning many aspects of life previously ignored in other studies. Diet and nutrition receive major emphasis here. In addition, the data have been used to determine hunting and fishing technology, food-preparation practices, ecological implications, ritual uses of animals, evidence of taming and domestication, animal products as a source of tools and personal ornaments, and indications of prehistoric trade. Also examined are changes in animal use through time, comparisons between archaeological sites, and comparisons of house-mounds with ceremonial/administrative contexts within sites.

1

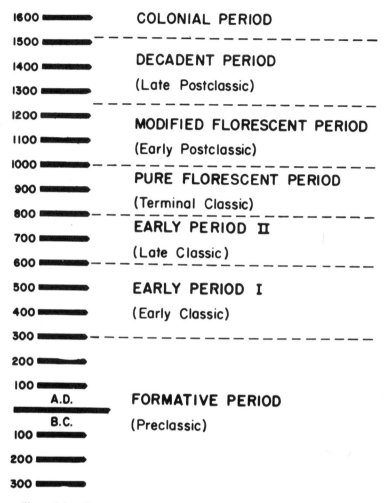

1600 ▬▶ COLONIAL PERIOD
1500 ▬▶ — — — — — — — — — — — — — — — — —
1400 ▬▶ DECADENT PERIOD
1300 ▬▶ (Late Postclassic)
— — — — — — — — — — — — — — — — — —
1200 ▬▶ MODIFIED FLORESCENT PERIOD
1100 ▬▶ (Early Postclassic)
1000 ▬▶ — — — — — — — — — — — — — — — —
PURE FLORESCENT PERIOD
900 ▬▶ (Terminal Classic)
800 ▬▶ — — — — — — — — — — — — — — —
EARLY PERIOD II
700 ▬▶ (Late Classic)
600 ▬▶ — — — — — — — — — — — — — — — —
500 ▬▶ EARLY PERIOD I
400 ▬▶ (Early Classic)
300 ▬▶ — — — — — — — — — — — — — — — —
200 ▬▶
100 ▬▶
A.D. FORMATIVE PERIOD
B.C. (Preclassic)
100 ▬▶
200 ▬▶
300 ▬▶

Figure 1.2. *Chronological periods on Cozumel.—From Sabloff and Rathje 1975b.*

The Cozumel Archaeological Project

Cozumel has often been dismissed as an unimportant outpost of the grander Maya tradition seen elsewhere on the mainland. Through the years, sites such as Tikal, Uxmal, and Chichén Itzá have captured the popular imagination with their "sacrificial wells", towering pyramids, sculptures, and ball courts. By comparison, Cozumel's poorly constructed, delapidated temples hardly seemed worth a second glance This attitude appeared justified by the fact that most of the visible prehistoric architecture on the island could be dated to the Late Postclassic or "Decadent" Period, a time when Maya civilization supposedly disintegrated; thus, Cozumel was dismissed as archaeologically insignificant, despite the fact that ethnohistoric documents indicate that the island was the location of the famous Ixchel pilgrimage shrine and that it was a port on a long-distance trade network (Tozzer 1941).

In 1972 and 1973, however, findings from the Cozumel Archaeological Project, led by William L. Rathje and Jeremy A. Sabloff, began to suggest that the picture was much more complex. It now appears that Cozumel's religious and commercial importance has more time depth than originally thought; indeed, Sabloff and Rathje assert (1975b: 22) that the "so-called Decadent Period actually was the culmination of the new commercially oriented cultural trends that began during the Florescent Period." The merchant elite of the Late Postclassic Period changed the prevailing cultural strategy from a Classic Period emphasis on building lavish temples, sculptures, and tombs to one of reinvesting the bulk of their capital in trade. Whereas Classic Maya society (perhaps best exemplified by Tikal) was based on religious symbolism and external indicators of personal status and wealth, by the Late Postclassic this had shifted to economic integration involving less conspicuous consumption and a wider distribution of material goods, many obtained by trade, among all social classes, a transition characteristic of Maya society as a whole. Cozumel itself contains few Classic Period remains with which to compare later developments (Sabloff and Rathje 1975b).

The excavations in 1972 and 1973 were designed to test a number of hypotheses concerning Cozumel's role in a large-scale trading network. The major emphasis was on confirming archaeologically a postulated shift during the Postclassic from a decentralized port-of-trade to a powerfully centralized trading port possessing external political clout. Fieldwork produced evidence that Cozumel was occupied as early as the Late Formative period and that it reached its greatest population and importance in the Late Postclassic—facts which lend support to the long-distance trade model (Sabloff and Rathje 1975b).

Since the 1800s, Cozumel has been visited by numerous archaeologists and others who identified many prehistoric sites (Sabloff and Rathje 1975a: 2). However, William T. Sanders was the only person to undertake controlled excavations on the island prior to the work of the Cozumel Archaeological Project (C.A.P.) in 1972–73. His fieldwork was done during a brief one-month stay in 1955 and was not exhaustive. The C.A.P. surveyed, recorded and located thirty-four sites, and partially excavated or tested at least twenty-two of these (Fig. 1.3). This work revealed that the five largest and most culturally significant sites on the island were San Gervasio (C-22), San Miguel (C-13), Buena Vista (C-18), El Cedral (C-15), and La Expedición (C-25).

San Gervasio (C-22) is by far the largest and most complex of the Cozumel sites. Located in the north-central portion of the island, it can be subdivided into at least seven dispersed groups, including several hundred buildings, complexes, and housemounds covering approximately 125 acres. Numerous *sacbes,* prehistoric stone-lined roads,

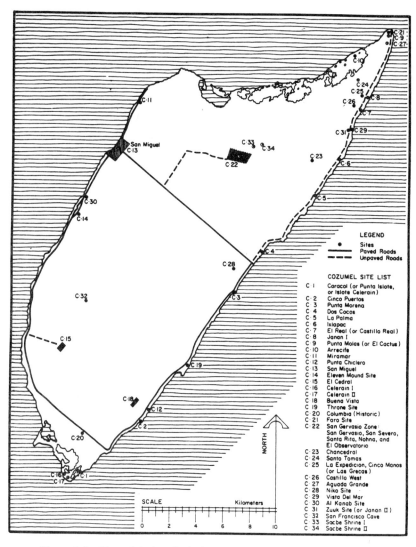

LEGEND

•	Sites
———	Paved Roads
– – –	Unpaved Roads

COZUMEL SITE LIST

C·1 Caracol (or Punta Islote, or Islote Celerain)
C·2 Cinco Puertos
C·3 Punta Morena
C·4 Dos Cocos
C·5 La Palma
C·6 Ixlapac
C·7 El Real (or Castillo Real)
C·8 Janan I
C·9 Punta Molas (or El Cactus)
C·10 Arrecife
C·11 Miramar
C·12 Punta Chiclero
C·13 San Miguel
C·14 Eleven Mound Site
C·15 El Cedral
C·16 Celerain I
C·17 Celerain II
C·18 Buena Vista
C·19 Throne Site
C·20 Columbia (Historic)
C·21 Faro Site
C·22 San Gervasio Zone: San Gervasio, San Severo, Santa Rita, Nohna, and El Observatorio
C·23 Chancedral
C·24 Santo Tomas
C·25 La Expedicion, Cinco Manos (or Las Grecas)
C·26 Castillo West
C·27 Aguada Grande
C·28 Niko Site
C·29 Vista Del Mar
C·30 Al Kanab Site
C·31 Zuuk Site (or Janan II)
C·32 San Francisco Cave
C·33 Sacbe Shrine I
C·34 Sacbe Shrine II

SCALE   Kilometers

0   2   4   6   8   10

NORTH

Figure 1.3. Map of Archaeological Sites on Cozumel.—From Sabloff and Rathje 1975.

lead out in all directions from San Gervasio to other sites, implying a central position politically and perhaps ceremonially; this is supported by the site's architectural complexity. The residences and civil-religious complexes closely resemble those at Mayapán, indicating the close cultural and trading ties between these two sites during the Late Postclassic (Freidel 1976; Gregory 1975; Sabloff and Rathje 1973).

La Expedición (C-25) is located near the northeastern tip of the island about half a mile inland from the coast. This was apparently a medium-sized population center that included a major pyramid temple, two shrines, and many massive rubble platform structures which may have had a storage function (Freidel 1976).

San Miguel (C-13) on the northwest coast represents the major port city on the island, prehistorically and in modern times. It was probably one of the largest prehistoric population centers on Cozumel. Most of the site has been destroyed by modern settlements and an airport, but ethnohistoric documents describe pyramidal mounds, colonnaded structures, shrines, residences, and *sacbes* connecting San Miguel with other sites; a few pyramidal substructures and a large rectilinear platform are all that remain today. Because of the architectural seriation of "talking idol" temples on the island, it appears that the focus of the Ixchel (Moon Goddess) cult may have been moved to this site during the Late Postclassic from San Gervasio (Connor 1975; Freidel 1976: 343–44).

El Cedral (C-15), the other important settlement on the west coast, is located less than two and a half miles inland from the southern coast. This is a fairly large dispersed settlement comprising a formal plaza group, two shrine groups, isolated shrines, and household groups. Architectural peculiarities indicate that this was a very conservative settlement with only indirect involvement in the island's long-distance trade (Freidel 1976).

Buena Vista (C-18) is located in the south-central portion of the island. This site contrasts with San Gervasio in the north by being tightly nucleated and by containing a large area (over 100,000 square meters) of rubble platform construction. These platforms are similar to those at La Expedición, though on a much larger scale, and may represent storage areas for the exchange and resupply transactions central to Cozumel's trading system (Rathje and Phillips 1975). The site also contained isolated shrine structures and two ceremonial platforms with various structures on them.

The bulk of the excavation carried out on the island in 1972 and 1973 was focused on three sites—San Gervasio (C-22), Buena Vista (C-18), and La Expedición (C-25)—that show the diversity of sites on Cozumel. One measure of the excavations done at the various sites is the number of artifacts or faunal remains recovered from each (Table 1.1). In many cases, though certainly not all, the quantity of artifacts as well as the number of animal bones are in direct proportion to the number of pits and trenches excavated at each site. Some proveniences

**Table 1.1   Distribution of Cozumel Artifacts
and Faunal Materials by Site**
(as of July 1979)

SITE	NO. EXCAVATION UNITS WITH FAUNAL REMAINS[1]	NO. ARTIFACTS/%	NO. BONES/%	MNI/%
C-9	1 pit	1/ 0.02	14/ 0.07	1/ 0.04
C-12	3 pits	6/ 0.10	11/ 0.05	4/ 0.17
C-2	4 pits	10/ 0.17	17/ 0.08	9/ 0.38
C-31	1 pit	109/ 1.81	795/ 3.85	90/ 3.81
C-27	7 pits, 7 trenches	253/ 4.20	507/ 2.45	59/ 2.50
C-13	2 pits, 1 trench	324/ 5.37	1,137/ 5.51	128/ 5.42
C-15	2 pits	354/ 5.87	675/ 3.27	41/ 1.73
		17.53%	15.28%	14.06%
C-25	28 pits, 14 trenches	865/14.35	3,147/15.24	478/20.24
C-18	41 pits	1,104/18.31	3,105/15.04	479/20.28
C-22	85 pits	2,853/47.33	11,241/54.44	1,073/45.43
12 other sites[2]		149/ 2.47	— —	— —
		79.99%	84.72%	85.94%
Total		6,028/100%	20,649/100%	2,362/100%

[1]Some sites include proveniences in addition to excavation units (surface collections, complex floors, etc.).
[2]Twelve sites produced no faunal remains, so they are not listed separately here.

were simply richer per cubic meter than others, either in faunal material or artifacts. Still, a definite dichotomy can be seen between C-18, C-25, and C-22 and the remaining seven sites containing animal bones. The former sites were intensively excavated (forty-one, forty-two, and eighty-five pits or trenches, respectively), and thus it is no surprise that nearly 85 percent of all animal bones on Cozumel (almost 86 percent of the minimum number of individuals) come from these sites. This relationship is also reflected in the number of artifacts; nearly 80 percent of them were recovered from these same three sites.

Geography, Climate, and Environmental Considerations

Cozumel is geologically one of the earth's youngest formations. The island is a coralline limestone block, separated from the mainland probably by faulting. It rose above sea level during the Pliocene or the Pleistocene. The Canal de Cozumel separates the island from the mainland; its 3,000-foot depth apparently eliminates the possibility of an earlier land bridge with the mainland (Edwards 1957; Davidson 1975; West 1964a).

The island rises a maximum of forty-five to fifty feet above the sea. It exhibits a karst topography because of its coralline origins, with caves and sinkholes similar to those of northern Yucatán visible in various stages of development (Davidson 1975). Drainage of rainwater is almost entirely underground, as is common in limestone areas. The major sources of potable water which would have been available to prehistoric residents of Cozumel are *aguadas* (potholes which hold rainwater), *cenotes* (deep, generally cylindrical sinkholes with a groundwater-fed pool at the bottom), and *cuevas con agua* (grotto-like formations which trap water beneath an overhang) (Davidson 1975).

The climate of Cozumel is heavily influenced by the warm waters which surround it and the unusually consistent easterly trade winds. These factors, plus the island's relatively small size, have produced a generally homogeneous and moderate environment (Davidson 1975). The climate is characterized by a small annual range of relatively high mean monthly temperatures and a definite winter dry period. Two periods of maximum rainfall occur on the island from May to June and from September to October, separated by a two-month midsummer dry spell *(veranillo)*. *Nortes*, or cyclonic rainfall associated with high winds and cold fronts, occur periodically from November to March. On occasion hurricanes hit the island.

The dominant vegetation on Cozumel is a low latitude dry forest or *monte* which covers 80 percent of the island. Trees generally reach a height of approximately fifty feet, although some in the southeast are higher and form almost a true rain-forest canopy; this accounts for only 3 percent of the land cover on the island. *Monte* areas have incomplete canopy development. This allows sufficient sunlight to penetrate that a tough scrub undergrowth clutters the forest floor and makes travel off-trail difficult. Other types of vegetation on Cozumel include secondary-growth thorn thickets, mangrove and other swamp growth along the lagoons, and coarse grass savannas (Davidson 1975).

Major Emphases of the Present Study

Faunal analysis in Mesoamerica has been largely conspicuous by its absence. Despite several decades of archaeological research in the Maya area, relatively little meaningful work has been done as of the early 1980s with the animal remains excavated from these sites. Zoological research was conducted in connection with the excavation of Tikal and Uaxactun, for example, but the results revealed information more pertinent to biogeography than to the study of prehistoric human behavior. As Pohl (1976) points out, faunal remains from most excavated sites were turned over to zoologists who merely produced lists of identified species to be included in site reports. However, a few publications have appeared which include an analysis of excavated faunal samples. Some of these sites are Mayapán (Pollock and Ray 1957); Zacaleu (Woodbury and Trik 1953); Altar de Sacrificios (Olsen 1972); Cancún (Wing 1974); and Seibal (Olsen 1978). The Cancún report is the only one dealing with an island site, and it is based on a very small sample from the

Formative period only. Pohl's study of five sites in the Petén is one of the few attempts so far to compare the fauna from several different major Maya excavations and to attempt to draw meaningful conclusions about patterns of animal utilization. However, interest in Mayan use of animals seems to have grown; the fauna of several recently excavated sites in northern Belize—such as Cerros, Colha, and Cuello—were being analyzed in 1983.

The Cozumel faunal sample is unique in several ways. First, the sheer volume of animal bone is much greater than that from any other Maya site so far reported. The next largest collection appears to be the fauna from Mayapán, which includes fewer than 7,000 bones from fewer than fifty-five species. The present study encompasses some 20,649 specimens representing at least seventy-seven different species (see Table 1.2 for a summary of the excavated fauna by general category). One of the advantages of such a large sample is that any conclusions or inferences drawn have a much greater probability of being reliable, that is, statistically significant. In addition, the Cozumel fauna appear to be much more complete than that from other sites. The comparatively high numbers of such often-absent fauna as bats, amphibians, small birds, and several thousand fish bones make this perhaps one of the most varied and representative samples of the archaeological record

Table 1.2   Summary of All Excavated Cozumel Fauna

CATEGORY OF FAUNA	TOTAL NO. BONES/%	TOTAL MNI/%
Crabs	183/ 0.89	92/ 3.90
Sharks	75/ 0.36	53/ 2.24
Stingrays	26/ 0.12	10/ 0.42
Reef fishes	8,371/40.54	799/33.83
	8,655/41.91	954/40.39
Amphibians	283/ 1.37	38/ 1.61
Dogs	645/ 3.12	93/ 3.94
Peccaries	1,221/ 5.91	191/ 8.09
Other mammals	5,633/27.28	420/17.78
	7,499/36.32	704/29.80
Turtles	1,842/ 8.92	340/14.39
Iguanids	1,577/ 7.64	231/ 9.78
Crocodiles	35/ 0.17	14/ 0.59
Indeterminate reptiles	381/ 1.85	— —
	3,835/18.57	585/24.77
Birds	377/ 1.83	81/ 3.43
Total	20,649/100%	2,362/100%

obtained anywhere in the New World, undoubtedly because thorough screening was carried out on most of the excavated backdirt, which was not done at the majority of the Maya sites previously mentioned. Bone preservation may also have been somewhat better on Cozumel than elsewhere.

That ten different sites are represented in this collection is also unusual. It provides a unique opportunity for comparing faunal utilization between sites, as well as for intrasite correlation. It is possible, for instance, to examine differences in animal exploitation between Buena Vista (C-18), a nucleated platform complex inhabited chiefly by administrators and other officials, and San Gervasio (C-22), a dispersed, largely residential community inhabited by a variety of socioeconomic groups. Another aspect of the present sample is its relative time depth in comparison with most other Maya sites. Although it is true that the majority of faunal remains have been dated to the Late Postclassic and historic contexts, some material exists from every time period to as early as the Late Formative.

Generally, there are seven major classes of information which can be obtained from archaeological faunal analysis: food-gathering preferences, patterns, and techniques; butchering and other food-preparation practices; environmental or ecological implications; religious and ceremonial uses of animals; animal bone as a source of tools and other artifacts; evidence of domestication; and indications of prehistoric trade (see Hamblin 1975). The Cozumel material, with its large quantity and diversity of fauna, is an ideal data base with which to examine all of these aspects of prehistoric culture. The dietary or nutritional contribution of animals to ancient economics has often been viewed as the most important component of faunal analysis; in most cases this emphasis is appropriate. To the Maya, however, animals also appear to have been of tremendous social and religious or symbolic importance, in addition to playing a central role in the diet (Pohl 1976: 3–5). In fact, it would be fair to say that animals constituted an integral part of the entire Maya world-view.

Since the Cozumel Archaeological Project focuses primarily on identifying patterns of prehistoric trade, one of the major concerns here is to identify any non-native fauna which occur in these ten sites. Such species, found outside their normal geographic ranges, lend support to Sabloff and Rathje's theory that Cozumel was an important trading center, especially in the Late Postclassic. Unfortunately, however, the presence of such animal remains cannot be used to distinguish between a decentralized port-of-trade and a highly centralized trading port, although the time period in which they occur may be of significance.

Dietary preferences in an island environment are another important focus of the present study. Patterns appear here which are significantly different from those at other Maya sites, due at least in part to ecological parameters. A tentative determination of possible hunting techniques and whether or not certain age groups of animals were being selected is also made here. Food preparation practices are examined by a study of the numbers of butcher marks and burned or otherwise heat-affected bones present for each species.

Animal remains from elite ceremonial/administrative precincts and other cultural contexts such as housemounds, are compared, with the acknowledgment that the same group of people may have been responsible for the refuse in both contexts. Some of the animal bones from ceremonial sites (especially burials) may actually be part of the fill dirt brought in from other areas, although these areas are probably elite, and some of the bones may represent the remains of funeral feasts rather than those of animals deliberately interred with elite persons.

The role of domesticated animals (for example, dogs and turkeys) with respect to the Cozumel economy and the evidence that other species (such as coatimundis and peccaries) may have been tamed or kept in pens are also discussed. An attempt is made to determine whether the presence of several other domestic species (sheep, horses, and chickens) may represent some of the earliest Spanish animals brought to the New World, or if they are more likely modern intrusives. Several of the various classes of fauna, particularly the birds, amphibians, and some reptiles, are used to deduce past environmental conditions on Cozumel and any changes which may have occurred.

Finally, the uses of animals for tools or other artificats, as well as for ceremonial/religious purposes, are explored. Ethnohistoric documents and comparative data from other Maya sites are used to argue that many species present in the Cozumel sample were used in such contexts—animals as diverse as birds with brightly colored plumage, deer, marine toads, peccaries, stingrays, and sharks.

2. Computer Analysis, Minimum Number Calculations, and Other Technical Considerations

CERTAIN PROCEDURES are followed by most zooarchaeologists in the collection, cleaning, and recording of specimens. The Cozumel project, however, was unique in some respects and required the use of specific techniques not common to every faunal sample. During the 1973 field season on Cozumel all excavated dirt was screened with quarter-inch mesh. Screening was not consistently done during the 1972 season, although it was begun immediately whenever large concentrations of artifacts or bone appeared in a specific pit or trench. The 1972 season included only a relatively small proportion of the total excavation on the island (less than 20 percent), since the major focus of research was the survey and testing of certain sites. Therefore, the present sample contains the majority of all faunal material available from the excavated areas. This conclusion is supported by the fact that thousands of small fish bones, numerous amphibians, small bird bones, and two very fragile bat skulls were identified from these remains.

Many different comparative faunal collections were used to identify the Cozumel material (Table 2.1). Each specimen was identified to the closest possible taxonomic category. Fragmentary or undiagnostic bones often could be determined to the genus, family, and even order level. The designations *cf.* and *?* are employed when there is reason to believe that an element belongs to a certain species (*cf.*) or other taxon (*?*) but could not be so confirmed owing to the nature of the specimen (see, for example, Table 3.1). Although a preliminary faunal list was compiled to aid in narrowing down possible species, no identifications were made solely on the basis of an animal's known geographic range.

11

Table 2.1 Faunal Collections Used to Identify Cozumel Bones

INSTITUTION AND LOCATION AS OF 1980; CURATOR OR OWNER	FAUNA IDENTIFIED
National Park Service, Western Archaeological Center. Arizona State Museum, Tucson, Arizona Prof. Stanley J. Olsen	Mammals, birds, toads and turtles
Ornithology Collection, Department of Ecology and Evolutionary Biology, University of Arizona, Tucson, Arizona Dr. Amadeo M. Rea	Birds
Vertebrate Faunal Collection, Florida State Museum, Gainesville, Florida Dr. Elizabeth S. Wing	Fishes, crabs
U.S. National Museum, Smithsonian Institution, Washington, D.C. Dr. Storrs Olson	Birds
Personal collection, Tucson, Arizona Stanley J. Olsen	Mammals, crocodiles, and iguanids
Personal collection, Tucson, Arizona Dr. Amadeo M. Rea	Birds
Personal collection, Gainesville, Florida Dr. Pierce Brodkorb	Birds (especially parrots)
Personal collection, Prescott, Arizona Dr. Lyndon L. Hargrave	Birds (particularly turkeys)
Personal collection, Tucson, Arizona Dr. Thomas Van Devender	Turtles, amphibians, iguanids
Personal collection, Tucson, Arizona Kevin Moody	Turtles
Personal collection, Tucson, Arizona Nancy L. Hamblin (provided by John B. Sparling, Boca Raton, Florida)	Crabs

The taxonomic designations used here for various animal species are usually those most commonly used by American archaeologists as of the early 1980s.

Measurements were taken on certain elements of three species of mammals—collared peccaries (skulls only), dogs (skulls and limb bones) and cottontail rabbits (lower jaws only). All measurements followed the specifications in Von Den Driesch (1976).

Computer Analysis and Statistics

Computer analysis is used in this study to compile the information yielded by the complex mass of faunal data in a manner such that meaningful patterns can be readily discerned and basic statistics provided. A computer code was designed by the author for use in analyzing the Cozumel fauna because existing formats were not specific or inclusive enough to fit the data without extensive modification or were not applicable to the kind of programming or computer hardware available. The computer code used included nine variables for specifying archaeological provenience and fifteen variables for describing each specimen (Fig. 2.1). The coding system is alpha-numeric. All of the data available on each faunal specimen (except measurements) were coded and then checked for accuracy. Keypunchers subsequently entered these data on computer cards or diskettes (in the case of the reptiles) and then verified the work.

Analysis of the data was carried out using a Cyber 175 computer. SPSS (Statistical Package for the Social Sciences) was the programming employed, specifically subprograms "Frequencies," "Breakdown" and "Crosstabs." These subprograms automatically provided basic descriptive statistics such as mean, standard deviation, and variance, but the cumulative bone counts and simple percentages were most useful for the present study.

The use of a computer to analyze massive amounts of faunal data need not involve complex statistical techniques unless these are appropriate to a given research design. In fact, the very nature of faunal data and the lack of any one reliable method for quantifying such data make the use of certain statistical techniques misleading and undependable. In this case, the essential task was to collate, compile, and organize the data into potentially usable form. When bone measurements were taken, mean, standard deviation, variance, F-Test, and T-Test were calculated. Such techniques are appropriately used in cases where two or more groups of raw numerical data are to be compared.

Minimum-Number Calculations

For some time researchers have been looking for a reliable method of comparing relative numbers of animal remains found in sites. One method has been simply to use the number of identified elements per

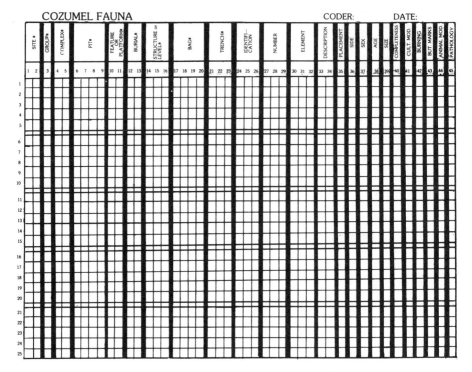

Figure 2.1. Computer Coding Form for Cozumel Fauna.

taxon, but several difficulties are encountered in doing so. The major problem is that there is no way of knowing which fragments belong to one animal skeleton and which belong to separate individuals; thus, there is a need for measurable units of comparison which are clearly independent of each other.

The actual number of identifiable skeletal elements also varies from species to species (for example, pigs have nearly twice as many identifiable foot bones as deer or sheep, and carnivores have even more), so that a simple bone count will bias the figures in favor of the animals with more recognizable parts. Another relevant factor is a phenomenon which has been labeled the "schlepp effect" (Perkins and Daly 1968) and which may operate to bias the raw bone count at a site in favor of the smaller animal species, in that "the larger the animal and the farther from the point of consumption it is killed, the fewer of its bones will get "schlepped" back to the camp, village, or other area" (Daly 1969: 149).

A second method involves weighing the skeletal remains from each taxonomic unit found in a site. Unfortunately, there are several major problems with this approach. As was true of using simple bone counts, the schlepp effect and variations in the number of identifiable elements per species may act to bias the results. Equally serious is the difficulty encountered when some bones from a site are mineralized (and thus heavier than normal) or leached out (and thus lighter), both of which phenomena occurred with no predictable pattern in the Cozumel fauna. A related problem is the appearance of such relatively light elements as skull or scapula fragments in either disproportionately high or low numbers within a specific sample (Reed 1970).

In North America particularly, most faunal analysts now use a third method, the Minimum Number of Individuals (or MNI) to measure the relative abundance of taxa found in archaeological sites. Shotwell (1955: 272) has defined this as "that number of individuals which are [sic] necessary to account for all of the skeletal elements (specimens) found in the site." Originally, this method involved separating the most abundant element of each species into right and left sides of the body, and then using the greater number as the unit of calculation (White 1953, 1956). Since all lefts will not necessarily match all of the rights, this will usually introduce a slight error on the conservative side. One way of correcting for this is by examining the sizes and relative ages of all the elements before attempting to match them up (Daly 1969; Flannery 1968; Grayson 1973; Bokonyi 1970).

According to Grayson (1973) and Thomas (1971) the use of the minimum-number method allows more detailed inferences to be made from a faunal collection and also establishes a basis for more elaborate statistical techniques. This method also provides units which are necessarily independent of each other, and the schlepp effect is at least partially corrected for in that even a single element indicates the presence of a whole animal. Problems arise, however, when different investigators introduce variations in their application of this method. Grayson (1973, 1974) notes that if one determines MNIs by subdividing a site's fauna on the basis of both vertical stratigraphy and horizontal excavation units (the maximum distinction method), a relatively large MNI will be obtained. Conversely, if one treats all the faunal materials from a site as one group, ignoring both natural stratigraphy and excavation units (the minimum distinction method), the resulting MNI will be relatively small. Chi-square tests run on the same data processed by these two different variations have resulted in significant differences at the .01 level. Another source of difficulty lies in the relationship between minimum numbers and sample size; specifically, the use of MNIs tends to exaggerate the importance of the rarer animals (Payne 1972; Grayson 1978) so that sufficiently large samples are required. One problem is that there can be no easy definition of a "sufficiently large" sample, since this can vary widely with the individual faunal sample. The number of taxa in a given site, the various ratios of MNIs to number of identified elements per taxon, and the use of the maximum distinction method for calculating MNIs all have a measurable statistical effect on adequate sample size. At least two approaches to correcting for this problem have been proposed, but more recent statistical work (Grayson 1979) suggests that no amount of correction factors can adequately compensate for an inherently flawed method such as MNIs.

Weighing the bones of the Cozumel fauna was out of the question owing to the wide variations observed in mineralized and leached or badly weathered specimens from the different sites. It also appeared inappropriate to return to the simple bone-count method, for the reason discussed above. Despite its problems, the MNI method does provide a way for comparisons to be made with the work of other faunal analysts, most of whom used this method as of the early 1980s. Furthermore, we had no better procedure to ascertain how many individual animals were represented at a site—a crucial factor if accurate deductions concerning prehistoric faunal use are to be made. Therefore MNIs were used, but subject to certain conditions. First, a compromise between the maximum and minimum distinction methods was employed. Since most excavated proveniences within the Cozumel sites are distinctly separate cultural units (e.g., a temple versus an administrative complex 300 yards away), combining all faunal material from separate areas did not seem logical. MNIs were thus calculated (within each site) separately by pit, trench, or other unit of excavation, but the levels within these units were ignored since many were either culturally mixed layers or arbitrary excavation levels. If two excavation units were close together (for example, two pits inside a temple structure), the fauna from these were grouped together for the purpose of MNI calculation. Using the method described by S. Bokonyi (1970) the bones of each taxon were then subdivided and matched not only on the basis of how many left and right elements were present, but also on age groups and sizes of the individual specimens. In most cases, MNIs were calculated separately for all taxa through the family level of identification. This allowed general comparison of data with those of other investigators in the Maya area. MNIs for bird families were omitted because of the vast difference among the species represented under these families and the resultant lack of meaning for such MNIs. No order-level (or higher) calculations were done for MNIs, or for taxa preceded by *cf.* and *?*, since these determinations would be essentially meaningless.

As a hedge against the problems inherent in using this method, MNIs were used solely as a control—along with simple bone counts—when conclusions were being drawn from the data. It is probable that sophisticated statistical techniques, such as chi squares, based on MNIs would be unreliable in the extreme, given the numerous flaws in this method. Furthermore, no estimates of the biomass represented by the Cozumel fauna were attempted, because these would hinge directly on MNIs with all of their inherent weaknesses, and such calculations of meat weights consumed at prehistoric sites are practically valueless for analytic utility (see, for example, Fagan 1966; Guilday 1970; Hamblin, Dirst and Sparling 1978). Factors such as preservation, absence of bone from sites because of cultural formation processes (such as cooking methods and disposal elsewhere), and differing methods of calculation all affect the reliability of such figures. Adequate biological studies are also required on the live weights of local fauna, scarce data for Mexican animals in general and almost totally absent for Cozumel fauna. (Many mammal species on the island are noticeably smaller and more slender than their mainland counterparts.)

Dating of the Cozumel Sites

Ceramic remains recovered from the Cozumel excavations had not been exhaustively analyzed as of the early 1980s. A preliminary attempt to determine a chronology for at least some of these proveniences was made for use in analyzing artifacts, shells, and faunal material. This was done by noting the pottery types present in excavated pits and trenches and assigning a date for them whenever possible. For example, Mayapán Black-on-Cream and Tulúm Red are both Late Postclassic pottery types, while Puuc Slate is considered Early Postclassic. If no potsherds appeared, or if there was a conflicting mixture of types, no date was assigned. Arthur Vokes analyzed each provenience by separate levels, which often resulted in several different dates within the same pit or trench. The approach used by David A. Phillips for artifact analysis was to assign dates (used in this study) on the basis of each separate bag; this sometimes provided dates in cases where a level-by-level analysis would not have.

Taphonomy and Cultural Factors

Taphonomy is a concept used by many paleontologists and some archaeologists to describe the various natural processes of deposition and preservation which influence the transformation of a live animal into an accumulation of buried skeletal remains (Efremov 1940: 74). Differences in the longevity of various skeletal elements, the relative acidity or humidity of the soil, and the degree of exposure to erosion and animal modification (insects, rodents, and carnivores) are some of the relevant factors here. Pohl (1976: 69–81) provides an excellent discussion of this topic.

Numerous cultural formation processes have also been at work in any archaeological context affecting the resulting corpus of faunal material. It has been said that in a certain sense, bones are artifacts, since they have passed "through the cultural filter" (Daly 1969: 152; Reed and Braidwood 1960: 165; Reed 1970: 210). As noted by Cleland (1966), animal remains from archaeological sites represent not only a piece of nature but more significantly, the relationship between culture and the natural environment. Every society is faced with a range of choices in its selection of animal species within the limits of environmental setting and technological level. Beyond this generalization, there are specific behaviors which directly affect the numbers of faunal remains at any given site. The "schlepp effect" has already been mentioned. Among the Maya, gifts of food, particularly meat, are used today, as they probably were in the past, to solidify social relationships. This might have resulted in the displacement of certain faunal elements within a site, or even between sites. Food preparation practices and use of bone for tools or other artifacts also act to destroy bone or render it at times unidentifiable (Daly 1969; Michelsen 1967). The term "cultural modification" is used throughout this book to signify any physical evidence of human activities that appears on animal remains—butcher marks, engraving, incising, hole-drilling, burning, polishing, and the like.

It is difficult to measure the exact degree to which all of these factors, both natural and cultural, have affected the Cozumel fauna. However, soil composition and environment may not have been significant influences, as they have been in other Mayan sites, since comparatively large numbers of small and fragile bones are well-preserved here. The great majority of the Cozumel fauna further appears unaffected by such disturbances as burning, animal behavior, or artifact manufacture. A preponderance of skull elements of most of the species encountered here may be partially due to differential preservation, as well as to cultural selection processes such as ceremonial use of peccary heads, and decorative use of dog and shark teeth.

3. Fishes and Crabs

FISHES AND OTHER AQUATIC ANIMALS have only recently begun to receive attention by archaeologists. Indeed, of all animal remains, fishes have probably received the least attention. This is primarily due to the difficulty of identifying these species and the relative lack of comparative type-collections for most areas of the world.

Several kinds of information can be obtained from a study of fish remains. Prehistoric dietary preference is one category, the probable level of fishing technology another. Practices such as fish-drying or preservation might also be deduced from the absence of skull elements, since the heads are usually removed in such cases. Changes in local environment through time and exploitation of certain specific micro-environments can be investigated using fish bones (see Casteel 1972, 1974; Ryder 1970; Wing and Hammond 1974). Ceremonial significance of certain species, as well as cooking techniques, can also be deduced from the remains of these aquatic animals.

Fishes and crabs (*Pisces* and *Crustacea*) represent numerically the most significant of all the Cozumel fauna. With 8,655 specimens constituting 41.91 percent of the total Cozumel sample, these two classes of animals surpass even the mammals (7,499 bones). One aspect of this group is its great variety; forty different taxa are represented, including twenty-three species of fishes and crabs (see Tables 3.1 and 3.2). For ease of comparison and discussion, these were subdivided into four major categories: crabs, sharks, stingrays, and coral-reef fishes. The molluscan material has been studied separately by Arthur W. Vokes (1978).

Crabs

Two species of crustaceans are represented in the Cozumel sites: the blue crab (*Callinectes sapidus*) and the stone crab (*Menippe mercenaria*). The majority of the fragments were identified as blue crab (eighty-

Table 3.1   Cozumel Fishes and Crabs
Taxonomic List

Class: Crustacea
  Subclass Malacostraca
    Order Decapoda
      Suborder Reptantia
        Tribe Brachyura (true crabs)
          Callinectes sapidus (blue crab)
          Menippe mercenaria (stone crab)
Class: Chondrichthyes (cartilaginous fishes)
  Order Squaliformes (= Selachii)—(sharks)
    Family Orectolobidae (nurse sharks)
      Ginglymostoma cirratum (nurse shark)
    Family Carcharhinidae (requiem sharks)
      Galeocerdo cuvier (tiger shark)
      ? *Carcharhinus sp.*
      Carcharhinus sp.
      Carcharhinus maculipinnis (large black-tipped shark)
    Family Sphyrnidae (hammerhead sharks)
      Sphyrna sp.
      Sphyrna cf. S. mokarran (great hammerhead shark)
      Sphyrna cf. S. zygaena (common or smooth hammerhead shark)
  Order Rajiformes (= Batoidei)—(rays and skates)
    Family Dasyatidae (stingrays)
      Dasyatis americana (southern stingray)
Class: Osteichthyes (bony fishes)
    Family Muraenidae (moray eels)
      Muraena miliaris (goldentail moray)
      Enchelycore nigricans (viper moray)
    Family Sphyraenidae (barracudas)
      Sphyraena sp.
      Sphyraena barracuda (great barracuda)
    Family Serranidae (groupers and seabasses)
      Epinephelus sp. (groupers)
      Mycteroperca sp. (groupers)
    Family Lutjanidae (snappers)
      Lutjanus sp.
    Family Pomadasyidae (grunts)
      Haemulon sp.
    Family Labridae (wrasses)
      Bodianus sp. (hogfishes)
      Bodianus rufus (Spanish hogfish)
      Halichoeres sp.
    Family Scaridae (parrotfishes)
      Sparisoma sp.
      Sparisoma cf. S. viride (stoplight parrotfish)
      Scarus sp.
    Family Acanthuridae (Surgeonfishes)
      Acanthurus sp.
    Family Balistidae (triggerfishes)
      Balistes sp.
      Balistes cf. B. vetula (queen triggerfish)
      Melichthys niger (black durgon)
    Family Diodontidae (porcupinefishes and burrfishes)
      Diodon hystrix (porcupinefish)

Table 3.2   Total Summary of Cozumel Fishes and Crabs

TAXON	NO. SPECIMENS	%	MINIMUM NO. OF INDIVIDUALS	%
Brachyura	37	0.40	17	1.8
Callinectes sapidus	84	1.00	39	4.1
Menippe mercenaria	62	0.70	36	3.8
Squaliformes	6	0.07	6	0.6
Ginglymostoma cirratum	10	0.12	6	0.6
Galeocerdo cuvier	3	0.03	3	0.3
? *Carcharhinus sp.*	1	0.01	—	—
Carcharhinus sp.	25	0.29	18	1.9
Carcharhinus maculipinnis	1	0.01	1	0.1
Sphyrna sp.	26	0.30	16	1.7
Sphyrna cf. S. mokarran	2	0.02	2	0.2
Sphyrna cf. S. zygaena	1	0.01	1	0.1
Dasyatidae	17	0.20	7	0.7
Dasyatis americana	9	0.10	3	0.3
Osteichthyes	6,713	77.56	—	—
Muraenidae	18	0.20	7	0.7
Muraena miliaris	7	0.08	5	0.5
Enchelycore nigricans	6	0.07	6	0.6
Sphyraena sp.	54	0.62	14	1.5
Sphyraena barracuda	21	0.24	16	1.7
Serranidae	95	1.10	30	3.1
Epinephelus sp.	258	3.00	91	9.5
Mycteroperca sp.	54	0.62	29	3.0
Lutjanus sp.	33	0.40	21	2.2
Haemulon sp.	282	3.25	94	9.9
Labridae	7	0.08	4	0.4
Bodianus sp.	1	0.01	1	0.1
Bodianus rufus	1	0.01	1	0.1
Halichoeres sp.	7	0.08	6	0.6
? Scaridae	2	0.02	—	—
Scaridae	2	0.02	2	0.2
Sparisoma sp.	220	2.54	104	10.9
Sparisoma cf. S. viride	1	0.01	1	0.1
Scarus sp.	26	0.30	20	2.0
Acanthurus sp.	167	1.92	167	17.5
Balistidae	131	1.51	74	7.8
Balistes sp.	146	1.68	83	8.7
Balistes cf. B. vetula	7	0.08	5	0.5
Melichthys niger	12	0.14	11	1.2
Diodon hystrix	100	1.15	7	0.7
Total	8,655	99.95	954	99.7

four elements, as opposed to sixty-two for stone crabs). However, a minimum number count actually shows a more even distribution of the two species (thirty-nine individual blue crabs versus thirty-six stone crabs). In addition, thirty-seven specimens had to be assigned the general designation *Brachyura* (true crabs) due to their very fragmentary nature (see Table 3.2).

The remains represented parts of crab legs (cheliped, propodus, dactylus, manus, carpus, and merus), especially the claw elements. This is to be expected since these are the most solid and durable portions of a crab's body. The carapace (shell) tends to be paper-thin and very fragile, so that preservation factors may be operating. The fact that 137 of the total 183 crab elements (74.86 percent) are either heat-calcined, heat-darkened, or burned may indicate that preservation is a selective factor here; elements affected by heat are less likely to disintegrate into the chalky or powdery condition often seen in unaffected crab elements. Another interesting (but untestable) hypothesis is that many crabs were taken during their molting seasons when the new shells were not yet hard, these being referred to as "soft-shelled crabs"; thus, the absence of carapace fragments could lead to speculation on the seasonality of crab fishing on Cozumel. Such negative evidence, however, should not be relied upon. The operation of preservation factors seems more likely.

Both the blue and the stone crab would have been easily obtained in the shallow waters close to Cozumel's coastline. Blue crabs inhabit salt and brackish waters in marshes and swamps, muddy bottoms, estuaries, and open sea. The lagoons around the island are an ideal habitat. The sixteenth-century bishop Diego de Landa mentions an abundance of crabs in the lagoons of the Yucatán (Collier 1964: 139). The stone crab, by contrast, prefers to burrow in shallow areas below the low-tide mark and often digs around sea walls, retreating to holes and crevices or under rocks. Both species are edible. The large, heavy claw of the stone crab, in particular, is favored. Fishermen in Florida break off this claw and throw the crab back to grow another one for the market the following year (Schmitt 1965). The Cozumel Maya might also have employed this convenient practice, thus helping to explain the lack of even a single carapace fragment.

The relatively high frequency of heat-affected crab claws (137, or nearly 75 percent) suggests that many crabs were roasted over coals or fire. Most of these claws (120) are either charred or heat-darkened, while the remainder (17) are merely heat-calcined. Similar occurrences in an early Guatemalan coastal site led Coe and Flannery (1967) to theorize that some of the crabs had been boiled in soup pots; in fact, they found one crab pincer still adhering to the interior of a potsherd. The burnt claws were thought to have been roasted. There is evidence on Cozumel for both roasting and boiling. The forty-six fragments which do not show effects of heat may have been broken open and the meat

Table 3.5 Distribution of Cozumel Sharks

SITE	SPECIES	NO. SPECIMENS	%	MNI	%
C-13	*Galeocerdo cuvier*	1	1.33	1	1.88
	? *Carcharhinus sp.*	1	1.33	—	—
	Carcharhinus sp.	1	1.33	1	1.88
	Sphyrna sp.	4	5.33	2	3.77
C-2	(None)	—	—	—	—
C-15	Squaliformes	1	1.33	1	1.88
	Sphyrna sp.	1	1.33	1	1.88
C-18	Squaliformes	1	1.33	1	1.88
	Ginglymostoma cirratum	2	2.66	1	1.88
	Carcharhinus sp.	10	13.33	4	7.54
	Sphyrna sp.	6	8.00	5	9.43
C-22	Squaliformes	2	2.66	2	3.77
	Ginglymostoma cirratum	3	4.00	3	5.66
	Carcharhinus sp.	8	10.66	8	15.09
	Carcharhinus maculipinnis	1	1.33	1	1.88
	Sphyrna sp.	15	20.00	8	15.09
	Sphyrna cf. S. mokarran	1	1.33	1	1.88
	Sphyrna cf. S. zygaena	1	1.33	1	1.88
C-25	*Ginglymostoma cirratum*	3	4.00	1	1.88
	Galeocerdo cuvier	2	2.66	2	3.77
	Carcharhinus sp.	4	5.33	4	7.54
	Sphyrna cf. S. mokarran	1	1.33	1	1.88
C-27	(None)	—	—	—	—
C-31	Squaliformes	2	2.66	2	3.77
	Ginglymostoma cirratum	2	2.66	1	1.88
	Carcharhinus sp.	2	2.66	1	1.88
Total		75	99.91	53	99.87

graph. If the figures fall in an overlap area between two species (or families), a definite determination cannot be made. But when the measurements fall distinctly in the middle range of values for a given species, identification of the vertebrae is possible.

Sharks represent less than 1 percent of all fish and crab elements but account for approximately 5.5 percent when minimum numbers are calculated. A review of the relative frequencies (Table 3.7) shows clearly that the Carcharhinidae and Sphyrnidae dominate the sample. Including the tiger shark, these two families account for 78.66 percent of the bones (77.34 percent of the MNIs). Nurse sharks represent a mere 13.33 percent of the bones (11.32 percent of the MNIs). A few specimens (three teeth and three vertebrae) could be classified only as Squaliformes (sharks); the vertebrae were either too fragmentary or badly eroded, while the teeth were removed from the collection in Mexico.

Table 3.6   Cozumel Shark Elements and Modifications

SITE	SPECIES	ELEMENT	NO.	MODIFICATION
C-2	(None)	—	—	—
C-13	*Sphyrna sp.*	Vertebrae	4	—
	Carcharhinus sp.	Vertebra	1	—
	? Carcharhinus sp.	Vertebra	1	—
	Galeocerdo cuvier	Vertebra	1	—
C-15	*Sphyrna sp.*	Vertebra	1	Hole Drilled
	Squaliformes	Tooth	1	—
C-18	*Ginglymostoma cirratum*	Vertebrae	2	—
	Sphyrna sp.	Vertebrae	6	—
	Carcharhinus sp.	Vertebrae	10	5-Hole Drilled
	Squaliformes	Vertebra	1	Hole Drilled
C-22	*Carcharhinus sp.*	Tooth	1	Hole Drilled
	Carcharhinus sp.	Vertebrae	7	—
	Carcharhinus maculipinnis	Tooth	1	—
	Ginglymostoma cirratum	Vertebrae	3	—
	Sphyrna sp.	Vertebrae	15	1-Hole Drilled
	Sphyrna cf. S. mokarran	Vertebra	1	Hole Drilled
	Sphyrna cf. S. zygaena	Vertebra	1	—
	Squaliformes	Vertebra	1	Hole Drilled
	Squaliformes	Tooth	1	—
C-25	*Ginglymostoma cirratum*	Vertebrae	3	—
	Sphyrna cf. S. mokarran	Vertebra	1	—
	Charcharhinus sp.	Vertebrae	4	—
	Galeocerdo cuvier	Vertebra	1	—
	Galeocerdo cuvier	Tooth	1	—
C-31	*Ginglymostoma cirratum*	Vertebrae	2	—
	Squaliformes	Vertebra	1	—
	Squaliformes	Tooth	1	—
	Carcharhinus sp.	Vertebrae	2	—
Total			75	

The nurse shark *(Ginglymostoma cirratum)* is a generally sluggish, bottom-dwelling species which resides relatively close to shore in sun-warmed waters (McCormick, Allen and Young 1963). Most nurse sharks are small, although they have reportedly reached a maximum of fourteen feet (Randall 1968). The animal often lies on the bottom feeding on squid, shrimp, crabs, spiny lobsters, sea urchins, and small fishes. This habit makes them easy to capture by reaching into shallow water and grabbing them by hand. Other means of fishing for nurse sharks include the use of a spear or a hook and line. One reason this species may occur with such low frequency in the Cozumel sample is because it is a rarely seen tropical shark, appearing commonly around offshore reefs and only sporadically straying inshore (Hoese and Moore 1977). The Cozumel Maya apparently did not exert themselves to obtain fish—

Table 3.7   Cozumel Sharks
Total for All Sites

SPECIES	NO. SPECIMENS	%	MNI	%
Ginglymostoma cirratum (nurse shark)	10	13.33	6	11.32
Galeocerdo cuvier (tiger shark)	3	4.00	3	5.66
Carcharhinus spp.[1] (requiem sharks)	27	36.00	19	35.84
Sphyrna spp.[2] (hammerhead sharks)	29	38.66	19	35.84
Squaliformes (sharks)	6	8.00	6	11.32
Total	75	99.99	53	99.98

[1] Includes ? *Carcharhinus sp.*, *Carcharhinus sp.*, and *Carcharhinus maculipinnis*.
[2] Includes *Sphyrna sp.*, *Sphyrna cf. S. mokarran*, and *Sphyrna cf. S. zygaena*.

they appear to have used species close to the island and to have ignored the deep-ocean fish farther away.

The Carcharhinidae (requiem sharks) represent the largest family of sharks. Most of the eighteen species which occur in Caribbean waters are dangerous to man and can be found along the shoreline in tropical, subtropical, or open sea (Tinker and DeLuca 1973). Generally, these sharks can be captured in shallow inshore waters by the use of a hook and line or by spear fishing. Only two carcharhinids were identified in the Cozumel sample (the tiger shark and the large black-tipped shark), while the majority could only be determined to the generic level *(Carcharhinus sp)*.

The tiger shark *(Galeocardo cuvier)* is a strong, active, voracious fish with an extremely varied diet. It is considered dangerous to man. Tiger sharks will savagely attack bathers or each other and will often wreck fish nets and gear. Considering their aggressive nature and the fact that a thirteen- to fourteen-foot tiger shark weighs between 1,000 and 1,300 pounds, it is understandable that only three individuals appear in the Cozumel sample. This relative scarcity may indicate a pattern of avoidance, since the tiger shark is one of the most common sharks in the tropics (particularly the Caribbean) and often appears close to shore.

The large black-tipped or spinner shark *(Carharhinus maculipinnis)* is an inshore species. It generally travels in schools, reaches a maximum of eight feet in length, and apparently is more common in the Gulf of Mexico than in the Caribbean (Hoese and Moore 1977; McCormick et al. 1963); this may explain why only one element of this species was found in the Cozumel sites.

The hammerhead (Sphyrnidae) is one of the most common sharks found in warm waters (Tinker and DeLuca 1973). The Cozumel sites included the hammerhead in numbers approximately equal to the Carcharhinid sharks (Table 3.7). Like the requiem sharks (Carcharhinidae), hammerheads can be speared or taken with a hook and line. None of the hammerheads was definitely assigned to species, although two great hammerhead and one common or smooth hammerhead specimens were tentatively identified (*Sphyrna cf. S. mokarran* and *Sphyrna cf. S. zygaena,* respectively). The great hammerhead *(Sphyrna mokarran)* is the largest species in this family, reaching at least eighteen feet in length. It is circumtropical in its distribution and is likely to be found over inshore reefs. By contrast, the common or smooth hammerhead *(Sphyrna zygaena)* is generally a smaller species (usually measuring nine to eleven feet, although some have been measured up to fourteen feet in length). It occurs along shorelines and also far at sea.

The number of shark elements exhibiting any kind of cultural modification is relatively small; only eleven, or 14.66 percent, had holes drilled in them (see Tables 3.6 and 3.8). Of these, one is a drilled shark tooth, while the remaining ten are vertebrae with holes drilled through their centers as if for stringing on a necklace or bracelet (see Olsen 1971: 4). A similarly drilled fossil shark tooth listed as a "pendant" was reported from a cache at Zacaleu, Guatemala (Woodbury and Trik 1953). Five additional shark teeth appear in the Cozumel sample. Although these are unmodified, they may be significant, since Landa refers to "very sharp teeth of fishes" being used for arrowheads (Tozzer 1941: 121).

Borhegyi (1961), who surveyed several archaeological sites in Mexico and Guatemala where shark teeth had been found, reports that Maya sites are characterized by mostly non-perforated teeth, found either as burial offerings or in votive vases and caches. He believes that their common association with other marine objects, such as sea shells, coral, echinoderms, and stingray spines, suggests a primarily ceremonial significance for them. Further, it appears that shark teeth were used sparingly as ceremonial offerings in the Mexican and Mayan area throughout all time periods. They are found as early as the Preclassic at La Venta, all the way up through the late Postclassic at Mayapán. The drilled shark vertebrae and teeth from Cozumel occur in a variety of cultural contexts (Table 3.8). Only three elements appear in burials (two unmodified shark teeth and one drilled vertebra); a total of six drilled vertebrae occur in household midden or rubble-fill contexts; the remaining seven were associated with ceremonial/administrative structures and complexes (three drilled vertebrae, one drilled tooth, and three unmodified teeth). This indicates that the use of these items was not necessarily restricted to any one aspect of Cozumel life. All of the datable proveniences were assigned to the Late Postclassic.

In general, most of the shark species are distributed throughout most of the sites on the island (Table 3.5). Where a species is absent,

Table 3.8 Proveniences of Cozumel Shark Artifacts and Shark Teeth

SITE	PROVENIENCE	DATE	SPECIES	ELEMENT	NO.	MODIFICATION
C-15	pit 179, burial 31	n.d.	*Sphyrna sp.*	Vertebra	1	Hole Drilled
	pit 179, burial 31	n.d.	Squaliformes	Tooth	1	—
C-18	pit 100 (midden)	LPC	*Carcharhinus sp.*	Vert.	1	Hole Drilled
	pit 97 (rubble fill)	LPC	*Carcharhinus sp.*	Vert.	4	Hole Drilled
	pit 100 (midden)	LPC	Squaliformes	Vert.	1	Hole Drilled
C-22	Group 3, pit 144	LPC	*Carcharhinus sp.*	Tooth	1	Hole Drilled
	pit 154	LPC	*C. maculipinnis*	Tooth	1	—
	pit 154	LPC	*Sphyrna sp.*	Vert.	1	Hole Drilled
	pit 156	LPC	*S. cf. S. mokarran*	Vert.	1	Hole Drilled
	pit 154	LPC	Squaliformes	Tooth	1	—
	Group 2, pit 136	LPC	Squaliformes	Vert.	1	Hole Drilled
C-25	pit 31, Str. 2-1-A	LPC	*Galeocerdo cuvier*	Tooth	1	—
C-31	pit 250, burial 39	n.d.	Squaliformes	Tooth	1	—
Total					16	

this can be explained in each case by small sample size—either the total number of fishes in general at the site is relatively low (as in C-2, C-15, and C-27), or the species in question occurs in such low frequencies everywhere that its distribution appears restricted as a result (e.g., *Galeocerdo cuvier*).

The Cozumel sharks were probably eaten. Borhegyi (1961: 280) asserts, "It may be assumed that the pre-Columbian Maya fishermen of Yucatán hunted sharks not only for their teeth, but also (or even primarily) for their livers and their meat." E. H. Thompson (1932) relates the story of a shark-fishing expedition in northwestern Yucatán in which he participated some years after his arrival in 1885. He accompanied two native Maya fishermen in a small dugout canoe. With a minimum of simple equipment (a lance, two wooden mallets, some large hooks, chains, and long coiled ropes), the two men managed to capture seven sharks in one night of hunting. The mallets and lance were used to dispatch each shark after it had swallowed a hook embedded in bait and been allowed to wear itself out struggling. Thompson mentions that the sharks were fished to obtain their livers, and he describes boiling shark livers in earthen pots to obtain oil. Borhegyi (1961: 280) states that this account was more than just an isolated instance: That two fishermen, armed with primitive fishing gear and wooden mallets, were easily able to catch seven sharks longer than their own canoe in only a few hours "suggests a well-integrated and probably age-old tradition of shark fishing." John Lloyd Stephens, in his *Incidents of Travel in Central America, Chiapas, and Yucatán* describes a shark hunt from shipboard. He also states that in Campeche, shark meat was sold "regularly in the market and eaten by all classes" (Stephens 1841: 462).

Shark liver is significant for its nutritive value, iodine, and high fat-soluble vitamin content. A specialist in Maya nutrition, Dr. Nevin Scrimshaw, informed Borhegyi that "consumption of shark liver would be a very rich source of vitamin D in the diet and would also make a significant contribution to the protein and B-complex content of a diet which otherwise consists primarily of corn and beans. Indeed, such a practice could well make the difference between good nutrition and poor nutrition for a population group, even if it were only a biweekly occurrence" (Borhegyi 1961: 281). Borhegyi believes that the consumption of shark meat and oil-rich shark liver in pre-Columbian times may have helped prevent many nutritional diseases and protein deficiencies.

The Cozumel shark material contains only sixteen artifacts and unmodified shark teeth (21.33 percent), indicating that the majority represents food refuse. None of the elements indicates cooking processes, but it would be simple to cut huge chunks of shark meat away from the vertebral column in order to cook it. In fact, it is possible that many of the sharks caught by Cozumel fishermen were butchered on the beaches, so that the few shark elements found in these sites represent only a small percentage of the total shark consumption. Even if shark elements other than teeth, calcified vertebrae, or perhaps dermal ossicles were originally transported to some sites, their cartilaginous nature would not permit preservation.

Stingrays

Like sharks, rays are distinguished from other fishes by a cartilaginous skeleton. All members of the stingray family (Dasyatidae), of which thirty species are known, are armed with one or more venomous spines in their whiplike tails. Most have only a single tailspine, but some have two, three, or more, the point of which can be eight to fifteen inches long. This spine is covered by a thin sheath which is pushed back toward the base when it is thrust into a victim. Along the edges of the stingers' underside run two deep grooves within which flows a venomous secretion, the method of whose injection is still under debate—whether by actual venom gland, or by spongy tissue extending the length of the grooves. Stingrays are plentiful in coastal shallows, particularly in warmer climates. They are chiefly bottom dwellers who often lie partially concealed in the mud. Rays are especially fond of molluscs, clams, and oysters, but they also eat worms, crustacea, and occasionally small fishes (Hoese and Moore 1977; Randall 1968; McCormick et al. 1963; Tinker and DeLuca 1973).

Only one species of stingray was definitely identified from the Cozumel sites (the southern stingray, *Dasyatis americana*), although several others may be present in the area (Randall 1968). The distinctive tailspines permitted this determination. The vertebrae, however, could be identified only to the family level (Dasyatidae). The southern stingray *(Dasyatis americana)* reaches a width of at least five feet and a body length of approximately four and a half feet. It is mostly an inshore ray, occurring out to the edges of offshore reefs. Alternatively, they might have been easily speared in the shallow waters by Cozumel fishermen. Landa describes the killing of stingrays by bow and arrow as they lay hidden in the mud (Tozzer 1941: 191).

Stingrays were probably not captured for food, but were used by the Maya as implements in ceremonial scarifications and bloodlettings—to pierce the tongue, nose, ears, and to mutilate the penis (J. E. S. Thompson 1966: 218; Tozzer 1941: 190–191; Borhegyi 1961; Lange 1971). There also seems to be a strong correlation between the occurrence of shark teeth and stingray spines in caches, burials or offerings (Borhegyi 1961; Wing and Steadman 1980). Borhegyi therefore suggests that the unperforated shark teeth in Mayan sites may also have been used for similar bloodletting and penitential purposes.

Less than 1 percent of the Cozumel fishes and crabs consists of stingrays (twenty-six elements) and approximately 1 percent of the MNI (Table 3.2). Most of the elements are vertebrae (65.3 percent); only nine (34.6 percent) are tailspines (Table 3.9). Most elements were found in burial contexts (twenty out of twenty-six, or 76.9 percent). All but

Table 3.9   Distribution of Cozumel Stingrays

SITE	SPECIES	ELEMENT	NO. BONES	MNI
C-15	*Dasyatis americana*	tailspines	5	1
C-22	Dasyatidae	vertebrae	17	7
	Dasyatis americana	tailspines	4	2
Total			26	10

one of the tailspines (88.8 percent) and twelve of seventeen vertebrae (70.58 percent) occur in burials. Stingray spines are also associated with burials at the nearby site of Tancah (Miller 1977: 102). In two-thirds of the Cozumel proveniences where stingray spines occur, so do unperforated shark teeth (see Tables 3.8 and 3.10); thus Cozumel stingrays and shark teeth generally follow the pattern previously established for other Mayan sites. However, the suggestion (Borhegyi 1961: 283) that stingrays may have been caught by accident, since sharks are often caught with stingray barbs imbedded in their jaws, is probably incorrect. If it were so, one would not expect to find stingray vertebrae, especially not in the numbers exhibited by the Cozumel sites. An interesting pattern emerges if the stingray elements are analyzed by site. Of the eight sites containing fish and crab remains, only two produced stingrays. The majority (80.76 percent) come from San Gervasio (C-22), a site comprising primarily elite residences, administrative complexes,

Table 3.10   Proveniences of Stingray Elements

SITE AND PROVENIENCE	DATE	NO.	MNI
A. Tailspines			
C-15, pit 179, burial 31	N.D.	5	1
C-22, Group 3, pit 154 (midden)	LPC	1	1
C-22, Group 6, pit 216 (tomb)	PR	3	1
Total		9	3
B. Vertebrae			
C-22, Group I, pit 49 and 117 (burials)	LPC	3	1
C-22, Group II, pit 131	LPC	1	1
C-22, Group III, pit 154 (midden)	LPC	2	1
C-22, Group IV, pit 178 (burial)	PF	3	1
C-22, Group VI, pit 194 and 194A (Altar, tomb)	TC	6	1
C-22, Group VI, pit 195A (near stairway, Str. C)	mixed	1	1
C-22, Group VI, pit 219	TC	1	1
Total		17	7

Total stingray elements in burials = 20 out of 26, or 76.9%.

and ceremonial precincts. The remaining tailspines are all from one elite burial at El Cedral (C-15). Perhaps the other large sites with ceremonial contexts and burials may have contained such elements at one time, but they have since been looted. (This is known to have occurred at some sites.) Or perhaps it was fortuitous that the burials at other sites with stingrays in them were not excavated.

Reef Fishes

Of all the Cozumel fishes and crabs, reef fishes are the largest and most diverse. Twenty-five taxa, including at least fifteen distinct species, comprise nearly 97 percent (or almost 84 percent of the MNIs) of all excavated fish and crab elements (see Tables 3.2 and 3.3).

Unfortunately, a high percentage (80.19 percent) of these reef fishes could be classified only as Osteichthyes (bony fishes). This is because of the relatively high proportions in the sample of such elements as vertebrae, non-diagnostic fish spines, and undetermined fish fragments (see Table 3.11). Together, these three categories make up 79.87 percent of the reef fishes. Most fish spines and miscellaneous fragments cannot be closely identified. However, some investigators believe that fish vertebrae can sometimes be used to make identifications to the family level, if not to genus and species (Casteel 1976: 73; Follett 1963). This may be true if the fish fauna from a site show great diversity in habits and morphology or where the family is monotypic. The nature of the Cozumel fishes, however, is such that nearly all of them inhabit the coral reefs near the island and exhibit great similarities in skeletal

Table 3.11   Cozumel Reef Fishes:
Distribution of Skeletal Elements

ELEMENT	NUMBER	%
Skull elements[1]	1,334	15.93
Vertebrae	2,773	33.12
Pelvic Girdle[2]	77	0.91
Diagnostic Fish Spines[3]	273	3.26
Non-diagnostic Fish Spines	2,166	25.87
Indeterminate	1,748	20.88
Total	8,371	99.97

[1]Includes: maxillae, dentaries, premaxillae, teeth, skulls, occipital condyles, basioccipitals, basibranchiostagels, parasphenoids, quadrates, vomers, hyomandibulars, articulars, operculars, preoperculars, pharyngeals, infrapharyngeals, and fused cranial complexes.

[2]Includes: pelves, ischia, and pelvic girdles.

[3]Includes: first and second dorsal spines, caudal spines, and caudal spine support apparatuses.

morphology. Therefore, these elements were simply identified as *Osteichthyes* (bony fishes). However, 1,684 elements, or 20.1 percent could be assigned to family level and the majority to genus or species as well (see Table 3.2). This number appears sufficiently large so that at least some inferences can be drawn.

Work by Casteel (1972, 1974, 1976) indicates that fish remains can be used to deduce seasonality of fish kills, based mainly on fish scales and vertebrae, and to estimate the live weights of these animals from the vertebrae and otoliths. Neither of these was attempted for the Cozumel fishes for several reasons. First, no fish scales or otoliths were found in the Cozumel sample, probably because flotation was not performed on the excavated dirt. This leaves only vertebrae for seasonality and live-weight determinations. Both of these determinations depend heavily on the successful identification of the element to genus if not to the species level. Casteel (1976) discusses in detail his single and double regression methods, stressing the necessity for good-sized samples of fish of each species and their associated bone measurements from a wide range of sizes, in order to produce a representative mathematical curve from which to estimate live weights. The identity of the species is obviously required in order for the correct growth curve to be applied to the measurement data. This could not be accomplished with the Cozumel fish vertebrae.

Determining the seasonality of fish kills is best accomplished in areas where there are definite seasonal differences in temperature, so that annuli can easily be distinguished on fish bones (Casteel 1972). However, in tropical and subtropical zones (including Cozumel) where temperature varies little from season to season, annulus formation seems to depend more heavily on other factors such as gonad maturation and seasonal deterioration of the food supply, although the exact causal factors are far from clear. It appears that for each species in such areas, very specific data must be obtained in order to determine exactly what the annular rings mean. As of the early 1980s such data were not available for tropical reef fishes.

Coral reefs provide the setting for the most diverse of all fish communities. In fact, they are among the most biologically productive of all natural communities (Lowe-McConnell 1977; Johannes 1976). More ecological niches exist here than in almost any other biotope. Corals can grow only where the mean annual temperature is at least 20°C (68°F) and preferably 23°C (73.4°F). Since coral reef communities are often many years old, they are likely to have provided a stable environment for the resident fishes over long periods of time; this stability probably explains the typically complex interrelationships among species inhabiting the reefs. Some reef fishes typically feed on algae or corals. Other species consume invertebrates; still others are large or small fish-feeders (see Fig. 3.1).

The moray eels (Muraenidae) are typically nocturnal reef-dwellers feeding principally on fishes. The larger morays may have flesh which

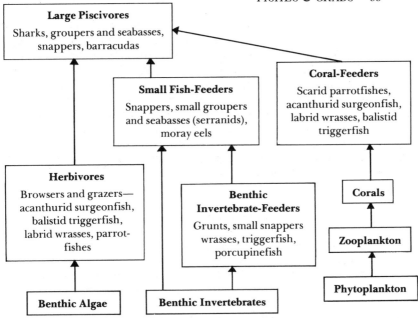

Figure 3.1. Simplified food web showing trophic relationships among coral reef fishes. Adapted from Lowe-McConnell 1977: 35 with additional information from Randall 1968.

is poisonous to eat (Hoese and Moore 1977). It seems significant, therefore, that the only two morays identified from Cozumel are the goldentail moray *(Muraena miliaris)* and the viper moray *(Enchelycore nigricans),* two of the smallest members of this family, reaching a length of 2 and 2.5 feet, respectively (Randall 1968). These two species occur almost equally in the sample, although there are a number of vertebrae which were determined only to the family level (Muraenidae). Altogether, the morays account for less than 1 percent of the bones (0.35 percent) and only 1.8 percent of the MNIs (Table 3.2). They were apparently not of great importance to the Cozumel fishermen. They could have been easily speared or obtained in the shallow waters by hook and line.

Of the three species of barracudas (Sphyraenidae) known from the Caribbean, only one appears in the Cozumel sample—the great barracuda *(Sphyraena barracuda),* which, though edible, is responsible for more cases of *ciguatera* poisoning in the Caribbean than any other fish. According to Randall (1968), *ciguatera* poisoning causes weakness, diarrhea, and other physical symptoms, sometimes terminating in coma or death. However, it is the large individuals of this species in particular which are implicated here (the record size being 5.5 feet), while the Cozumel barracudas were noticeably small individuals no more than two to three feet in length. In 1888, Tarleton Bean collected fishes on

Cozumel and obtained this species of barracuda (*Sphyraena picuda* = *Sphyraena barracuda*), which he refers to as "the fish best known to the people of Cozumel for food purposes, apparently . . . [and] which we found to be an excellent table-fish" (Bean 1890: 194). This species is common around reefs, which probably explains its selection by the Cozumel Maya. Great barracudas could have been captured in the shallows with the use of hook and line or spear. The possibility that other barracudas were also present in this collection cannot be entirely ruled out since fifty-four vertebrae could only be assigned to the generic level (*Sphyraena sp.*). All barracudas together total less than 1 percent of the fish bone sample (.88 percent), or only 3.2 percent of the MNIs, which implies that the fish preferences of prehistoric islanders differed significantly from those of the nineteenth-century inhabitants; barracudas were not a favorite of the prehistoric Maya on Cozumel.

The only two genera of the Serranidae (groupers and sea basses) present in the sample were both groupers—*Epinephelus* and *Mycteroperca*—identified only to the genus level. These groupers begin life as males and metamorphose into females when they are larger. Typically bottom dwellers, most of these fish inhabit rocky areas and reefs (Hoese and Moore 1977). Groupers are among the most commercially important tropical food fishes in modern times, despite the fact that a few of the larger species (including the genus *Mycteropera*) have been known to cause *ciguatera* poisoning when eaten (Randall 1968). Perhaps this explains why the *Epinephelus* groupers far outnumber *Mycteroperca sp.* in the Cozumel sites; there are 258 bones of the former and only 54 of the latter. (Another ninety-five bones are currently assigned only to the family level (Serranidae). Since all of these groupers could be procured by hook and line or by spearing, this disparity indicates a pattern of cultural selection—perhaps one based on the prudent avoidance of *ciguatera* poisoning. Altogether, the groupers comprise the most numerous family of reef fishes found in the Cozumel sites. They account for 4.7 percent of all fish bone, or 15.7 percent of the MNIs (Table 3.2). The Cozumel fishermen must have placed a relatively high value on groupers in comparison to the other reef fishes.

The snappers (Lutjanidae) are usually benthic fishes which are native to offshore reefs as well as to deeper waters, depending on the species (Hoese and Moore 1977). The larger species, especially the cubera and dog snappers, are known to produce *ciguatera* if taken from toxic sectors of reefs (Randall 1968). This fact is apparently reflected in the very low frequency of snappers on Cozumel (only thirty-three bones, representing a mere 0.4 percent of all fishes, or 2.2 percent of the MNIs). These were identified only to the generic level, *Lutjanus sp.*, so that it is not known exactly which species of snappers were being consumed. The relative lack of such an important and edible family of easily obtainable fishes (Randall 1968) implies that they were being selected against, for whatever reason.

The grunts (Pomadasyidae) are a family of reef fishes numerically important in the Cozumel sample. The only genus represented is *Haemulon*, and it accounts for 3.25 percent of all Cozumel fishes (or 9.9 percent of the MNIs). Grunts are well represented on Caribbean reefs with respect to number of species as well as number of individuals. In the daytime they may be seen in dense aggregations on small isolated reefs (Lowe-McConnell 1977). Despite the fact that many species are small in size, grunts are usually consumed enthusiastically (Randall 1968). This pattern evidently held true as well for the prehistoric inhabitants of Cozumel.

Wrasses (Labridae) are represented in the Cozumel sites by only sixteen bones, making up a low .18 percent of all fish bone, or 1.2 percent of the MNIs. This seems unusual since this is one of the largest families of tropical fishes, and some of the species are quite numerous on coral reefs (Hoese and Moore 1977). Several of the wrasses (represented by seven pharyngeals) were not identified beyond the family level (Labridae), although two were determined to the genus *Bodianus* and seven were assigned to *Halichoeres sp.* One of the former was identified as the Spanish hogfish *(Bodianus rufus).* This species is common on offshore reefs in water ranging from ten to one hundred feet in depth. As there would seem to be no particular problem in obtaining wrasses (hooks and lines, spears, or shallow-water traps could have been used), it is puzzling that they occur in such low frequencies here. A cultural preference for other species seems the logical explanation. Interestingly enough, their very close relatives, the parrotfishes (Scaridae), were taken in comparatively high numbers on Cozumel.

Parrotfishes represent one of the most popular families in this sample. They account for 2.9 percent of all fish bone, or 13.3 percent of the MNIs (Table 3.2). These herbivorous fishes are abundant on the reefs of shallow tropical seas. Parrotfishes are superior competitors among the plant-feeding reef animals, which probably explains why they are often the dominant fishes (Randall 1968). The overwhelming majority (88 percent—221 bones) of the Cozumel parrotfishes belonged to the genus *Sparisoma*, with one tentatively identified as the stoplight parrotfish *(Sparisoma cf. S. viride).* This particular species attains a length of twenty inches and a weight of 3.5 pounds. Hoese and Moore (1977) term this a rare species known from offshore reefs. Relatively few (26 bones) were assigned to the genus *Scarus* even though these species are not considered rare or even uncommon in the area. The parrotfishes in general were likely speared or trapped in relatively shallow waters.

Surgeonfishes (Acanthuridae) represent another fairly numerous family among the Cozumel shallow-water fishes. Their bones account for only 1.92 percent of the total sample, but this represents 17.5 percent of the MNIs because surgeonfishes possess one very diagnostic skeletal element—a retractable caudal spine with associated support apparatus—which resulted in a relatively high number of individuals being identified, as compared to other fishes whose elements are not as diagnostic. The fact that no other elements of the skeleton (such as pelves or skull elements) were identified as acanthurid suggests that the Cozumel Maya may have obtained these fish for ceremonial purposes (e.g., bloodletting, like the stingray spines) instead of for food. Otherwise, it seems reasonable to expect that at least a few skull elements, particularly the very distinctive teeth, would appear in the sample. None of the specimens could be determined beyond the genus level (*Acanthurus sp.*).

Triggerfishes (Balistidae) represent the second most important group of reef fishes excavated from Cozumel. They make up 3.4 percent of the total fish bones, or 18.1 percent of the MNIs (Table 3.2). As with the surgeonfishes, the minimum numbers are relatively high because triggerfishes possess two very diagnostic dorsal spines attached to and supported by a fused cranial complex. Although the number of these distinctive spines was high, other portions of the skeleton were present for this family, especially the skull elements and diagnostic pelves. Most of the specimens (153) were assigned to the genus *Balistes*, although 131 were left at the family level (Balistidae). Several bones, or five individuals, were tentatively identified as the queen triggerfish (*Balistes cf. B. vetula*). Generally, triggerfishes are edible, but this relatively large species has occasionally caused illness when consumed (Randall 1968). Eleven individuals (twelve bones) were identified as the black durgon (*Melichthys niger*). This species is most common in the clear waters of outer-reef areas at depths of fifty feet or more, suggesting that the Cozumel fishermen may have had to exert more effort than usual to get this fish. Another possibility is that the black durgons were collected in the tideways as dead animals. In any case, the distinctive spines were likely attractive to the Maya, as was true of the stingrays and possibly the surgeonfishes.

The only species of the Diodontidae (porcupinefishes and burrfishes) identified from the Cozumel sample is the porcupinefish (*Diodon hystrix*). It is unlikely that these fish were caught for food; the only parts of skeleton which appear here are the distinctive spines, implying that perhaps prehistoric use of the animal was for ornamental, and even ceremonial, purposes. This species was of only minor importance on Cozumel, since it represents a low 1.15 percent of the fish bones (or .7 percent of the MNIs).

A summary of the relative importance of the various reef fishes (Table 3.12) shows that the Cozumel sample is dominated by several major families. The top five are groupers, triggerfishes, grunts, parrotfishes, and surgeonfishes, which altogether make up 88.97 percent of the MNIs. A comparatively minor role is played by the remaining five families (moray eels, barracuda, snappers, wrasses, and porcupinefishes). These account for only 10.99 percent of the MNIs, excluding the indeterminate general category of bony fishes.

Table 3.12   Cozumel Reef Fishes:
Relative Importance by Family

TAXON	NO. SPECIMENS	%	MNI	%
Osteichthyes (bony fishes)	6,713	80.19	—	—
Muraenidae (moray eels)	31	0.37	18	2.25
Sphyraenidae (barracudas)	75	0.89	30	3.75
Serranidae (groupers and seabasses)	407	4.86	150	18.77
Lutjanidae (snappers)	33	0.39	21	2.62
Pomadasyidae (grunts)	282	3.36	94	11.76
Labridae (wrasses)	16	0.19	12	1.50
Scaridae (parrotfishes)	251	2.99	127	15.89
Acanthuridae (surgeonfishes)	167	1.99	167	20.90
Balistidae (triggerfishes)	296	3.53	173	21.65
Diodontidae (porcupinefishes and burrfishes)	100	1.19	7	0.87
Total	8,371	99.95	799	99.96

Despite the lengthy list of fishes excavated from Cozumel, an impressive number recorded from the area are missing. A list derived from the sixteenth-century Spanish chroniclers Oviedo and Landa reports mullets *(Mugil spp.)*, fresh-water mullet *(Agonostomus sp.)*, mojarras *(Gerres spp.)*, snook *(Centropomus spp.)*, jacks *(Caranx spp.)* soles *(Achirus spp.)* and sardines *(Sardinella spp.)* as pre-Conquest items of food and commerce for the Yucatán Maya (Collier 1964: 139). None of these species appears in the Cozumel sites. Collier also mentions two other families of probable importance to the aboriginal economy—snappers (Lutjanidae) and anchovies (Engraulidae). The latter do not appear in the Cozumel sample. Snappers do, but they seem to be of relatively minor importance, since they represent less than 1 percent of the fish bones. This low frequency may again reflect the fact that the larger species of snapper are known to produce *ciguatera* poisoning if fished from toxic areas of reefs. Presumably, the Cozumel fishermen learned to avoid this.

Some indication as to why these species were evidently not being used on Cozumel may be found in the ecological requirements of the animals. Mullets, for instance, are more common in brackish water than in sea water of full salinity, particularly the adults of the species. The freshwater mullet, naturally, could not exist at all on Cozumel. Of the snooks, only one species is mentioned as "occasionally seen in reef areas near mangroves" (Randall 1968: 89) which implies that the animal was not available in any quantity. Jacks are not considered residents of reefs, even though they may briefly pass through the reef community when feeding on the resident fishes. Similarly, soles do not inhabit the reefs since they are usually confined to turbid water. The three genera of herrings which are likely to be encountered in the clear, shallow water of reefs do not include the one mentioned as a food item by Collier (1964); even if these three genera had been used on Cozumel, their small and delicate bones might not have been preserved. (This is probably the case since Bean [1890: 206] reported two members of one of these genera in his survey.) The mojarras are usually found on sand or mud bottoms in shallow water, and only three species are reported by Randall (1968) as possibly occurring on or near Caribbean coral reefs. Several different species of mojarra *(Gerres spp.)* were collected by Bean. Apparently, either the inhabitants of Cozumel did not prefer mojarra or these fish were comparatively scarce on the reef. Finally, only one species of anchovy is likely to occur inshore over reefs (Randall 1968). Even if this tiny fish had been used prehistorically, its soft bones would not be preserved, especially if the fish had been eaten whole, as is done today.

Other fishes known to occur on the island but which do not appear in the present sample include trunk fishes (Ostraciontidae), angelfishes (Pomacanthidae), gobies (Gobiidae), and damselfishes (Pomacentridae). None of these is mentioned as a food item by Bean (1890), although he does discuss others which were so used on the island. Randall (1968: 273) refers to only one of these four families, the trunkfishes, being eaten. However, these fish secrete a very strong toxic substance which can kill other fishes, and human consumption can result in illness. If the Cozumel fishermen avoided trunkfishes for this reason, they would be following the same pattern observed for other species known to be poisonous.

When the distribution of reef fishes is analyzed by site a clear pattern emerges (Table 3.13). In every case, the reef fishes represent the predominant majority of all fishes and crabs. These species average 95.24 percent of the bone sample, or 67.37 percent of the MNIs. The

Table 3.13   Importance of Reef Fishes by Site

SITE	NO. SPECIMENS	% OF TOTAL FISHES AND CRABS IN SITE	MNI	% OF TOTAL FISHES AND CRABS IN SITE
C-2*	1	100.00	—	—
C-13	765	98.70	70	93.33
C-15*	31	81.57	1	25.00
C-18	1,210	96.80	178	87.68
C-22	4,268	96.49	315	79.34
C-25	1,426	96.48	160	85.10
C-27*	53	94.64	13	81.25
C-31	617	97.31	62	87.32

*Sample size relatively small.

latter figure is lower than it should be owing to the statistical effect of some sites with small sample sizes, which tends to artificially lower the average. It is obvious that in sites with a decent sample size (C-13, C-18, C-22, C-25, and C-31) the importance of the reef fishes clusters tightly between 98.7 percent and 96.48 percent of total bones, and ranges from 93.33 percent to 79.34 percent of the MNIs. The low end of this MNI range occurs at C-22 (San Gervasio); it may be explained by the comparatively high percentages of crabs, stingrays, and sharks at this site. This suggests special dietary and ceremonial behavior by the occupants of San Gervasio, many of whom were members of the elite (Sabloff and Rathje 1975c).

None of the Cozumel fish and crab species can be considered pelagic—that is, they are not deep-water or oceanic species. Instead, they are all typical inhabitants of the coral reef environment, most of them (including the sharks) either living in or spending a fair amount of time in shallow inshore waters. The fishing technology required on Cozumel was therefore not complex. It is well known that the Maya had considerable boat-building expertise; Bernal Díaz refers to canoes on the northeastern coast of Yucatán capable of holding forty men (Roys 1943: 50; Lange 1971). Borhegyi (1961: 276) cites an early sixteenth-century description by Peter Martyr of a Maya fishing expedition near Cozumel: "Off the coast of Yucatán and well on the way from the island of Cozumel, the Spaniards encountered a canoe filled with fishermen. There were nine of them, and they fished with golden hooks." A mural from the Temple of the Warriors at Chichén Itzá illustrates boats and fishing activities, as do some scenes on incised bone found in a tomb below Temple 1 at Tikal (Wing and Hammond 1974). A creel for fish is shown on one of these incised bones, although the nature of the fishing gear is not apparent. Landa refers to the use of trammel nets, sack nets, hooks, harpoons, and bows and arrows used by the Maya (Tozzer 1941: 156, 190, 191). Wing and Hammond suggest that the quantities of notched pottery "net-sinkers" found at many Classic sites, including Lubaantun, imply the use of seine nets. Pohl (1976: 273) also refers to Preclassic and Postclassic artifacts identified as net sinkers from the site of Topexte, and Postclassic "fishline weights" found at both Macanche and Barton Ramie, although she acknowledges that their function is still a matter of debate. Notched potsherds were also found at the site of Tancah on the east coast of the Yucatán, and it has been suggested that they were used "with henequen nets to entrap large parrotfish which congregate near the mouths of the many underwater limestone caves from which fresh water pours into the sea" (Miller 1977: 100–101). Apparently, large shoals of fish, such as parrotfish, come to the mouths of these caves to feed on plant life and are eaten by still larger carnivorous fish. Miller (1977) watched the east-coast Maya fishermen on many occasions walk out into the shallow water to the tops of these caves and throw out a net with sinkers attached to trap the fish.

Well over 1,000 net sinkers *(mariposas)* occurred in the Cozumel sites (Phillips 1979); in fact, these items were the most numerous of all the artifacts recovered from the island. Thus the Cozumel fishermen probably used nets in combination with hooks, lines, spears, and possibly fish traps. The great majority of reef fishes previously discussed are reportedly obtainable by hook and line or by spearing. However, Bean's collecting expedition of 1888 indicated that for most of the species he captured on Cozumel, "hook fishing was essentially a failure" (Bean 1890: 193). He states that some species, such as the queen triggerfish *(Balistes vetula)* and trunkfish, were caught by angling, and a few in gill nets (two parrotfishes, *Scarus spp.*). His greatest success, however, was obtained using a seine net twenty-five fathoms (150 feet) in length. This may be what the island's prehistoric fishermen had already discovered centuries earlier. A fishing strategy emerges that was characterized by the use of canoes or small boats and the probable deployment of several different fishing methods, depending on the habits of the target species.

The percentage of burned bones is very low—less than 1 percent of all reef fishes (Table 3.14)—implying that fish were either filleted before cooking, or that they were boiled in soups and stews and only occasionally roasted directly over a fire. The burned bones seem to cover a normal cross-section of several major fish families.

The presence of a significant percentage of skull elements in these sites (nearly 16 percent) indicates that fish-drying was not practiced on Cozumel, at least not to any great extent, since the heads likely would have been removed and discarded elsewhere. In that the most commonly preserved fish bones are vertebrae, the appearance of skull elements totaling almost 16 percent of the present sample is quite significant. The reef fishes exhibited no pathologies or butcher marks, and only .16 percent were carnivore-chewed (5 bones) or rodent-gnawed (9 bones). None was culturally modified in any way.

Table 3.14   Distribution of Burned Reef Fishes

TAXON	NUMBER BURNED	
Bony Fishes (Osteichthyes)	18	
Serranidae	1	
Epinephelus sp.	7	
Sparisoma sp.	2	
Haemulon sp.	1	
Balistidae	2	
Balistes sp.	1	
Total	32	= 0.38 % of all reef fishes

One feature of the reef fishes is the relatively high proportion (43.4 percent of the MNIs) represented by species possessing distinctive dorsal, caudal or body spines: surgeonfish, triggerfishes and porcupinefish. Given the significance of the stingray spine in Maya religious contexts these other species might have been attractive to the Maya for similar reasons. Since these fish also provide good eating, perhaps there was a dual purpose involved in their selection. That spines constitute the majority of all elements present for these species certainly is cause for suspicion. However, other factors contributing to this result might be differential preservation (triggerfishes in particular have very heavy, durable spines) and the fact that other skeleltal elements are comparatively undiagnostic.

Another pattern is the avoidance of reef fishes which can cause poisoning. Barracudas, large moray eels, the larger groupers (especially *Mycteroperca spp.*) and snappers *(Lutjanus spp.)* are the most dangerous as far as *ciguatera* poisoning is concerned (Randall 1968: 3). These species, all of which are considered excellent food fish, played only minor roles in the Cozumel diet. Altogether they account for only 2.3 percent of all reef fish bones, or 12.26 percent of the MNIs. This seems significantly low for species so numerous and easily available in a coral reef environment. It is especially noteworthy that only smaller members of the species *Sphyraena barracuda* (great barracuda) were selected, when the larger individuals are known to be primarily responsible for *ciguatera* poisoning. Trunkfishes (Ostraciontidae) are often consumed in the West Indies, although they do secrete a toxic substance which may cause illness in humans. The Cozumel fishermen apparently preferred to pass them up entirely, since not a single specimen occurs in the present sample.

Religious, Dietary, and Trade Implications of Marine Fauna

Most fishes and crabs in the sample could be dated to the Late Postclassic and historic periods (Table 3.15). Even if all of the bones in the mixed and undatable categories were arbitrarily assumed to represent earlier periods, the Late Postclassic material would still dominate the sample; therefore, the general patterns of marine fauna use can be regarded as primarily Late Postclassic patterns.

Besides their use as food, there is evidence that fish functioned symbolically in the counting system, and that they also played a part in Maya religion. Thompson (1944) discusses in some detail the appearance of fish and fish heads in Maya glyphs (in the Dresden Codex, sculpture, ceramics, and elsewhre) and concludes that the animal was used as a symbol for counting. Linguistic evidence lends support to this hypothesis. The Maya word for counting is *Xoc (or Xooc)*, but in Yucatec, the word also appears to stand for an ill-defined group of

Table 3.15 Distribution of Cozumel Fishes and Crabs by Time Periods

TIME PERIOD	NO. SPECIMENS	%	MNI	%
LPC and Historic	5,847	67.56	543	56.92
Postclassic	335	3.87	59	6.18
Pre-Decadent	73	0.84	20	2.10
Pre-Postclassic	59	0.68	18	1.89
Pure Florescent	192	2.22	35	3.67
Mixed and no date	2,149	24.83	279	29.24
Total	8,655	100.00	954	100.00

NO. SPECIMENS: {335, 73, 59, 192} 659/7.61%

MNI: {59, 20, 18, 35} 132/13.84%

large fish (especially sharks) or whales (Roys 1933). Thompson notes that some of the glyphs do display the prominent serrated teeth and elongated snouts which are characteristic of sharks. Since the characteristics of these fish glyphs are quite variable, he states (1944: 17) that *Xoc* probably does not represent any one species or group of fish, but was more likely "a large mythological creature with no immutable characteristics, and with a tendency to become anthropomorphized."

The religious significance of fish is referred to by Landa; he describes a number of deities and rituals related to this group of animals (Tozzer 1941: 155–156). Landa writes of fishermen anointing their fishing implements prior to an expedition where many fish were caught. He also refers to sacrifices and offerings made by fishermen at a shrine before putting out to sea., Similarly, Roys (1943: 19) mentions temples near the seashore frequented by hunters and fishermen. Of particular interest is his reference to fishing shrines on Cozumel as well as the east coast of Yucatán. Lange (1971: 633) believes that the positioning of another temple on Cozumel purportedly in honor of the rain god suggests that there was a much closer relationship between Maya water deities and maritime interests than previously thought. The water these deities symbolized and cared for may not have been rain only, but the sea as well. There is evidence for this reasoning if one traces the derivation of the Maya rain god Chac back to its roots in Olmec civilization (see Lange 1971: 633 for a detailed account). In addition, the moon goddess Ixchel shared a central position on Cozumel with Chac and the fishing deities. She was an important deity, especially for the east coast Maya, and was associated with the moon, childbirth, procreation, weaving, medicine, shells, and water in general (Miller 1977; Lange 1971), all of these associations involving the concept of renewal. Since the moon rises in the east and appears to be born out of the sea, it is logical that this astronomical association of the moon goddess should be most important on the east coast of Yucatán. It is known that pregnant women consulted the famous Ixchel idol on Cozumel, where there was a major shrine to the moon goddess. According to Miller (1977: 107), "When a child is born, it emerges from an interior world of its mother. Perhaps the association of a newborn child and the moon seemingly reborn out of the belly of the earth in the eastern sky was a part of the metaphorical Maya belief in the association of the new moon with birth." Since the Maya devoted considerable efforts to tracking the cycles of the moon and were quite accomplished in the field of astronomy, it seems reasonable that they would have been familiar with the moon's tidal effects—a crucial factor in fishing and seafaring. Thus it would seem that at least part of the moon deity's significance to the Maya was derived from maritime associations (Lange 1971: 633).

Regardless of species, fish in general is highly nutritious. Relatively small amounts of marine resources per person would have provided the necessary protein balance in a diet dominated by plant products (such as corn, root crops, and beans) which had been grown on thin and perhaps nearly exhausted soils (Lange 1971). Fish is an excellent source of protein, not only in terms of quantity, but also in quality. A diet consisting of a moderate amount of incomplete protein can be transformed into one with an adequate amount of high-quality protein if even small amounts of fish are consumed (Mayer 1962). The protein content of edible fish portions has been noted at 15–20 percent when water is included. By dry weight, however, protein is usually over 50 percent and occasionally as high as 90 percent (Driver 1961: 63). Curing by drying, salting, or smoking has been found to have relatively little effect on the overall nutritive value of fish (especially protein), although the loss of some vitamins can occur as a result of processing and storage (Cutting 1962).

In addition to protein, fish is a source of unsaturated fats (compared to meats), calcium, potassium, phosphorous, iron, B-vitamins, Vitamin A, iodine, and such essential trace elements as copper, manganese, zinc, cobalt, fluorine, vanadium, molybdenum, chromium and selenium (Driver 1961: Guha 1962; Kuhnau 1962; Sever 1975). The vital role of these trace elements in the human body has only recently begun to be understood. Many act as catalysts for normal metabolic processes and maintenance of general health. Others are needed for fixing iron into blood hemoglobin for bone formation and action of hormones (Mn), protein metabolism (Co), integrity of the teeth (fluorine), regulation of the thyroid (iodine), protection of the liver (selenium), and the like. Zinc is an especially vital element; a deficiency of it results in markedly retarded growth and sexual development, as well as possible congenital malformations of the central nervous system (Sever 1975). Fish is a particularly valuable source of these elements, since isotope studies have shown they are concentrated in the muscle and viscera of fish from 100 to 10,000 times their original level in sea water (Kuhnau 1962).

The use of marine resources by the Maya may have had wider implications than merely the improvement of diet in certain local areas or the acquisition of sharks' teeth and stingray spines. Lange (1971) asserts that the population of a large portion of Yucatán was heavily dependent upon marine products as the primary protein source, especially in the Classic and Late Postclassic periods. Extensive studies of settlement-pattern data tend to refute this, at least as far as the specific time periods are concerned (Ball and Eaton 1972). Still, the existence of a diverse resource-exploitation pattern (including marine fauna), should no longer be doubted, as opposed to the old concept of nearly complete dependence on maize. Certainly the Cozumel data support the idea of a heavy reliance on marine fauna in the Late Postclassic.

The exploitation of marine resources may have been undertaken at least partially for the sake of long-distance trade. Roys notes (1943: 41) that "fish have always been good and abundant in Yucatán waters, and the people of the coast devoted most of their energy to fishing, both for their own consumption and for sale to the inhabitants of the interior." Because maize did not grow well there, the chief occupations along the coast were said to be fishing, salt-gathering, and commerce (Scholes and Roys 1948: 170–171). That fishing was an important industry in aboriginal Yucatán is emphasized by Landa, who reported that the catch was salted, dried in the sun, or roasted, depending on the kind of fish, and traded over considerable distances (Tozzer 1941: 190). Pollock and Ray (1957: 650) believe that this may explain the great quantity of saltwater fish bones present at Mayapán, a site located far inland from the sea. Similarly, the great numbers of net-sinkers found at Tancah on the east coast of the Yucatán led Miller (1977: 101) to infer that the local people were fishing for export as well as for their own needs. He does not specify exactly how many of these net-sinkers were excavated from Tancah, or if any other evidence existed to support the hypothesis of fish-trading.

Cozumel may have been involved in the trade of marine resources, although the evidence is certainly not conclusive. The Postclassic was a period dominated by waterborne trade (Sabloff 1977: 71). The Maya made practical use of the sea's "readily available protein and lanes of easy transport for great quantities of bulky and heavy trade goods over long distances" (Miller 1977: 97). Specifically, the Cozumel Archaeological Project has demonstrated the involvement of this island and the coast of Yucatán in the Postclassic maritime trade. One of the things remaining to be discovered as of the early 1980s is the medium of exchange. The great number of net-sinkers in the Cozumel sites might point towards fish-trading with the mainland. The great abundance of fish and crab remains, however, may only reflect a logical exploitation of the available sea resources for local consumption. The fact that there is no indication of fish-drying or preservation activities (since skull elements appear in adequate percentages) tends to cast some doubt on this hypothesis. On the other hand, fish caught for export would not necessarily leave any archaeological evidence if the heads were removed on the beach and discarded in the sea. The remaining body parts would also be absent since the preserved fish would have been traded elsewhere. Perhaps some of the fish excavated at Mayapán and other inland sites were originally caught on Cozumel.

4. Amphibians

AMPHIBIANS ARE OFTEN SCARCE, if not entirely absent, from archaeological contexts. For example, even the very large faunal sample from Mayapán (over 6,000 bones) contained only twenty-eight amphibian bones, representing four individual animals (Pollock and Ray 1957). The bones are very small and fragile, many of the limbs being mere hollow tubes with quickly perishable gelatinous capsules on the articular ends. Nevertheless, the Cozumel fauna produced 283 amphibian specimens representing at least thirty-eight individual animals of several species (Table 4.1).

Bufonids dominate the sample. The large marine toad, *Bufo marinus*, accounts for 88 percent of all amphibian bones, or 63.1 percent of the minimum number of individuals. Another 11 percent of the bone sample is represented by *Bufo sp.;* this taxon also accounts for 29 percent of the MNIs. Although this second category of toad bones could not be positively identified beyond the generic level, it is strongly suspected that these, too, are *Bufo marinus*. Another bufonid toad, *Bufo valliceps*, should be in the area (Stuart 1963: 26–27), but not a single specimen was so identified from the Cozumel sites; thus, it seems highly probable that the *Bufo sp.* bones are actually those of the large marine toad *(B. marinus)*, even though this has not been confirmed. If the figures for *Bufo sp.* and *Bufo marinus* are added together, the large bufonid toads represent 99 percent of the amphibian bones, or 92.1 percent of the MNIs present.

The remaining specimens include the indeterminate amphibian fragment, one bone belonging to the family Hylidae (tree frogs), and one from the family Leptodactylidae. The hylids are a family of predominantly arboreal, slim-waisted, small frogs with elongated hind limbs and rounded adhesive discs on the digits. In contrast, the leptodactylid frogs include land-dwelling, aquatic, and arboreal forms, all of which possess teeth in the upper jaw (Stebbins 1962, 1966).

Table 4.1   Cozumel Amphibians: Taxonomic Checklist

Class: Amphibia (amphibians)
  Order Salientia (frogs and toads)
    Family Bufonidae (true toads)
      Bufo marinus (marine toad)
      Bufo sp.
    Family Leptodactylidae (leptodactylid frogs)
      *? *Leptodactylus sp.* (either *labialis* or *melanonotus*)
    Family Hylidae (hylid tree frogs)
      Smilisca baudinii (= *Hyla baudinii* — Mexican tree frog)

*The single specimen (a tibiofibula) matched both *Leptodactylus labialis* and *L. melanonotus* very closely in size and in characters. However, *Eleutherodactylus laticeps* could not be entirely ruled out without a more complete comparative collection.

Environmental Indicators

Amphibians are often excellent indicators of restricted environmental conditions, since most frogs and toads have rather detailed and specific life requirements as compared to mammals, for example. Almost all amphibians lay their eggs in water or near it, and most pass through an aquatic larval stage, having developed gills. The presence of amphibians on Cozumel thus indicates water sources close to the sites studied. The question is whether or not these sources necessarily represented a permanent supply of water or were merely seasonal in nature.

The large marine toad *(Bufo marinus),* despite what its name suggests, spends only part of the time in the water. As a member of the family Bufonidae, it is both terrestrial and aquatic, as well as fossorial (Stebbins 1962). It occurs in both arid and humid lowland forests, particularly in the dry season, and is common in the vicinity of wells or ponds (Martin 1958). But these toads are also found in and around courtyards and houses, in gardens, by roadsides, and at the edges of mangrove swamps. In the daytime this nocturnal creature hides under fallen tree trunks, matted leaves, and stones, or burrows in soft earth. For breeding purposes, this species apparently does not require a permanent water source; the eggs, long gelatinous strings, are often laid in small, temporary pools of rainwater. Experiments have also shown that *B. marinus* eggs placed in low concentrations of seawater had reduced mortality and had somewhat accelerated development in the early stages; thus, the marine toad is more tolerant of salt water than most other amphibians (Wright and Wright 1949). The implication is that this species is well adapted for life on Cozumel. It could live in a variety of terrestrial, aquatic, and fossorial contexts, while breeding would require nothing more than limited pools of standing rainwater. The island has many *aguadas*, or rainwater pools in limestone outcrops. Exposure to salt water from one of Cozumel's numerous lagoons would not have been overly detrimental to the species, either.

Table 4.2   Cozumel Amphibians: Species Distribution

SPECIES	NO. BONES	PERCENT	MNI	PERCENT
Bufo marinus	249	88.00	24	63.1
Bufo sp.	31	11.00	11	29.0
? Leptodactylus sp.	1	0.35	1	2.6
Smilisca baudinii	1	0.35	1	2.6
Amphibian	1	0.35	1	2.6
Total	283	100.05	38	99.9

The Mexican tree frog, *Smilisca baudinii*, has a wide distribution throughout the Middle American lowlands. Primarily arboreal, it is also found in such varied habitats as small bushes, grassy or weedy clumps, ponds, palm trees, under boards, holes in trees, under tree bark, or the bases of large-leaved plants like "elephant ears" and banana trees. Breeding occurs after the rainy season begins and requires only a temporary shallow pool of rainwater (Martin 1958; Duellman 1970; Wright and Wright 1949). This species would have no difficulty surviving on Cozumel.

The leptodactylid poses more of a problem, since the species represented by the one bone specimen cannot be identified. If, as seems very improbable, it is *Eleutherodactylus sp.*, the animal would deposit its eggs in terrestrial situations—moist crevices in cliffs or in a pit under a rock. A comparison of collected skeletal materials makes it more likely that the specimen is *Leptodactylus sp.* This particular genus produces foam nests in pockets in the ground, and when the next rain comes, the newly hatched larvae are washed into nearby pools to continue their development (Stebbins 1962). While *Leptodactylus labialis* is often found near small temporary pools, poorly drained hollows or even open cultivated fields, *L. melanonotus* frequents permanent water (Martin 1958). On Cozumel some permanent water sources exist in the form of *cenotes* (natural groundwater-fed wells in the limestone) and *cuevas con agua* (water trapped in grotto-like formations beneath an overhang). Whichever species of leptodactylid frog is represented could logically have fit Cozumel's environmental parameters.

It is possible that these amphibians are intrusive in the Cozumel sites and thus not contemporary with the cultural context. This is a common occurrence at many archaeological sites, although here the great numbers and widespread distribution make this improbable.

Cultural Patterns

In addition to environmental considerations, it is possible to reconstruct a cultural pattern of amphibian utilization on the island. More than 94 percent of the bones (or 73.7 percent of the MNIs) are from burials in four different sites (see Tables 4.3 and 4.4). The overwhelming majority of this material was excavated from ceremonial contexts, implying that frogs and toads were more than food sources. This is supported by the fact that nearly all parts of the body are present (see Table 4.5). If amphibians were being exploited as a common food source one would expect the elements present to consist only of hind-limb bones, since this is the major meat-bearing portion of a frog or toad. Obviously the Cozumel data do not yield such a pattern. Conversely, if the animals were being used whole, one would expect to find percentages of body parts very similar to the natural proportions of such elements in a live amphibian skeleton. Thus, if forelimbs characteristically account for 17.1 percent of the bones in an intact toad skeleton, approximately that proportion of the archaeological sample should also consist of forelimbs, if the animals were being used in articulated form. In general, this appears to be the case. Skull elements and vertebrae are underrepresented in the archaeological sample (by −12.2 percent and −5.2 percent, respectively) while all of the limb bones and pelvic elements are somewhat overrepresented (ranging from +1.3 percent to +7 percent). Preservation factors may be an influence here, since amphibian skull elements particularly, as well as vertebrae, tend to be paper-thin and very fragile. Amphibian limb bones are more durable and the long hollow tubes often can still be identified even if broken. This might explain why forelimbs, hindlimbs, and pelvic elements appear in slightly higher numbers than would be expected in the live animal. The most significantly overrepresented skeletal element is the femur (+7 percent), but this is not high enough to warrant any conclusions about frog legs being selected for consumption on Cozumel. Rather, the overall pattern seems to be one of whole-animal use, for whatever purpose.

At least 96.1 percent of the bones (or 76.3 percent of the individual animals) are from Late Postclassic period deposits (Table 4.6). If burials only are examined, the percentage of Late Postclassic material is 97.4 percent (numbers of bones) or 82.76 percent (MNIs). This may be partly due to the overall scarcity of non-Late Postclassic proveniences excavated on Cozumel. However, it is notable that even in those few early contexts which are represented by amphibian remains, the numbers of bones tend to be very low in each case, while most Late Postclassic

Table 4.3 Archaeological Context of Cozumel Amphibians

	NO. BONES	% OF TOTAL	MNI	% OF TOTAL
Bones from burial contexts	268	94.7	29	76.32
Bones from non-burial contexts	2	0.71	2	5.26
Indeterminate	13	4.59	7	18.42
Total	283	100.00	38	100.00

Table 4.4 Distribution of Cozumel Amphibians in Burial Contexts

SITE	BURIAL	SPECIES	NO. BONES	MNI	TIME PERIOD
C-15	31	Bufo sp.	1	1	Mixed-Early Postclassic to Late Postclassic
C-18	18	*Bufo marinus*	1	1	Pure Florescent (Terminal
C-18	18	*Bufo sp.*	1	1	Classic or Early Postclassic)
C-18	18	*Smilisca baudinii*	1	1	
C-31	39	*Bufo sp.*	1	1	Mixed-Pure Florescent to Late Postclassic
C-22	26	*Bufo sp.*	1	1	Late Postclassic
C-22	27	*Bufo marinus*	214	15	Late Postclassic
C-22	27	*Bufo sp.*	11	2	Late Postclassic
C-22	27	*? Leptodactylus sp.*	1	1	Late Postclassic
C-22	30	*Bufo sp.*	1	1	Late Postclassic
C-22	35	*Bufo marinus*	29	3	Late Postclassic
C-22	35	*Bufo sp.*	4	1	Late Postclassic
Total			268	29	

Table 4.5 Cozumel Amphibians:
Distribution of Skeletal Elements

SKELETAL ELEMENT	NO. BONES	%	% OF INTACT AMPHIB. SKELETON	% DISCREPANCY
Skull Elements[1]	30	10.6	22.8	− 12.2
Vertebrae[2]	50	17.7	22.9	− 5.2
Forelimb Bones[3]	64	22.6	17.1	+ 5.5
Pelvic Girdle[4]	48	17.0	14.3	+ 2.7
Thighs (Femora)	36	12.7	5.7	+ 7.0
Hind Limb Bones[5]	52	18.4	17.1	+ 1.3
Indeterminate	3	1.1	—	—
Total	283	100.1	99.9	—

[1]Includes only fronto-parietals, pterygoids, squamosals, and nasals.
[2]Includes fused sacra and trunk vertebrae, but no atlases or axes.
[3]Includes scapulae, humeri, and radio-ulnae.
[4]Includes urostyles, ilia, and ischia.
[5]Includes tibio-fibulae, astragali, and calcanea.

proveniences produce relatively large amounts of bone (Tables 4.4, 4.6). Preservation problems may be involved to some extent. The particular pattern of amphibian use seen on Cozumel occurs primarily in the Late Postclassic, but the existence of similar patterns in earlier time periods cannot be ruled out. Indeed, information available from earlier contexts at other Maya sites supports the conclusion that this same pattern was one of long standing.

Hallucinogenic Drug Use

It might seem curious that there are many more amphibian bones on Cozumel than in other Maya sites, primarily belonging to the large marine toad and occurring predominantly in human burials. The reasons for these occurrences may be revealed in Marlene Dobkin de Rios' paper "The Influence of Psychotropic Flora and Fauna on Maya Religion" (1974), later supported by Peter Furst (1976). Among other things, Dobkin de Rios employs the regular appearance of the frog/toad motif in the Maya archaeological record (especially in religious or ceremonial contexts) to hypothesize that marine toads were used for ceremonial hallucinogenic purposes. The Cozumel data provide additional support for this thesis.

A noticeable characteristic of toads in the genus *Bufo* is their large, elongated parotid glands, located roughly in the shoulder area of the animal. These glands are especially large and prominent in *Bufo marinus*.

Table 4.6   Time Periods of Cozumel Amphibians

TIME PERIOD	NO. BONES	%	MNI	%
Late Postclassic (Decadent)	272	96.1	29	76.3
Pure Florescent (Terminal Classic or Early Postclassic)	5	1.8	3	7.9
Mixed: mostly Modified Florescent (Early Postclassic) through Late Postclassic (Decadent)	1	0.35	1	2.6
Mixed: mostly Pure Florescent (Terminal Classic or Early Postclassic)	1	0.35	1	2.6
Mixed: mostly Pure Florescent through Late Postclassic	1	0.35	1	2.6
No Date	3	1.1	3	7.9
Total	283	100.05	38	99.9

The poison secreted in these glands is well known for its swift and powerful effects; even small doses of the venom, if ingested by dogs, birds, and other animals, cause immediate convulsions and usually death (Wright and Wright 1949). A description of human toad-poisoning victims is supplied by Dr. William Northcote in his 1770 medical textbook: ". . . he is seized with an asthmatic shortness of breath, vomiting, cold sweats, convulsions, fainting, and at length with death, if not timely remedied" (Wasson and Wasson 1957: 71).

The substance responsible for these physical reactions is bufotenin, chemically an indole alkaloid in the form of a tryptamine derivative: 5-hydroxy-N,N-dimethyltryptamine, or 5-OH-DMT (Schultes and Hofmann 1973). The substance was named bufotenin because it was first isolated from the skin glands of toads (*Bufo spp.*), although it was later found to occur in plants and other animals as well. Specifically, bufotenin was found to be a component of snuff powder prepared by Haitians from *Piptadenia peregrina* seeds, which the natives used in their religious ceremonies to produce mystical states of consciousness (LaBarre 1970; Szara 1970; Schultes and Hofmann 1973). In 1956 the hallucinogenic activity of bufotenin was reported by Fabing and Hawkins (1956), who had injected humans with the substance intravenously. Oddly enough, some later studies found no hallucinogenic activity at all, even with higher doses (Schultes and Hofmann 1973). Still, some pharmacologists group bufotenin with a number of other related chemical compounds (tryptamine derivatives) known to produce tremors in animals and which are definitely hallucinogenic in man—DMT, psilocybin, and LSD, for example (Rech and Moore 1971). It may be significant that these tryptamine derivatives are all structurally related to serotenin, a substance which accumulates in the brain of many warm-blooded animals, where it plays a role in the biochemistry of central nervous system regulation. These tryptamine structures in hallucinogens may also be biochemically important in the metabolism of psychic functions (Schultes and Hofmann 1973); the pharmacological properties of these psychoactive drugs, including bufotenin, may interact with the dynamic mechanisms of certain pathways in the brain.

While Dobkin de Rios asserts (1974: 148–49) that "bufotenin is a hallucinogenic drug which has dangerous cardiovascular effects in man and is usable only in low dosages," and LaBarre (1970: 146) calls it "a violently hallucinogenic drug," pharmacologists cannot agree on bufotenin's precise effects on the human body. The fact that later groups tested with injected bufotenin failed to exhibit hallucinogenic activity may be explained in several ways. One possibility is that the drug's effects on the first group tested were only a fluke. The power of suggestion might account for the sensations experienced by some people in the experiment. Another possibility is that the effects of the drug are highly individualistic; that is, only people with a specific type of chemical pathway in the brain would experience hallucinations, while others might merely become nauseous or unconscious. A third alternative is that injecting the drug into the bloodstream may not be the best way to observe its effects on humans; perhaps ingesting it or inhaling it produces the optimum effect. Significantly, Peter Furst (1976: 165) notes that animal poisons, including the venom of *B. marinus,* should not be equated with the botanical hallucinogens; "the massive assault on the system brought on by bufotenin-containing *Bufo* venom is of a very different order than the shift from one state of consciousness to another triggered by bufotenin-containing snuff." Perhaps we might more appropriately refer to this substance by more neutral terms such as "psychotropic," "psychoactive," or "psychogenic," thus avoiding the issue of hallucinations entirely.

Whether or not bufotenin actually is hallucinogenic in man, it is a poison which can cause paralysis, convulsions, and death in mammals that ingest it (Wright and Wright 1949). In the 1600s the Dominican friar Thomas Gage reported that the Pokomam Maya of Guatemala made a fermented ritual drink called *chicha,* "which certainly is the cause of many Indians' death, especially where they use the toad's poison with it" (J. E. S. Thompson 1958: 225). Venomous toads were apparently steeped in the fermented beverage to give it extra potency (Furst 1976). Significantly, Stanley J. Olsen (1978) mentions in the faunal report for the Maya site of Seibal that a partial marine toad *(Bufo marinus)* skeleton was discovered inside a Fine Orange pottery vessel in a terminal Late Classic burial. Originally, this vessel was described by the excavator, Gair Tourtellot, as pertaining "to the culture of the invaders of the Maya realm" (Olsen 1978), although more recent findings indicate that Fine Orange pottery is actually an imported trade ware from the Gulf Coast area of Mexico. The fact that the toad skeleton appears in this burial vessel at Seibal, therefore, may be interpreted as a Maya funerary practice which happened to include the use of imported pottery.

It is possible that this find represents a toad which was steeped in a fermented beverage used for ritual purposes—in this case, for the funeral ceremonies of an important individual. Pohl (1976) believes that its presence may imply pharmacological uses in curing rituals. At any rate, it is undeniably a marine toad found in a burial context—exactly as the majority of amphibians were found on Cozumel.

According to the Mayapán report (Pollock and Ray 1957), the skull and skeleton of a single marine toad were found in a sealed chamber containing two human burials. The bones of at least two other toads (both *Bufo valliceps*) were also found in this chamber, along with a large quantity of other faunal remains. The investigators felt they could not be certain which animal bones represented midden material (i.e., food remains) and which may have been offerings with the dead. Nevertheless, this does follow the pattern of toads being found in burial contexts. These are probably Postclassic in date, since the great majority of the Mayapán material seems to be from the thirteenth to the fifteenth centuries. The only other amphibian remains at Mayapán were two bones of a ranid frog found in an open shaft in the substructure of a temple. Pollock and Ray thought it probable that their presence was intrusive, but the frog may have been part of a ritual sacrifice when the temple was built or dedicated. Similarly, two toad bones *(Bufo sp.)* were excavated from pyramid fill at Altar de Sacrificios (Olsen 1972). Again, these could be intrusive, but they might represent part of the ceremonies involved in laying the cornerstone, so to speak, of a religious building. Finally, it is noteworthy that the single amphibian bone found at the site of Dzibilchaltun was the skull of a marine toad which occurred in an Early Period (Classic) burial (Wing and Steadman 1980).

The significance of the marine toad in Mesoamerica apparently predates the Maya. At the Olmec ceremonial site of San Lorenzo in Veracruz, Michael Coe (1971) found an abundant quantity of *Bufo marinus* remains in middens dating to 1250–900 B.C. which he believes may indicate possible hallucinogenic use of the animal. Muriel Porter Weaver (1972: 50) also refers to the Olmecs' seeming predilection for marine toads and mentions that the consumption of *Bufo marinus* flesh produces hallucinations. Peter Furst believes that these toads at San Lorenzo were not ordinary food items, in view of their high poison content and their apparent sacred stature in Middle American religion. He concludes that "as animal manifestation of the Earth Mother, the toad could well have entered into magico-religious inebriation—as much, perhaps, for symbolic as for pharmacological considerations." (1976: 161). The Cozumel evidence indicates that the same may have been true for the Maya. Even today, preparations of *Bufo marinus* poison are still included in the pharmacopoeias of some *curanderos* (native curers) in Veracruz. Furst (1976) describes the process by which the toad is gently irritated to make it release the poison from its parotid glands. The poison is collected in small bowls and processed with secret techniques passed down through generations of *curanderos*. After repeated treatment over fire to remove or reduce the harmful elements, the remaining substance is hardened and rolled into pills for later use—one of the purposes being love magic.

According to Furst, these surviving practices help to explain the appearance of small, toad-shaped effigy bowls found in archaeological sites in Veracruz, adjacent areas of southeastern Mexico and Guatemala. It seems significant that the parotid glands containing the poison were customarily emphasized on these toad effigies by the prehistoric potters. Similarly, a well-known monumental Aztec basalt sculpture of a toad in the National Museum of Anthropology, Mexico City also emphasizes these parotid glands. At least one example of these "toad bowls" appears in a high-status Preclassic burial in Tomb I, Mound E-III-3 at Kaminaljuyu, Guatemala, in addition to several other vessels with quadrupedal figures resembling toads or frogs, plus several small toad or frog mortars of gray stone (Shook and Kidder 1952). Dobkin de Rios (1974: 150) also mentions the excavation of toad bowls and sculptures very similar to the Kaminaljuyu finds from Middle and Late Preclassic contexts in the El Trapiche Mound group in Chalchuapa, El Salvador, as well as a large stone frog/toad effigy of probable Late Preclassic date. However, Thompson (1974: 160) asserts that these toads with prominent poison glands rarely appear on wares other than plumbate pottery, the makers of which were probably not Maya. He argues that these potters commonly represented Mexican, not Mayan, deities on their plumbate vessels. Nevertheless, this may not necessarily present any obstacle to the present argument if one chooses to view Mesoamerican cultures and their religions as a continuum in time. That is, the appearance of toad bones in Late Postclassic Maya burials may merely represent the end of a long sequence of ancient religious practices which began in the Preclassic period with toad bowls and effigies inserted in burials. Thompson himself (1954) states that it is often difficult, if not impossible, to separate Mexican from Mayan religious elements. Besides, the toad bowls at least are evidently regarded as Mayan vessels, not Mexican, and one scholar has speculated that they could have been used to hold the toad's venomous exudate (Furst 1974: 154).

Religious Symbolism

The toad as a religious symbol is part of a widespread mythic complex in both North and South America in which the toad is regarded as the animal manifestation of a dualistic Earth Mother Goddess, at once destroyer and creator of life (Furst 1976). Sometimes the toad is the earth, and from her body supposedly sprouted the first food plants—in Mexico, maize. She also represents the mythological teacher of hunting skills and magic arts. In the complex Aztec cosmological scheme, for example, the toad being is Tlaltecuhtli, guardian of the earth, as well as a monstrous, devouring form. Furst asserts that the toad's being at once impressively fertile and cannibalistic (often feeding on smaller members of the same or related species, including offspring) must have reinforced or perhaps inspired its role as the Great Earth Mother. Toads also display one of the most dramatic metamorphoses of the entire animal kingdom: from aquatic, gill-breathing fishlike vegetarians into largely terrestrial, carnivorous quadrupeds, some of them capable of killing with powerful poisons. The toad thus appears to embody some of the principles known to be basic to American Indian thought: the ideas of transformation, dualism or complementary opposites, and the cycle of death and regeneration (Furst 1976).

In Maya religion, specifically, an important function of frogs or toads (it is not clear which) was as attendants and musicians of the Chacs, the Yucatec rain gods. The four Chacs are found in art representations attended by what Thompson asserts (1954: 230) are small frogs whose croaking announces rain. Since Chac was a man of great stature who taught agriculture and whom the Indians held to be the god of bread and water, thunder and lightning, the fact that the presence of frogs or toads announces rain forms a natural association with this god (Thompson 1970: 285). A study of the animal figures in the Maya codices (Tozzer and Allen 1910) shows that it is usually not clear whether the artist meant to portray frogs or toads. Tozzer and Allen use the terms interchangeably, since they believe it is impossible to know from the drawings which of these rain-association amphibians is depicted. These animals are represented in the Madrid Codex by stout tailless bodies, flattened heads, and toothless mouths. In some figures, it appears that marine toads are intended; the great breadth of the head and mouth plus the short, inflated body combine to produce a very toadlike appearance. Another figure is likely a frog—its legs are froglike, and it appears to be swimming in water. Frog in Maya is *uo*, also the name of the second month of the Maya year. The beginning of the month *uo* is August 5, under the Gregorian calendar, which is the height of the rainy season in the Maya area—the time when most amphibians breed.

Other instances of the amphibian motif appear in the Madrid Manuscript, which contains representations of tree frogs (family Hylidae), noted for their loud voices during the rainy season when they seek out pools of water in which to breed. The conspicuousness of these frogs at the beginning of the rainy season no doubt accounts for their importance in the Maya economy, especially since the tree-toad gods are often found associated with agriculture and the sowing of grain, which occurs at the beginning of the rainy season (Tozzer and Allen 1910: 310). It has been noted (Schellhas 1904: 39) that the frog god, pictured with the club-shaped fingers of a frog, is shown in the Madrid Codex sowing seed and making furrows with a planting stick. Interestingly, the Tablet of the Palace in Palenque contains a glyph detail showing the figure of a toad, which Greene (1967) interprets as representing the month *uo*. One of the major attributes of this sculpture, which she dates at approximately A.D. 645, is the poison gland represented by three circles at the back of its head.

5. Reptiles

THE COZUMEL REPTILES include turtles, iguanids, and crocodiles (see Table 5.1) and represent numerically the third most important class of animals in the sample. Information obtained from each of these reptile groups includes dietary preferences, food preparation practices, the skeletal elements recovered, the cultural contexts in which they were found, their possible ceremonial uses, and their distribution by site and by time period.

Turtles

Turtles are by far the most numerically significant group of reptiles found in the Cozumel sites. These animals constitute over 48 percent of all reptile bones, or nearly 60 percent of the MNIs (see Table 5.2). At least five different species are represented here, all of which inhabit water to varying degrees.

The box and freshwater turtles (Emydidae) are clearly predominant (see Table 5.3). Over three-fourths of the Cozumel turtles belong to this family, or approximately 72 percent of the MNIs. Emydids are unspecialized, flat-shelled, often brightly colored turtles which generally inhabit freshwaters and marshes (Pritchard 1967; Pope 1964). The majority of the emydids were identified as *Geomyda pulcherrima* (or *Geomyda cf. G. pulcherrima*). This species accounts for almost 45 percent of all Cozumel turtle elements, or more than 37 percent of the MNIs (see Table 5.4). This turtle is probably the one Wright (1970: 103) mentions as commonly seen on Cozumel in modern times; it is referred to by the natives as *tortuga de caja* (box tortoise). None of the members of the genus *Geomyda* is purely terrestrial or aquatic. Most have an average shell length of eight to nine inches, and they appear to be omnivorous (Pope 1964: 98). The only other emydid species identified from these sites, *Pseudemys scripta*, is an aquatic turtle with a shell size ranging

Table 5.1 Cozumel Reptiles: Taxonomic List

Class: Reptilia
  Order Squamata (lizards and snakes)
    Suborder Sauria (lizards)
      Family Iguanidae (iguanids)
        Anolis sp. (anoles)
        Ctenosaura similis (rock or false iguana)
        ? *C. similis* (rock or false iguana)
        Iguana iguana (green or common iguana)
        ? *I. iguana* (green or common iguana)
        Sceloporus sp. (spiny lizards)
  Order Crocodilia (crocodiles and alligators)
    Family Crocodylidae (crocodiles)
      Crocodylus sp.
      Crocodylus cf. C. acutus (American crocodile)
  Order Testudines (turtles)
    Family Kinosternidae (mud and musk turtles)
      Kinosternon cruentatum (red-spotted mud turtle)
      ? *K. cruentatum* (red-spotted mud turtle)
    Family Chelydridae (snapping turtles)
      Chelydra serpentina (common snapping turtle)
    Family Emydidae (box and freshwater turtles)
      Pseudemys scripta
      ? *P. scripta*
      Geomyda pulcherrima
      ? *G. pulcherrima*
    Family Cheloniidae (sea turtles)

Table 5.2 Cozumel Reptiles

TAXON	NO. BONES	%	MNI	%
Turtles	1,842	48.03	340	58.12
Iguanids	1,577	41.12	231	39.49
Crocodiles	35	0.91	14	2.39
Indeterminate Reptile bones*	381	9.93	—	—
Total	3,835	99.99	585	100.00

*Includes one ? reptile and one ? large reptile fragments.

Table 5.3 Cozumel Turtles: Distribution by Family

FAMILY	NO. BONES	%	MNI	%
Kinosternidae (mud and musk turtles)	357	19.38	83	24.41
Chelydridae (snapping turtles)	1	0.05	1	0.29
Emydidae (box and freshwater turtles)	1,404	76.22	245	72.06
Cheloniidae (sea turtles)	19	1.03	1	3.24
Testudines (turtles)	61	3.31	—	—
Total	1,842	99.99	340	100.00

up to several inches larger than that of *Geomyda* (at least in the Cozumel sample). This species appears to be much less important here, representing less than 9 percent of all turtles or nearly 13 percent of the MNIs (Table 5.4). Also found were a large number of shell fragments which could only be assigned to the family level (Emydidae). Most of these (372) could represent either *Geomyda* or *Pseudemys*, but some elements (43) were designated as large emydids because they approached the generally larger size range of *Pseudemys*.

The mud and musk turtles (Kinosternidae) are the next most important family, constituting over 19 percent of all turtle elements or more than 24 percent of the MNIs (Tables 5.3 and 5.4). All of these specimens were identified as *Kinosternon cruentatum* (or as ? *K. cruentatum*). These probably belong to the subspecies *K. cruentatum consors*, which

Table 5.4 Cozumel Turtles: Distribution of Species

TAXON	NO. BONES	%		MNI	%
Testudines	61	3.31		—	—
Kinosternon cruentatum	350	19.00	19.38	83	24.41
? *K. cruentatum*	7	0.38		—	—
Chelydra serpentina	1	0.05		1	0.29
Emydidae	372	20.20		60	17.65
Large emydidae	43	2.33		14	4.12
Pseudemys scripta	146	7.93	8.80	44	12.94
? *P. scripta*	16	0.87		—	—
Geomyda pulcherrima	799	43.38	44.90	127	37.35
? *G. pulcherrima*	28	1.52		—	—
Cheloniidae	16	0.87	1.03	11	3.24
? Cheloniidae	3	0.16		—	—
Total	1,842	100.00		340	100.00

has been reported in the Yucatán and specifically on Cozumel as well (Pritchard 1967). (The necessary comparative material was not available to confirm this.) As with all the Central and South American members of this family, the life history and habits of *K. cruentatum* are almost completely unknown (Pritchard 1967: 33). However, all kinosternids have four glands which open directly to the exterior at the edges of the shell and can produce a distinct and unpleasant odor (Pope 1964). Perhaps this characteristic, though not as pronounced in the mud turtles *(Kinosternon spp.)* as in the musk turtles *(Sternotherus spp.),* accounts for the lower numbers of *K. cruentatum* here as compared with the emydids. Still, Pope (1964: 70) cites Dr. Archie Carr in observing that the modern Miskito Indians of Nicaragua "roast a species of *Kinosternon* and eat it with relish." There is evidence to suggest similar treatment of this particular turtle by the Cozumel Maya.

Sea turtles (Cheloniidae) are the third most important family of turtles present in the Cozumel material. The few elements found here constitute only about 1 percent of all turtle remains, or a mere 3.24 percent of the MNIs (Tables 5.3, 5.4), even though the southeastern coast of Cozumel is a habitual breeding and living ground for the green turtle *(Chelonia mydas).* This area provides a rich bank of marine grasses and algae, plants upon which the green turtle grazes extensively (Pritchard 1967). This is the preferred soup turtle, whose flesh is reknowned for its flavor (Pope 1964). (In fact, a turtle meat-packing plant was in operation on Cozumel for some years [Wright 1970].) Sea turtle eggs are also a staple item in some areas of Latin America, and the shell has been reported to form the basis for a soup (Gans 1975). Since the shell of sea turtles is relatively poorly constructed and much less dense than that of other turtles, cooking practices may have destroyed most of the archaeological evidence for use of these turtles. If the Cozumel natives preferred the eggs of the green turtle, this would leave few traces in a prehistoric site. Another alternative is that eating sea turtle was taboo despite the animal's abundance in the area.

Although the few recovered fragmentary elements could not be identified beyond the family level, they probably belong to the green turtle. Two other sea turtles present in the general area cannot be entirely ruled out: the loggerhead *(Caretta caretta)* and the hawksbill *(Eretmochelys imbricata),* the latter being the major source of tortoise shell in recent times. Landa (in Tozzer 1941: 192) mentions sea turtles with shells "larger than large shields," referring to them as having plenty of flesh and being good to eat. Unfortunately, this description does not allow one to distinguish the species under discussion.

The last turtle appearing in this material is the common snapping turtle *(Chelydra serpentina),* of which only a single shell fragment is present (Tables 5.3, 5.4). This snapper prefers ponds with muddy bottoms and banks. An omnivore, it subsists on aquatic animals and plants as well as carrion. On land, this turtle (which can weigh up to sixty or seventy pounds) is aggressive, often striking at anything within reach (Pope 1964; Gans 1975; Pritchard 1967). Perhaps this behavior accounts for its scarcity in the Cozumel sample.

Almost 98 percent of the skeletal elements are portions of the upper or lower shell (Table 5.5). This is to be expected, since a turtle skeleton consists mostly of shell elements. Significantly, however, not a single skull fragment appeared in this sample, and limb bones and pelvic elements are poorly represented (less than 2 percent). Preservation factors may be at work here, or these elements may have been discarded elsewhere during food preparation. An unidentified turtle beak, erroneously removed from the collection in Mexico as an artifact, is evidently from one of the non-marine species and is not included here. That carapace (upper shell) elements greatly outnumber those of the plastron (lower shell) is normal, given the much greater number of separate bones which make up the former.

There is a fairly even distribution of turtle species over most of the island (Table 5.6), especially of those with larger sample sizes (emydids and kinosternids). The sea turtles and snapping turtle occur in such low numbers that their appearance in only a few sites cannot be considered significant.

Examination of the cultural contexts in which turtles appear (Table 5.7) indicates that those in burials and ceremonial/administrative contexts predominate. However, a significant proportion also occurs in housemounds, and enough turtles come from proveniences of unknown cultural significance that the percentages of elite and housemound turtles may actually be nearly equal. In any case, the exploitation of turtles on Cozumel appears to have been a widespread cultural pattern,

Table 5.5   Distribution of Turtle Elements

ELEMENT	NO. BONES	%	
All skull elements	—	—	
Limb bones and pelvic girdle elements[1]	36	1.95	
Plastron elements[2]	686	37.24	
Carapace elements[3]	1,101	59.77	97.99
Indeterminate turtle shell fragments	18	0.98	
Indeterminate	1	0.05	
Total	1,842	99.99	

[1]Includes hyoid, scapulae, humeri, ulnae, ilia, ischia, pubes and indeterminate limb bones.
[2]Includes all elements of the lower shell: epiplastra, hyoplastra, xiphiplastra, entoplastra, and indeterminate plastron fragments.
[3]Includes all elements of the upper shell: peripherals, nuchals (proneurals), neurals, pleurals, pygals, and suprapygals.

Table 5.6 Distribution of Turtles by Site

SITE	TAXON	NO. BONES	MNI
C-2	Emydidae	3	2
C-13	*Kinosternon cruentatum*	2	2
	Chelydra serpentina	1	1
	Emydidae	19	2
	Large emydidae	6	1
	Pseudemys scripta	2	2
	Geomyda pulcherrima	31	5
	Cheloniidae	2	1
	? Cheloniidae	1	—
Subtotal		64	14
C-15	? *K. cruentatum*	1	—
	Emydidae	14	1
	Geomyda pulcherrima	23	2
Subtotal		38	3
C-18	Testudines	1	—
	Kinosternon cruentatum	· 125	23
	? *K. cruentatum*	6	—
	Emydidae	66	14
	Large emydidae	9	3
	Pseudemys scripta	106	18
	? *P. scripta*	9	—
	Geomyda pulcherrima	77	24
	? *G. pulcherrima*	5	—
	? Cheloniidae	1	—
Subtotal		421	82
C-22	Testudines	39	—
	Kinosternon cruentatum	158	43
	Emydidae	166	31
	Large emydidae	23	7
	Pseudemys scripta	21	13
	? *P. scripta*	6	—
	Geomyda pulcherrima	424	50
	? *G. pulcherrima*	16	—
	Cheloniidae	8	6
	? Cheloniidae	1	—
Subtotal		862	150
C-25	Testudines	4	—
	Kinosternon cruentatum	43	10
	Emydidae	97	8
	Pseudemys scripta	12	9
	? *P. scripta*	1	—
	Geomyda pulcherrima	218	38
	? *G. pulcherrima*	7	—
	Cheloniidae	6	4
Subtotal		388	69

Table 5.6   Distribution of Turtles by Site (continued)

SITE	TAXON	NO. BONES	MNI
C-27	Testudines	1	—
	Kinosternon cruentatum	6	3
	Emydidae	7	3
	Large emydidae	3	2
	Pseudemys scripta	5	2
	Geomyda pulcherrima	18	7
Subtotal		40	17
C-31	Kinosternon cruentatum	16	2
	Large emydidae	2	1
	Geomyda pulcherrima	8	1
Subtotal		26	4
Total		1,842	340

regardless of social class. Pollock and Ray (1957: 648) note that the majority of the turtle remains at Mayapán were found in dwellings and that relatively few were associated with ceremonial buildings.

Turtles evidently played a role in the ceremonial life of the Maya. Scholars have mentioned these reptiles' being sacrificed, their appearance in the Maya Codices in association with certain constellations and as a hieroglyph for the seventeenth Maya month, their representation in ceremonial architecture and in animal effigy figures, and the use of turtle carapaces as musical instruments (Tozzer 1941: 114; Tozzer and Allen 1910; Schellhas 1904; Pollock and Ray 1957).

The majority of these turtles have been dated to the Postclassic, Late Postclassic, or historic periods; these account for over 68 percent of the turtle elements, or about 67 percent of the MNIs (Table 5.8). In contrast, only a little over 17 percent of the material (or approximately 7 percent of the MNIs) was excavated from proveniences dated earlier than the Postclassic. Material from undated contexts is insufficient to affect this pattern significantly.

That the use of turtles for food by the Maya was very common is implied by their frequent occurrence at such sites as Cancún, Mayapán, Altar de Sacrificios, Seibal, Dzibilchaltun, Lubaantun, Macanche, Flores, and Tikal. The seventeenth-century Dominican friar Thomas Gage mentioned that the Maya ate many water and land tortoises (J. E. S. Thompson 1958); Landa also refers to the tasty flesh of sea turtles (in Tozzer 1941: 192). Wing (1974: 187) cites Oviedo's description of capturing sea turtles—by dragnets, or, more often, by hand when the turtles are beached. The Cozumel turtles include 1,764 elements which were either burned or heat-darkened; these represent 95.77 percent of all turtle elements. This suggests that turtles were roasted in their shells directly over a fire or hot coals before eating. All eight sites where

Table 5.7   **Distribution of Turtles by Provenience**

PROVENIENCE	NO. BONES	%	MNI	%
Burials and ceremonial/ administrative contexts	752	40.83	114	33.53
Housemounds	492	26.71	82	24.12
Other*	598	32.46	144	42.35
Total	1,842	100.00	340	100.00

*These are proveniences not definitely assigned to either one of the above contexts. It is suspected, however, that many of these represent housemounds or domestic refuse.

turtles appear contain a high porportion of these heat-affected elements, and every species in the sample shows the same treatment. In her study of five Maya sites, Pohl (1976: 272) notes that the carapaces of several turtle species were often discolored and burned, and that turtles were still being roasted in the Petén in the late 1970s.

In addition, thirty-six shell fragments exhibited evidence of cultural modification. Thirty (from four different sites) had been cut or shaped in some manner, two (from San Gervasio, C-22) had holes drilled in them, three (from C-22) had been polished, and one (from C-22) had been incised or carved. All turtle species in the sample except the snapping turtle were represented by these modified elements. (Phillips [1979] refers to another shell fragment, questionably turtle, which was thought to have been culturally modified. His examination of the specimen in Mexico showed otherwise, so it is not included here.) The Mayapán site also produced turtle artifacts, one a plastron fragment which had been cut, the other a nearly complete box turtle shell with holes drilled at the front ends of both the carapace and plastron (Pollock and Ray 1957). Determining the context in which the Cozumel artifacts would have been used is difficult, since they are so fragmentary as to be unrecognizable. Possibly some were employed in ceremonial proceedings, since these reptiles did hold religious significance for the Maya.

Another twenty turtle elements (from three sites) had been either rodent-gnawed or carnivore-chewed. Finally, a single hypoplastron *(Kinosternon cruentatum)* excavated from a housemound at San Gervasio (C-22) showed evidence of pathological deformation.

Iguanids

Iguanids (Iguanidae) are second to turtles in numerical importance among Cozumel reptiles. This family of lizards includes more than 41 percent of the reptile bones, or almost 40 percent of the MNIs (Table

Table 5.8 Time Periods of Cozumel Turtles

TIME PERIOD	NO. BONES	%		MNI	%	
Late Postclassic and Historic	1,105	59.99	} 68.46	202	59.41	} 67.06
Postclassic	156	8.47		26	7.65	
Pre-Postclassic	263	14.28	} 17.21	18	5.29	} 7.06
Pure Florescent	54	2.93		6	1.76	
No Date	264	14.33		88	25.88	
Total	1,842	100.00		340	99.99	

5.2). Since many of the skeletal elements of the large iguanid lizards are not very diagnostic, the majority of this material could only be identified to the family level. These account for almost 68 percent of all iguanids or slightly more than 44 percent of the MNIs (Table 5.9).

Of those which could be determined further, the rock or false iguana (*Ctenosaura similis*) was clearly predominant, representing more than 25 percent of all iguanid bones, or nearly 44 percent of the MNIs (Table 5.9). Most of this large lizard's usual two- to four-foot length is tail (Wright 1970; Smith 1946; Minton and Minton 1973). This thick, fleshy tail is especially treasured for food in Central America, which may explain why most of the ctenosaurs in the Cozumel sample represent very large individuals—their longer tails would have provided more meat. This herbivorous lizard, also known as the black or spiny-tailed iguana, is mainly terrestrial. It habitually suns itself on rock fences and is very abundant around Mayan temples and pyramids, trees near ruins, and crevices among rocks (Minton and Minton 1973; Gaige 1936). Thus, this species would have been easily available to the inhabitants of Cozumel. Ctenosaurs may also have been preferred over other lizards because their meat is entirely white, a characteristic valued by the present-day Maya in south coastal Guatemala (Coe and Flannery 1967). Fr. Thomas Gage wrote that land iguanas (probably referring to ctenosaurs) run fast, climb trees like squirrels, and breed in the roots of trees or in stone walls. He also commented, "The sight of them is enough to affright one. Yet when they are dressed and stewed in broth with a little spice, they make a dainty broth, and eat also as white as a rabbit" (J. E. S. Thompson 1958: 224).

The common or green iguana (*Iguana iguana*) is second in importance among iguanids in the sample. This species accounts for less than 5 percent of the bones and under 11 percent of the MNIs. (Table 5.9) The green iguana is the largest lizard in the Americas, having been known to reach a 6-foot 7-inch length in the tropics (Gans 1975: 58); a

Table 5.9   Cozumel Iguanids: Distribution of Species

TAXON	NO. BONES	%	MNI	%
Large Iguanidae	1,065	67.53	102	44.16
? large Iguanidae	1	0.06	—	—
Anolis sp.	3	0.19	2	0.87
Ctenosaura similis	400	25.36	101	43.72
? *C. similis*	18	1.14	—	—
Iguana iguana	77	4.88	25	10.82
? *I. iguana*	12	0.76	—	—
Sceloporus sp.	1	0.06	1	0.43
Total	1,577	99.98	231	100.00

6½-foot iguana has a tail 5 feet long. However, the prospect of obtaining a fair amount of delectable tail meat may have been offset by the difficulty in capturing these lizards. Green iguanas, primarily arboreal creatures, are also excellent swimmers and will often jump 18 to 20 feet into the water from their perches in high trees along water courses. In some tropical forests, these iguanas climb to heights of 40 to 50 feet in the trees (Gans 1975; Pope 1964). The green iguana is considered a delicacy in many parts of Latin America, both for its eggs and its meat; in fact, it is sometimes called *gallina de palo* (chicken of the tree) (Minton and Minton 1973). During the lizards' most active period in the late afternoon,Guatemalan Indians in canoes often attempt to stun them with rocks or sticks thrown into the trees overhanging riverbanks (Coe and Flannery 1967). Bishop Landa mentions that the Maya "fish for them with slip knots fastened up in the trees and in their holes," referring to the use of snare traps (Tozzer 1941: 191). The egg-laying season (around March), when the females descend from their trees to the ground, is one of the best times to capture green iguanas, and the natives in Guatemala pursue the lizards intensely with dogs in hopes of obtaining the sixty to eighty eggs an adult female can lay (Coe and Flannery 1967; McBryde 1947). As Pohl (1976: 235) points out, "iguana eggs are exceptionally high in calcium and vitimin A, and they have a high caloric value." Mexican Indians also claim that iguana meat is most flavorful in March and April. This lizard can be kept alive a long time (Bishop Landa says from twenty to thirty days) without food or water as long as it is not overheated, and thus represents a convenient source of meat in the tropics (Minton and Minton 1973). The relative scarcity of this species in the Cozumel sites may reflect a combination of several factors: difficulty of capture (when compared with the easily available ctenosaurs), preference for the all-white ctenosaur meat, and use primarily of green iguana eggs rather than meat.

The anoles, a very large and complex genus of small- to medium-sized lizards (seven-inch maximum), are mainly arboreal and can change color rapidly (Smith 1946; Gans 1975; Pope 1964). In certain areas they frequent human habitations, which probably explains the presence of the three *Anolis sp.* specimens (representing two individuals) at the site of San Gervasio (Table 5.9). These lizards may have been consumed, but such a low number of remains indicates that they are intrusive.

The single spiny lizard *(Sceloporus sp.)* specimen, also found at San Gervasio, is probably intrusive as well (Table 5.9). This genus generally inhabits rocks, trees, fence posts, and walls of old buildings (Pope 1964; Wright 1970), a lifestyle which could easily account for its appearance in the present sample.

Vertebrae account for the majority of all iguanid skeletal elements present (Table 5.10). Since these lizards are mostly tail, one would expect to find more vertebrae than other elements. Similar results might also

Table 5.10   Skeletal Elements of Cozumel Iguanids

SKELETAL ELEMENT	NO. BONES	%	
Skull elements[1]	170	10.78	21.18
Mandibles, maxillae, and dentaries	164	10.40	
Major limb bones[2]	313	19.85	
Foot and toe bones (including claws)	102	6.47	
Vertebrae[3]	640	40.58	
Miscellaneous[4]	161	10.21	
Indeterminate	27	1.71	
Total	1,577	100.00	

[1]Includes premaxillae, skulls, occipital condyles and complexes, frontals, exoccipitals, prefrontals, parietals, quadrates, palatines, pterygoids, jugals, and postorbitals.
[2]Includes humeri, radii, ulnae, femora, tibiae, and fibulae.
[3]Includes axes, caudals, sacrals, presacrals, and chevrons.
[4]Includes ribs, scapulae, clavicles, interclavicles, innominates, ilia, ischia, and pubes.

occur if the tail portion were selected for use and other body parts discarded elsewhere. However, that a substantial proportion of the sample consists of skull elements, mandibles and maxillae (over 21 percent), and major limb bones (nearly 20 percent), and that all other body parts are also present, indicates use of the whole animal. The limb bones, especially, would contain a fair amount of meat; many iguanids present here have legs the size of domestic chickens.

Table 5.11 presents the distribution of iguanids by site. The two species considered to be intrusive, *Sceloporus sp.* and *Anolis sp.* are present only at San Gervasio (C-22). Ctenosaurs appear in every site. In general, the larger the sample size at a given site, the more likely bones of the relatively scarce *Iguana iguana* were to occur.

The majority of iguanids are found in burials and ceremonial contexts rather than housemounds (Table 5.12). This same trend was observed for the overwhelming majority of the more than 2,000 iguanid bones excavated at Mayapán (Pollock and Ray 1957). As the authors of that report have noted, the burrowing nature of iguanids may be responsible to some degree for this distribution pattern. However, the very great percentage of heat-affected elements present in the Cozumel sites contravenes the idea that a significant portion of these animals are intrusive in the burials and ceremonial rubble where they were found. A substantial amount of material occurs in proveniences about which the cultural context is unknown, and this could modify these results somewhat (see Table 5.12), especially if many of the unknown proveniences were actually housemounds. Still, this would not negate the fact that a large number of iguanids were found in ceremonial/ad-

Table 5.11 Distribution of Iguanids by Site

SITE	TAXON	NO. BONES	MNI
C-2	Iguanidae	5	3
	Ctenosaura similis	1	1
Subtotal		**6**	**4**
C-12	Iguanidae	2	2
	Ctenosaura similis	7	2
	? *C. similis*	2	—
Subtotal		**11**	**4**
C-13	Iguanidae	3	2
	Ctenosaura similis	1	1
	? *C. similis*	1	—
Subtotal		**5**	**3**
C-15	Iguanidae	120	3
	Ctenosaura similis	8	2
	? *C. similis*	3	—
	Iguana iguana	19	2
Subtotal		**150**	**7**
C-18	Iguanidae	173	21
	Ctenosaura similis	64	24
	? *C. similis*	5	—
	Iguana iguana	34	7
	? *I. iguana*	5	—
Subtotal		**281**	**52**
C-22	Iguanidae	673	49
	? Iguanidae	1	—
	Anolis sp.	3	2
	Ctenosaura similis	231	41
	? *C. similis*	3	—
	Iguana iguana	16	10
	? *I. iguana*	6	—
	Sceloporus sp.	1	1
Subtotal		**934**	**103**
C-25	Iguanidae	47	17
	Ctenosaura similis	72	24
	? *C. similis*	2	—
	Iguana iguana	5	5
	? *I. iguana*	1	—
Subtotal		**127**	**46**
C-27	Iguanidae	6	3
	Ctenosaura similis	3	2
	? *C. similis*	1	—
	Iguana iguana	3	1
Subtotal		**13**	**6**
C-31	Iguanidae	36	2
	Ctenosaura similis	13	4
	? *C. similis*	1	—
Subtotal		**50**	**6**
Total		1,577	231

Table 5.12   Distribution of Iguanids by Provenience

PROVENIENCE	NO. BONES	%	MNI	%
Burials and ceremonial/ administrative contexts	1,141	72.35	89	38.53
Housemounds	73	4.63	29	12.55
Other*	363	23.02	113	48.92
Total	1,577	100.00	231	100.00

*These are proveniences not definitely assigned to either one of the above contexts, although it is suspected that many of these represent housemounds or domestic refuse.

ministrative contexts. That iguanids did have considerable importance in Mayan religion is well documented. According to Landa, they were used extensively as sacrifices, as an alternative food source when religious rules otherwise forbade meat consumption, and also in medicine (Tozzer 1941: 122, 148, 154, 164, 191). Iguanids appear in the Maya Codices almost exclusively as ceremonial offerings (Tozzer and Allen 1910: 318).

Nearly 65 percent of iguanid elements (almost 69 percent of the MNIs) have been dated to the Postclassic, Late Postclassic, and historic periods (Table 5.13). Less than 9 percent of the bones, or about 8 percent of the MNIs, are from periods earlier than the Postclassic. The relatively small amount of undated material is not sufficient to affect the general pattern significantly. The increased use of iguanids by the Maya in the Postclassic, particularly the Late Postclassic, may represent a wider pattern than just on Cozumel; the huge quantities of iguanid remains at Mayapán have also been dated primarily to the Late Postclassic (Pollock and Ray 1957). In contrast, a survey of other Maya sites (especially those with earlier time periods) produces very few iguanids.

A total of 168 elements (distributed over four sites) were immature, including nine bones which were fetal to very immature. This represented only 10.65 percent of all iguanid elements, which indicates a preference for the adult animals. Very likely, this resulted from a desire for the greatest meat yield; most of the individuals in the Cozumel sample (both ctenosaurs and iguanas) were very large adult animals.

Significantly, 1,100 elements (69.75 percent of all iguanids) were burned or heat-darkened. Many of the animals apparently were roasted over a direct flame before being eaten or offered in sacrifice.

No evidence of cultural modification or butchering was found on any of these lizards. Carnivore-chewed and rodent-gnawed elements accounted for only 5.77 percent (91) of all iguanid bones from eight sites.

The number of pathologies was relatively high compared to all the other animal species in the Cozumel sites. Altogether there were twelve

Table 5.13 Time Periods of Cozumel Iguanids

TIME PERIOD	NO. BONES	%		MNI	%	
Late Postclassic and Historic	980	62.14		145	62.77	68.83
Postclassic	38	2.41	64.55	14	6.06	
Pre-Postclassic	35	2.22		8	3.46	
Pure Florescent	97	6.15	8.56	9	3.90	8.22
Terminal Classic	2	0.13		1	0.43	
Early Period (Classic)	1	0.06		1	0.43	
No Date	424	26.89		53	22.94	
Total	1,577	100.00		231	99.99	

such specimens among the iguanids, only two of which appeared to be congenital bone deformations. These were a matched pair of ribs (left and right) from El Cedral (C-15) with an abnormal swelling at their articular ends. The other ten (from six sites) represent mostly limb bones, all of which had been broken and rehealed before death. These included five tibias, two radii, one ulna, one indeterminate longbone shaft, and one ilium. Observation of iguanid behavior during the archaelogical fieldwork on Cozumel leads to the conclusion that at least some of these lizards (probably ctenosaurs) are clumsy and ill-suited to climbing in trees. Dr. William L. Rathje reports seeing iguanids fall awkwardly out of trees many times, almost hitting the people working below. It may be significant that none of the pathological bones was identified as *Iguana iguana*, the species whose habits are primarily arboreal and which should therefore be adept at balancing in trees. Four of the broken and rehealed bones are definitely ctenosaurs (which are primarily terrestrial), while the remainder were identified only to the family level (Iguanidae). An alternative explanation can be offered, however. Coe and Flannery (1967) refer to the Guatemalan Indian practice of tying together the feet of captured iguanas and keeping the lizards in their houses until selling or eating them. If the Cozumel Maya also did this, some of the animals might have sustained broken limbs while struggling to escape. They might also have been injured during capture (especially if caught in snare-traps), or their captors might even have broken the lizards' legs deliberately in order to prevent escape. If so, the fact that the bones are rehealed would imply that the iguanas were kept alive for quite a long time before being killed and eaten.

Crocodiles

Crocodiles rank a distant third in numerical importance among the identified reptiles. The fourteen individuals (thirty-five bones) which appear in these sites represent less than 1 percent of all reptile bones, or fewer than 3 percent of the MNIs (Table 5.2).

Probably only one species, the American crocodile *(Crocodylus acutus)*, is present in the sample. This is the most widespread crocodile in Latin and South America, where it is distributed over the lowlands, particularly on the coasts (Stuart 1964). Morelet's crocodile *(Crocodylus moreleti)* is a more inland species and has a comparatively limited distribution, occurring only in rivers flowing into the ocean (Wright 1970). Most of the Cozumel crocodile elements were so fragmentary as to allow determination only to the generic level (see Table 5.14).

The great majority (nearly 63 percent) of these specimens were fragments of mandibles, maxillae, dentaries, and some other skull elements (Table 5.15). However, several vertebrae, limb bones, and a tar-

Table 5.14   Species Totals of Cozumel Crocodiles

SPECIES	NO. BONES	%	MNI	%
Crocodylus sp.	26	74.29	12	85.71
? Crocodylus sp.	7	20.00	—	—
Crocodylus cf. C. acutus	2	5.71	2	14.29
Total	35	100.00	14	100.00

sal element were also present. Only one bone represented an immature animal—a fragmentary caudal vertebra *(Crocodylus sp.)*. Since the meat-laden tail of this reptile is customarily consumed for food (the rest of the animal is usually considered too pungent [Pohl 1976: 179]), one might wonder why the present sample does not contain more caudal vertebrae. Perhaps these elements were discarded elsewhere after use. More likely, the very small sample size (a total of only thirty-five bones) has affected the distribution of skeletal elements. Also, the skull elements may have been used in religious ceremonies, as was apparently true at Seibal (Pohl 1976: 179).

Crocodiles are found in five sites, generally in proportions relative to the size of the total faunal sample excavated (Table 5.16). These sites represent every geographic part of the island, so that no distinctive patterns are evident.

The majority of crocodiles were excavated from housemounds; relatively few came from burials or other ceremonial contexts (Table 5.17). The number of indeterminate proveniences could modify this statement somewhat, although many of these are suspected to be housemounds as well.

More than 88 percent of crocodile elements (or nearly 86 percent of the MNIs) have been dated to the Postclassic, Late Postclassic, or

Table 5.15   Skeletal Elements of Cozumel Crocodiles

SKELETAL ELEMENT	NO. BONES	%	
Skull elements	9	25.71	62.86
Mandibles, maxillae, and dentaries	13	37.14	
Vertebrae (caudals and 2 other vertebrae)	4	11.43	
Major limb bones (femur and humerus)	2	5.71	
Tarsals	1	2.86	
Indeterminate	6	17.14	
Total	35	99.99	

Table 5.16   Distribution of Crocodiles by Site

SITE	TAXON	NO. BONES	MNI
C-13	*Crocodylus sp.*	1	1
	? *Crocodylus sp.*	2	—
Subtotal		3	1
C-18	*Crocodylus sp.*	13	2
	Crocodylus cf. C. acutus	1	1
Subtotal		14	3
C-22	*Crocodylus sp.*	8	6
	Crocodylus cf. C. acutus	1	1
	? *Crocodylus sp.*	2	—
Subtotal		11	7
C-25	*Crocodylus sp.*	3	2
	? *Crocodylus sp.*	3	—
Subtotal		6	2
C-27	*Crocodylus sp.*	1	1
Total		35	14

historic periods (Table 5.18). None comes from contexts dated earlier, and only a few are undated (not enough to affect these results).

No evidence of cultural modification occurred on Cozumel—unlike, for example, the worked mandible and drilled teeth which appeared at Altar de Sacrificios (Olsen 1972). There were no pathologies, no butcher marks, no evidence of burning, and no modifications by animals (carnivore-chewing or rodent-gnawing).

The use of crocodiles in sacrifices is mentioned by Landa, who discusses the ceremonial burning of the animal's heart by priests (in Tozzer 1941: 163). Other internal organs were apparently used in the late 1970s in potions by the Maya in Belize (Pohl 1976: 179). Crocodiles also appear frequently in the Maya Codices in connection with the planet Saturn (Tozzer and Allen 1910).

Table 5.17   Distribution of Crocodiles by Provenience

PROVENIENCE	NO. BONES	%	MNI	%
Burials and ceremonial/ administrative contexts	4	11.43	2	14.29
Housemounds	18	51.43	5	35.71
Indeterminate contexts	13	37.14	7	50.00
Total	35	100.00	14	100.00

Table 5.18 Time Periods of Cozumel Crocodiles

TIME PERIOD	NO. BONES	%		MNI	%	
Late Postclassic and Historic	27	77.14 ⎫		9	64.29 ⎫	
Postclassic	4	11.43 ⎬ 88.57		3	21.43 ⎬ 85.72	
No Date	4	11.43		2	14.28	
Total	35	100.00		14	100.00	

Table 5.19   Distribution of Indeterminate Reptiles by Site

SITE	TAXON	NO. BONES
C-22	Reptile	4
	? Reptile	1
C-25	? large reptile	1
C-18	Reptile	375
Total		381

Indeterminate Reptiles

A large number (381) of reptile longbone shafts and other fragments occurred in three of the Cozumel sites (Table 5.19). These bones could not be closely determined, although almost all are probably turtles or iguanids. Only one fragment, classified as ? large reptile, was likely a crocodile. There was no indication that any of these elements belonged to snakes: had any serpent vertebrae been present, these diagnostic elements would have been easily recognizable. The snake has tremendous symbolic importance in Maya religion and art, appearing repeatedly, often as a rattlesnake, in the Maya Codices in association with various deities (Schellhas 1904; Tozzer and Allen 1910). However, these

Table 5.20   Proveniences of Indeterminate Reptiles*

PROVENIENCE	NO. BONES	%
Burials and ceremonial/ administrative contexts	375	98.43
Housemounds	4	1.05
Indeterminate contexts	2	0.52
Total	381	100.00

*Includes one ? reptile and one ? large reptile bones.

Table 5.21   Time Periods of Indeterminate Reptiles*

TIME PERIOD	NO. BONES	%	
Late Postclassic	376	98.69	99.74
Postclassic	4	1.05	
No Date	1	0.26	
Total	381	100.00	

*Includes one ? reptile and one ? large reptile bones.

reptiles are found only rarely in Maya sites (the occurrence of a single rattlesnake vertebra at Seibal is apparently typical [Olsen 1978]). Moreover, whether or not any snakes actually live on Cozumel is uncertain. Native informants told the author (January 1978) that they had never seen or heard reports of any on the island.

Most of these indeterminate reptiles (more than 98 percent) appear in burials and ceremonial/administrative contexts, while only about 1 percent were excavated from housemounds (Table 5.20). Close to 100 percent were dated to the Postclassic and Late Postclassic periods (Table 5.21). Little can be said about these results, since the species represented are not known.

6. Birds

ALTHOUGH THE COZUMEL avian remains are only fourth in numerical importance, the twenty-six species (thirty-eight taxa) identified here represent the most diverse class of fauna excavated on the island (see Tables 6.1, 6.2; also Hamblin and Rea 1979). This great variety makes Cozumel unique among Maya sites. Other sites have neither such a diverse avifauna nor, generally, the volume of bird bone encountered here (Olsen 1972, 1978; Pohl 1976; Wing 1974, 1975; Wing and Steadman 1980; Woodbury and Trik 1953). At Mayapán, which produced a very large avian collection (more than 1,100 identified bones), only eight different taxa are represented (Pollock and Ray 1957).

Findings derived from bird remains can be used to explore several different fields of archaeological interest. The present data are used to compare the use of avifauna at each site by examining the differing exploitation of ecological zones or ecozones, as well as in the areas where two such zones overlap (ecotones). In addition, the relative significance of various birds in the Cozumel diet, the possible uses of certain avian species for ceremonial/religious and other non-food purposes, and the presence of a long-distance trade network between Cozumel and other parts of Mexico and Central America are discussed.

Utilization of Ecological Zones

The sites where bird bones are found have two points in common (see Table 6.3). Found at all six sites are species which characteristically inhabit old rain forests (see Table 6.4). The great curassow *(Crax rubra)*, which occurs in five of the sites, requires old rain forest—in other words, secluded portions of dense, undisturbed, humid tropical forest (Edwards 1972; Blake 1953; Peterson and Chalif 1973). These conditions are

Table 6.1 Birds of Cozumel: Taxonomic Checklist

Pelecaniformes
  Sulidae (boobies and gannets)
    Sula leucogaster (brown booby)
  Fregatidae (frigate birds)
    ? *Fregata magnificens* (magnificent frigate bird, or man-o'-war bird)

Ciconiformes
  Ardeidae (herons and bitterns)
    Ardea cf. A. herodias (great blue heron)
    Ardea (Hydranassa) tricolor (Louisiana heron)
    Dichromanassa rufescens (reddish egret)
    Nycticorax (Nyctanassa) violacea (yellow-crowned night heron)
  Ciconiidae (storks)
    Mycteria americana (wood stork)
    ? *Mycteria americana* (wood stork)

Falconiformes
  Accipitridae (hawks)
    Accipiter bicolor (bicolored hawk)
    Buteo cf. B. magnirostris (roadside hawk)

Galliformes
  Cracidae (curassows, guans, and chachalacas)
    Crax rubra (great curassow)
    Crax sp. (great curassow)
    ? *Crax sp.* (great curassow)
  Phasianidae (quails, pheasants, and peacocks)
    ? *Dactylortyx thoracicus* (singing quail)
    Gallus gallus (domestic chicken)
    ? *Gallus gallus* (domestic chicken)
  Meleagrididae
    Meleagris gallopavo (domestic or common turkey)
    ? *Meleagris gallopavo* (domestic or common turkey)
    Meleagris (Agriocharis) ocellata (ocellated turkey)
    ? *Meleagris (Agriocharis) ocellata* (ocellated turkey)

Gruiformes
  Rallidae (rails, gallinules, and coots)
    Prophyrula martinica (purple gallinule)
    Fulica americana (American coot)

Charadriiformes
  Scolopacidae (woodcocks, snipe, and sandpipers)
    Tringa cf. T. melanoleucus (greater yellowlegs-sandpiper)

Columbiformes (pigeons)
  Columbidae
    Columba leucocephala (white-crowned pigeon)
    ? *Columba leucocephala* (white-crowned pigeon)
    ? *Columba sp.*

Table 6.1   Birds of Cozumel: Taxonomic Checklist (continued)

Psittaciformes
  Psittacidae (parrots)
    Ara cf. A. militaris (green or military macaw)
    Ara macao (scarlet macaw)
    Ara sp.
    Aratinga sp. (parakeet)
    Amazona xantholora (yellow-lored parrot)
    Amazona cf. A. xantholora (yellow-lored parrot)
    ? *Amazona xantholora* (yellow-lored parrot)

Strigiformes
  Tytonidae (barn owls)
    Tyto alba (barn owl)

Piciformes
  Picidae (woodpeckers, etc.)
    Celeus cf. C. castaneus (chestnut-colored woodpecker)

Passeriformes
  Icteridae (meadowlarks, blackbirds, and troupials)
    Scaphidurus (Psomocolax) oryzivorus (giant cowbird)
    Quiscalus (Cassidix) mexicanus (great-tailed grackle)
    ? *Quiscalus (Cassidix) mexicanus* (great-tailed grackle)
    Quiscalus (Cassidix) sp. (grackle)

no longer present on the island, and the endemic Cozumel race of the species *(Crax rubra griscomi)* is on the brink of extinction if not already vanished (Paynter 1955; Delacour and Amadon 1973). Mayan agricultural practices over a long period of time have evidently resulted in a gradual habitat modification. Further support for this habitat change comes from San Miguel (C-13), the only site without the curassow. Here, two other rain-forest species appear, the bicolored hawk *(Accipiter bicolor)* and the chestnut-colored woodpecker *(Celeus cf. C. castaneus)*, neither of which occurred on Cozumel as of the early 1980s.

The other factor common to all the sites is the presence, and usually the predominance, of turkeys. At all but two sites, Zuuk (C-31) and Buena Vista (C-18), both common and ocellated turkeys occur. The absence of *M. gallopavo* (the common turkey) from these two sites may be only an artificial consequence of the very small sample size—eleven bones from Buena Vista and only five from Zuuk. Neither of the two turkeys appears to be native to the island. *M. gallopavo* was originally imported from the pine-oak uplands of northern Mexico (Leopold 1959), while the ocellated turkey occurs on the Yucatán Peninsula and inhabits open decidous forest, savannas, *milpas*, and other clearings, as well as the edges (but not the interior) of dense rain forest (Paynter 1955). Once brought to the island from the mainland, this species should have flourished, since these are precisely the environmental conditions on modern Cozumel and apparently in the Late Postclassic as well (Sabloff and Rathje 1975c).

The inhabitants of four of these sites used birds from only half of the possible habitats on the island, disregarding such non-native species as the turkeys (Tables 6.3, 6.4). The San Miguel (C-13) material includes two rain-forest birds (the hawk and the woodpecker) and an unidentified marine species. El Cedral (C-15) yields one old rain-forest species (the curassow), and possibly one from the woods/fields ecotone; one bone is questionably a parrot (?Psittaciformes). Buena Vista (C-18) contains the curassow (old rain-forest species) and two birds which require woods/fields ecotone: a pigeon (Columbidae) and a roadside hawk *(Buteo cf. B. magnirostris)*. Zuuk (C-31) also contains the curassow and a pigeon (Columbiformes)—old rain forest and woods/fields ecotone.

The other two sites, however, yield birds that cover the entire spectrum of ecozones on the island. From San Gervasio (C-22) come four birds inhabiting beach/stream areas *(Tringa cf. T. melanoleucus*—a sandpiper, *Porphyrula martinica*—purple gallinule, *Fulica americana*—American coot, and *Ardea tricolor*—Louisiana heron); five species requiring the woods/fields ecotone (? *Dactylortyx thoracicus*—singing quail, *Columba leucocephala*—white-crowned pigeon, *Amazona xantholora*—yellow-lored parrot, *Tyto alba*—barn owl, and *Quiscalus mexicanus*—great-tailed grackle); one old rain-forest bird—the curassow *(Crax rubra);* and one marine species—the magnificent frigate bird (? *Fregata magnificens)*. Similarly, La Expedición (C-25) contains four species from the beach/stream habitat *(Ardea cf. A. herodias*—great blue heron, *Dichromanassa rufescens*—reddish egret, *Mycteria americana*—wood stork, and *Nycticorax violacea*—yellow crowned night heron); four birds inhabiting the woods/fields ecotone *(Columba sp.*—a pigeon, *Amazona xantholora*—yellow-lored parrot, *Scaphidurus oryzivorus*—giant cowbird, and *Quiscalus sp.*—a grackle); the curassow *(Crax rubra)* requiring old rain forest; and one marine species *(Sula leucogaster*—brown booby).

Obviously, such variety in the number of different habitats used and the number of species involved is a radical departure from the other four sites. The variety cannot be attributed to differential access to environmental zones, since La Expedición is a northeastern coastal site on the island, whereas San Gervasio is a north-central interior site away from the coast. The other four sites are similarly varied—two are coastal and two are interior. Besides, the island is small enough (a maximum of twenty-four miles long by eight miles wide) that the inhabitants of all the sites should easily have been able to obtain birds from all ecozones. Sample size cannot totally account for this variety, either, since El Cedral, which has the largest bird bone sample (133 bones), is a site where only two habitat zones were being used. However, comparatively little earth was moved at this site.

A cultural reason for this variation seems likely. This conclusion is supported by the fact that the two sites with the largest variety of bird

Table 6.2 Cozumel Birds: Total MNIs and Bone Counts

TAXON	NO. BONES	%	MNI	%
Sula leucogaster (brown body)	1	.3	1	1.2
? Fregata magnificens (magnificent frigate bird)	1	.3	—	—
Ardea cf. A. herodias (great blue heron)	2	.5	1	1.2
Ardea (Hydranassa) tricolor (Louisiana heron)	2	.5	1	1.2
Dichromanassa refescens (reddish egret)	10	2.7	1	1.2
Nycticorax (Nyctanassa) violacea (yellow-crowned night heron)	1	.3	1	1.2
Mycteria americana (wood stork)	5	1.3	1	1.2
? Mycteria americana (wood stork)	1	.3	—	—
Accipiter bicolor (bicolored hawk)	1	.3	1	1.2
Buteo cf. B. magnirostris (roadside hawk)	2	.5	1	1.2
Galliformes	3	.8	—	—
Large Galliformes	88	23.3	—	—
? Large Galliformes	7	1.9	—	—
Cracidae	2	.5	—	—
? Cracidae	2	.5	—	—
Crax rubra (great curassow)	28	7.4	14	17.2
Crax sp.	4	1.1	2	2.5
? Crax sp.	2	.5	—	—
? Dactylortyx thoracicus (singing quail)	1	.3	—	—
Gallus gallus (domestic chicken)	3	.8	3	3.7
? Gallus gallus (domestic chicken)	1	.3	—	—
Meleagrididae	14	3.7	—	—
? Meleagrididae	2	.5	—	—
Meleagris gallopavo (domestic turkey)	46	12.2	12	14.8
? Meleagris gallopavo (domestic turkey)	8	2.1	—	—
Meleagris (Agriocharis) ocellata (ocellated turkey)	54	14.3	15	18.5
?M. (Agriocharis) ocellata (ocellated turkey)	10	2.7	—	—
Porphyrula martinica (purple gallinule)	1	.3	1	1.2

Taxon	n	%	n	%
Fulica americana (American coot)	1	.3	1	1.2
Charadriiformes	1	.3	—	—
Tringa cf. *T. melanoleucus* (greater yellowlegs)	1	.3	1	1.2
Columbiformes	5	1.3	—	—
? Columbiformes	9	2.4	—	—
Columbidae	1	.3	1	1.2
Columba leucocephala (white-crowned pigeon)	2	.5	4	5.0
? *Columba leucocephala* (white-crowned pigeon)	5	1.3	—	—
Columba sp.	1	.3	—	—
? *Columba* sp.	1	.3	1	1.2
? Psittaciformes	12	3.2	4	5.0
Ara cf. *A. militaris* (green or military macaw)	1	.3	1	1.2
Ara macao (scarlet macaw)	1	.3	1	1.2
Ara sp. (macaw)	4	1.1	2	2.5
Aratinga sp. (parakeet)	1	.3	1	1.2
Amazona xantholora (yellow-lored parrot)	4	1.1	1	1.2
Amazona cf. *A. xantholora* (yellow-lored parrot)	1	.3	1	1.2
? *Amazona xantholora* (yellow-lored parrot)	1	.3	2	2.5
Tyto alba (barn owl)	1	.3	4	5.0
Celeus cf. *C. castaneus* (chestnut-colored woodpecker)	2	.5	1	1.2
Scaphidurus (*Psomocolax*) *oryzivorus* (giant cowbird)	5	1.3	—	—
Quiscalus (*Cassidix*) *mexicanus* (great-tailed grackle)	1	.3	—	—
? *Quiscalus* (*Cass.*) *mexicanus* (great-tailed grackle)	1	.3	—	—
Quiscalus (*Cassidix*) sp. (grackle)	1	.3	—	—
Marine Bird	1	.3	—	—
Large Non-galliform Bird	2	.5	—	—
Large Bird	3	.8	—	—
Medium-large Bird	2	.5	—	—
Medium-small Bird	2	.5	—	—
Small Bird	3	.8	—	—
Total	377	100.00	81	99.5

Table 6.3 Distribution of Cozumel Birds by Site

SITE	TAXON	NO. BONES	MNI
C-13	*Gallus gallus*	1	1
	? *Gallus gallus*	1	—
	Meleagris (Agriocharis) ocellata	23	1
	? *Meleagris (Agriocharis) ocellata*	1	—
	Accipiter bicolor	1	1
	Celeus castaneus	1	1
	Meleagrididae	1	—
	? *Meleagris gallopavo*	1	—
	Indeterminate marine bird	1	—
	Indeterminate large bird	1	—
Subtotal		32	4
C-15	Large Galliformes	75	—
	Meleagrididae	1	—
	Meleagris gallopavo	30	4
	Meleagris (Agriocharis) ocellata	6	3
	? *Meleagris (Agriocharis) ocellata*	3	—
	Crax rubra	12	3
	Crax sp.	3	1
	? Psittaciformes	1	—
	Indeterminate medium-small bird	2	—
Subtotal		133	11
C-18	Large Galliformes	1	—
	Meleagrididae	1	—
	Meleagris (Agriocharis) ocellata	1	1
	? *Meleagris (Agriocharis) ocellata)*	1	—
	Crax rubra	3	2
	Columbidae	1	—
	Buteo cf. B. magnirostris	2	1
	Indeterminate large bird	1	—
Subtotal		11	4
C-22	*Tyto alba*	1	1
	Tringa cf. T. melanoleucus	1	1
	Porphyrula martinica	1	1
	Fulica americana	1	1
	? *Fregata magnificens*	1	—
	Ardea tricolor	2	1
	Amazona zantholora	1	1
	Amazona cf. A. xantholora	1	1
	Aratinga sp.	1	1
	Cassidix mexicanus	5	4
	? *Cassidix mexicanus*	1	—
	Columbiformes	3	—
	? Columbiformes	8	—
	Columba sp.	4	3
	? *Columba sp.*	1	—

Table 6.3   Distribution of Cozumel Birds by Site (continued)

SITE	TAXON	NO. BONES	MNI
	Columba leucocephala	1	1
	? *Columba leucocephala*	2	—
	Charadriiformes	1	—
	Large Galliformes	3	—
	Galliformes	1	—
	? Large Galliformes	7	—
	Crax rubra	7	6
	Crax sp.	1	1
	Cracidae	2	—
	? *Crax sp.*	1	—
	? *Dactylortyx thoracicus*	1	—
	Meleagrididae	8	—
	? Meleagrididae	1	—
	Meleagris gallopavo	11	6
	? *Meleagris gallopavo*	6	—
	Meleagris (Agriocharis) ocellata	15	4
	? *Meleagris (Agriocharis) ocellata*	2	—
	Gallus gallus	2	2
	Indeterminate small bird	3	—
	Indeterminate medium-large bird	2	—
	Indeterminate non-galliform bird	1	—
	Indeterminate large bird	1	—
Subtotal		111	35
C-25	*Sula leucogaster*	1	1
	Ardea cf. A. herodias	2	1
	Dichromanassa rufescens	10	1
	Mycteria americana	5	1
	? *Mycteria americana*	1	—
	Ara. cf. A. militaris	1	1
	Ara macao	12	4
	Ara sp.	1	1
	Amazona xantholora	3	1
	? *Amazona xantholora*	3	—
	Nycticorax sp.	1	1
	Scaphidurus oryzivorus	2	2
	Cassidix sp.	1	1
	Columbiformes	1	—
	Columba sp.	1	1
	Large Galliformes	9	—
	Galliformes	2	—
	Meleagrididae	3	—
	? Meleagrididae	1	—
	Meleagris gallopavo	5	2
	? *Meleagris gallopavo*	1	—
	Meleagris (Agriocharis) ocellata	9	6
	? *Meleagris (Agriocharis) ocellata*	2	

Table 6.3 Distribution of Cozumel Birds by Site (continued)

SITE	TAXON	NO. BONES	MNI
	Crax rubra	6	3
	? *Crax sp.*	1	—
	Indeterminate large non-galliform bird	1	—
Subtotal		85	27
C-31	Columbiformes	1	—
	? Columbiformes	1	—
	? *Meleagris (Agriocharis) ocellata*	1	—
	? Cracidae	2	—
Subtotal		5	—
Total		377	81

species, San Gervasio and La Expedición, are two of the largest and most culturally important sites on the island. San Gervasio was the major interior settlement throughout the history of Cozumel, perhaps serving as the island's main administrative center. It was an administrative center, a cult center for the oracle, and, in the Late Postclassic, a residential/commercial district. La Expedición, the major religious center on the northeast coast, appears to have been a ceremonial center designed for short-term festivals in which either local people or transient pilgrims participated. Its formal plaza group complements San Gervasio's administrative center. One writer concluded that "if festivals were a medium for the transmission of political and economic policy, [those at La Expedición] . . . could have provided an effective means of disseminating information from the capital of San Gervasio to the northeast coast communities as well as a means of solidifying bonds between this sub-region of the island and the capital on a much more frequent basis than that provided by festivals in the capital itself" (Freidel 1976: 275, 339). Thus, these two sites apparently were strongly linked and probably represent the two most important sites on the island for elite ceremonial and civil administrative functions. The avifauna reflect this.

Relative Dietary Importance of Various Avian Species

Determining which faunal elements at an archaeological site represent food species is always difficult. In this study, birds selected were those which ethnographic data indicated were used as food, or which had a fair amount of usable meat. Eliminated were those which were probably used mainly for ceremonial/religious or other cultural purposes. Since this may exclude some birds which were actually consumed (in

Table 6.4 Habitats of Cozumel Birds
*probable food species **no longer on Cozumel

TAXON	MARINE	BEACH AND STREAM	WOODS/FIELDS ECOTONE	OLD RAIN FOREST	DOMESTIC OR TRADE	IN-TRUSIVE
Sula leucogaster (brown booby)	x					
? Fregata magnificens (magnificent frigate bird)	x					
Ardea cf. A. herodias (great blue heron)		x				
Ardea (Hydranassa) tricolor (Louisiana heron)		x				
Dichromanassa rufescens (reddish egret)		x				
Nycticorax (Nyctanassa) violacea (yellow-night heron)		x				
Mycteria americana (wood stork)		x				
Accipiter bicolor (bicolored hawk)**		x				
Buteo cf. B. magnirostris (roadside hawk)			x	x		
*Crax rubra (great curassow)				x		
*? Dactylortyx thoracicus (singing quail)**			x	x	?	
*Gallus gallus (domestic chicken)						x
*Meleagris gallopavo (domestic turkey)					x	
*Meleagris (Agriocharis) ocellata (ocellated turkey)					x	

Table 6.4 Habitats of Cozumel Birds (continued)
*probable food species **no longer on Cozumel

TAXON	MARINE	BEACH AND STREAM	WOODS/ FIELDS ECOTONE	OLD RAIN FOREST	DOMESTIC OR TRADE	IN- TRUSIVE
Porphyrula martinica (purple gallinule)		x				
Fulica americana (American coot)		x				
Tringa cf. T. melanoleucus (greater yellowlegs-sandpiper)		x				
*Columba leucocephala (white-crowned pigeon)						
*Columba sp. (pigeons)			x			
Ara sp. (macaws)			x		x	
Ara cf. A. militaris (green or military macaw)					x	
Ara macao (scarlet macaw)					x	
Aratinga sp. (parakeet)					x	
Amazona xantholora (yellow-lored parrot)					x	
Tyto alba (barn owl)**			x			
Celeus castaneus (chestnut-colored woodpecker)**			x	x		
Scaphidurus oryzivorus (giant cowbird)**			x			
*Quiscalus (Cassidix) mexicanus (great-tailed grackle)			x			
*Quiscalus (Cassidix) sp. (grackle)			x			

addition to other uses in clothing decoration and in rituals), the following list should be considered conservative. The birds regarded as food species on Cozumel are the curassow *(Crax rubra),,* the singing quail *(Dactylortyx thoracicus),* the domestic chicken *(Gallus gallus)*—which is assumed to be a modern intrusive, the common turkey *(Meleagris gallopavo),* the ocellated turkey *(Meleagris ocellata),* the white-crowned pigeon *(Columba leucocephala),* other pigeons *(Columba sp.),* and the blackbirds *(Scaphidurus oryzivorus*—giant cowbird, *Quiscalus mexicanus*—the great-tailed grackle, and *Quiscalus sp.).* Only one bone in the entire avian collection shows evidence of butchering (an ocellated turkey), so this criterion is of limited value in confirming or rejecting possible food species.

The food species represent from 51 to 100 percent of all bird bones present in each site, with an overall average of 82 percent (Table 6.5). Thus, most of the avian remains on the island appear to represent exploitation of these animals for food. Galliform birds, a group which includes both species of turkeys, the curassow, the chicken, and the quail, are the most important avian food items at every site. These species represent from 60 to 100 percent of all the avian food bones, an average of 84.6 percent overall. Within this group, turkeys are by far the most important (averaging 45.7 percent overall), followed by the curassow, which averages 23.3 percent in the five sites where it occurs. Only one quail bone (? *Dactylortyx thoracicus)* appears (at San Gervasio), so this bird apparently was not a significant food item.

The four chicken bones from two different sites are too few to indicate an important food source, but their presence in itself is significant. Carter (1971) has suggested, primarily on the basis of linguistic similarities and comparative diffusion rates, that one or more varieties of chickens were present in Central and South America well before the time of European contact. Serious doubt is cast on this theory, however, by the fact that as of the early 1980s, no chicken remains had occurred in pre-Hispanic archaeological sites except as surface finds of much more recent origins. In fact, the four bones found in the Cozumel material are apparently the only ones excavated from any middle American prehistoric site. If chickens were as common and widespread in pre-Hispanic Latin America as Carter believes, one would expect to find much larger quantities of such material, or at least nominal representation of this species in many more sites. Furthermore, the Cozumel chickens were found in the top levels of pits in sites where modern contamination is very likely. The two bones from San Miguel (C-13) have been dated Late Postclassic-historic, meaning that European items were present at this level, as well as Mayan artifacts. This strongly suggests that these remains are post-Hispanic. The two chicken bones from San Gervasio (C-22) came from the top levels of a pit dated Late Postclassic. In 1980 a ranch stood on the site and sightseers often came to look at the ruins—ample opportunity for someone to drop the remains of a fried chicken lunch into the site. Chickens were also raised at the

Table 6.5 Distribution of Food Species by Site

SITE	% OF AVIAN BONES REPRESENTED BY FOOD SPECIES	% OF AVIAN BONES REPRESENTED BY GALLIFORMES[1]	% OF AVIAN FOOD BONES REPRESENTED BY TURKEYS[2]	% OF AVIAN FOOD BONES REPRESENTED BY CURASSOWS	% OF AVIAN FOOD BONES REPRESENTED BY COLUMBIFORMES (PIGEONS)	% OF AVIAN FOOD BONES REPRESENTED BY ICTERIDS[3]
San Miguel (C-13)	87.50	99.60	92.60	0	0	0
El Cedral (C-15)	97.50	99.90	30.70	11.50	0	0
Buena Vista (C-18)	72.20	87.50	37.50	37.50	12.50	0
San Gervasio (C-22)	84.60	72.40	46.00	11.60	20.20	6.30
La Expedición (C-25)	51.10	88.10	47.40	15.80	4.40	6.70
Zuuk (C-31)	100.00	60.00	20.00	40.00	40.00	0
Average	82.15	84.58	45.70	23.28*	19.28*	6.50*

*These averages *exclude* sites with values of zero.
[1] Galliformes include curassows, singing quail, domestic chickens, common turkeys, and ocellated turkeys.
[2] Turkeys include both the ocellated and common species.
[3] Icterids (blackbirds) include both giant cowbirds and great-tailed grackles.

ranch. Another possibility is that these remains may represent Spanish chickens, although Spanish artifacts which would lend support to this idea are absent. In sum, all four of the Cozumel chicken bones are probably intrusive, but whether they are modern or early Spanish chickens cannot be determined.

After Galliformes, the next most important group of birds in the Cozumel diet is Columbiformes (pigeons or doves). These are not present in all of the sites, but in the four where they do occur they account for an average of nearly 19.3 percent of the avian food bone. Grackles are apparently the least important of the presumed food species, since they appear in only two of the sites and represent an average of merely 6.5 percent. (Grackles are considered food items because they are large-bodied birds, readily obtainable at clearings, and not likely to be collected for their dark brown or black feathers.)

Since turkeys are the most significant avian food item on the island, and since both of the species were imported from the mainland, these birds may have been raised on Cozumel as either domestic animals or tame captives. The common turkey, *Meleagris gallopavo*, was domesticated and distributed throughout Mexico before the Conquest (Leopold 1959: 275). Schorger (1966) cites Oviedo to show that the Indians on Cozumel presented turkeys to the Grijalva expedition of 1518. The Cortez expedition of 1519 reported that domestic turkeys were widely distributed in the Maya lowlands. Forty of the animals were taken from the Indians' homes when the Cortez expedition landed on Cozumel (Schorger 1966: 6). A major problem has been that many of the Spanish terms in the ethnographic literature confuse the ocellated with the common turkey. The ocellated turkey *(M. ocellata)* has, however, never been domesticated, since its offspring fare poorly in captivity (Schorger 1966), and possibly owing to the superiority of its flight capabilities over those of the northern turkey (Leopold 1959). Therefore, the common turkey *(M. gallopavo)* was probably raised on Cozumel, although this does not preclude the possibility that the ocellated turkey was also periodically captured and tamed (but not domesticated) for later use as food. The presence of at least six immature individuals (thirty-six bones) from four different sites on the island supports this hypothesis. Two of these individuals were so immature (one was approximately five days old, the other one to five months) that species could not be determined. But the remaining four individuals were all ocellated turkeys, which certainly suggests capture of the animals at a very young age, if not hatching in captivity. Landa (Tozzer 1941: 202) specifically mentions that the Indians stole the eggs of certain large birds and raised the fowl tame after they were hatched.

The presence of pen-like stone circles in some of the sites may support the idea of captive birds. These enclosures range in diameter from 5 to 15 meters and have walls of dry-laid masonry up to a maximum preserved height of 1.5 meters (Freidel and Leventhal 1975: 69). Soil samples obtained from two of these stone circles at Buena Vista were tested, (see Table 6.6). The total ppm (parts per million) of soluble salts and soluble nitrates were both much higher inside the circles than in the control samples taken just outside. According to Ted McCreary (personal communication 1978), both salts and nitrates are common components of animal waste products (urine and manure), so such high values for these elements may indicate that animals were being kept in these enclosures. Lower kjeldahl values (organic nitrogen and ammonia) inside the circles indicate less microbial decomposition (probably of vegetation) there than outside the circles. The orthophosphates are also lower inside the circles, which means the phosphorus available to plants was not as great as outside the circles. The presence of animals in these enclosures might account for these facts. These circles may also have had multiple uses. Wallace (1978) has amassed evidence which suggests that at least some were used as enclosures for raising bees.

Landa (Tozzer 1941: 127) mentions that women raised fowl for food and for sale, and there is ethnographic reference to cooked turkeys being sold in the markets (Schorger 1966: 12). Pohl (1976: 213) suggests that some animals (including birds) may have been tamed by the women as a contribution to the domestic economy. Not all of these were necessarily turkeys: Schorger (1966: 8, 13) cites various references to the capturing and raising of curassows and chachalacas, and Landa mentions the raising of doves and white mallard ducks (Tozzer 1941: 201). Curassows and doves do appear in the Cozumel sites.

Ceremonial/Religious and Other Non-Food Uses of Birds

Since thirty different birds from Cozumel are identified to at least the generic level, and only about one-third have been designated as probable food species, the uses of many species have not been determined. Many

Table 6.6　Test Results on Soil Samples from Buena Vista Stone Circles

SAMPLE	SOLUBLE SALTS (ppm)[1]	SOLUBLE NITRATES (N) (ppm)[1]	KJELDAHL (ORGANIC N_2 & NH_2), ppm[2]	ORTHO-PHOSPHATES[3]
Circle #4	1,673	27.00	17,000	18.50
Control #4[4]	1,519	15.00	20,400	23.50
Circle #6	1,519	41.25	18,310	9.50
Control #6[4]	1,379	35.50	23,800	11.75

[1]Both salts and nitrates are components of animal urine and manure; note high values for these two elements inside the stone circles.

[2]Lower organic Nitrogen and ammonia values inside the circles indicate less microbial decomposition (probably of vegetation) taking place there.

[3]This indicates the amount of phosphorus in the soil available to plants; note the lower values inside the circles.

[4]Control samples were taken from the soil just outside each of the stone circles tested.

of these were probably used for ceremonial/religious or other non-food purposes. Landa refers repeatedly to the sacrificial offering of birds, their blood, their hearts, and their feathers (Tozzer 1941: 23, 109, 124, 163, 165). Some animals offered as ritual sacrifices in the Maya religion were "persented whole, some living and some dead, some raw and some cooked" (Tozzer 1941: 114). An apparently common ritual was the decapitation of a turkey as a sacrifice to the gods (Tozzer 1941: 141, 145, 147; Tozzer and Allen 1910: 325, 326, 327). Using a turkey's head as a sacrifice obviously would not preclude consuming the rest of the animal. It may be significant that the only two bird skulls found of any species were both common turkeys *(M. gallopavo),* and these were in an elite burial context at El Cedral. Tozzer and Allen (1910: 325) also refer to the frigate bird, pictured in the Maya Codices, as an offering or sacrifice; this bird was considered useful for medicinal purposes as well (Tozzer 1941: 203). Brightly colored bird feathers were used in male puberty rites and to decorate clothing, headdresses (specifically the turkey and the military macaw), banners, helmets, and shields. In addition, a certain "bird with rich plumes" was used as money (Tozzer 1941: 89, 106, 127; Tozzer and Allen 1910: 324, 328, 338, 345).

Notably, the Cozumel avifauna includes five brightly colored members of the parrot family, all but one of which was imported to the island. The feathers of these species (which include the green and scarlet macaws, a parakeet, and the yellow-lored parrot) were probably used for decoration. Many other species found in the Cozumel sites were also probably used for their feathers, such as the great blue heron, the Louisiana heron, and the owl (mentioned in Tozzer and Allen 1910: 324, 338 as being used in headdresses). In addition, the yellow-crowned night heron, the reddish egret, the wood stork, and the bicolored and roadside hawks were very likely captured for feathers. The owl is also cited as an animal of "mythologic significance" (Schellhas 1904: 45), so possibly it was used in ritual contexts as well as for decoration. Pygmy owls are very common in caches in the Rio Bec region (Pohl, personal communication 1979).

Only 9.8 percent of all the bird bone was burned or heat-darkened. This probably reflects cooking practices, especially since most of the bones involved are curassows, turkeys, and pigeons—all of which are considered food species. In addition, eight of the bones represent at least five different parrots and macaws, implying that these were either used as food or sacrificially burned. Excavations conducted by the Instituto de Anthropología e Historia de Guatemala in group G at Tikal also produced a number of burned bird bones. Specifically, Pohl mentions (1976: 272) a mealy parrot *(Amazona farinosa)* which was very charred and had evidently been roasted over a direct flame. A heat-darkened owl bone was also found, Distinguishing between use of these birds for food or for ceremonial purposes appears to be impossible; perhaps they were used for both.

The majority of bird bones were excavated from burials and ceremonial/administrative contexts (more than 65 percent of the bones, or nearly 62 percent of the MNIs—see Table 6.7). Only about 3 percent of the bones (or approximately 6 percent of the MNIs) occur in housemounds. The remainder are from indeterminate contexts, but these would not be a sufficient quantity to affect the general pattern. However, this does not necessarily imply non-food uses for over 65 percent of the Cozumel birds. It may only mean that birds were used (for whatever purpose) by the people inhabiting elite precincts and hence were deposited there. Still, a certain proportion was undoubtedly used as ritual offerings or for other ceremonial purposes.

As for other cultural uses of the Cozumel birds, bone artifacts are notably lacking. Only three pieces of worked bone can definitely be identified as avian. All three are turkey and have been cut or shaped for artifactual manufacture. However, Phillips (1979) lists four shell and bone beads (one discoidal and three elongate, removed and catalogued in Mexico) which he suggests are probably bird bone shafts inserted in a perforated shell bead.

Implications for Long-Distance Trade

The Cozumel sites appear to be the first in the Mayan lowlands to contain the common turkey, *Meleagris gallopavo*, in archaeological context. Previously, only the ocellated turkey, *Meleagris (Agriocharis) ocellata*, had been definitely identified from Mayan sites in the region (Schorger 1966: 8). On Cozumel, where common turkeys are definitely present at four sites and perhaps at a fifth (one bone is ? *M. gallopavo*), they always accompany ocellated turkeys in the same contexts. The northern species (*M. gallopavo*) is represented by forty-six bones, indicating at least twelve distinct individuals in many different proveniences—too many to be attributed to chance or intrusion.

The major result of this analysis has been confirmation of the existence of a long-distance trade network between Cozumel and other parts of Mexico and Central America. The presence of the common turkey (*M. gallopavo*) indicates contact with northern Mexico (even if only indirectly), since the original range of the bird extended no farther south than the Isthmus of Tehuantepec or even, some sources indicate, than

Table 6.7   Proveniences of Cozumel Birds

PROVENIENCE	NO. BONES	%	MNI	%
Burials and Ceremonial/ Administrative Contexts	247	65.52	50	61.73
Housemounds	12	3.18	5	6.17
Indeterminate	118	31.30	26	32.10
Total	377	100.00	81	100.00

Michoacan in Western Mexico and central Veracruz on the east (Leopold 1959, Schorger 1966).

In addition, three different species of macaws, none native to the island are present in these sites. The scarlet macaw *(Ara macao)*, a rain forest species of southern Mexico, is not found even on the Yucatán Peninsula (Paynter 1955) and thus was unquestionably a trade item on Cozumel. It is represented by twelve bones of at least four distinct individuals. One bone is probably that of a military macaw *(Ara cf. A. militaris)*, a wide-ranging northern Mexican species which was presumably a trade item since it is "absent from humid forests of [the] Caribbean lowlands" (Forshaw 1973). One element, a femur, has been designated as *Ara sp.* Although only the distal one-half to one-third of this bone is present, it appears to be osteologically distinct from either the military or scarlet macaw. It may be *Ara ambigua* (a Central American species) and thus a trade item, although it is possibly an extinct or previously undescribed non-Yucatecan species. In addition, one parakeet bone *(Aratinga sp.)* is definitely neither the species common on the Yucatán Peninsula *(Aratinga astec)* nor *A. holochlora,* a larger species of the Caribbean and Pacific lowlands. It, too, represents either a trade item or an extinct species.

Percentages of Skeletal Elements and Dating of Bird Bones

The majority of the avian skeletal elements (over 48 percent) are major limb bones (Table 6.8). Since these are the major meat-bearing portions of the body, this might indicate a concentration on birds primarily as food sources. However, these are also the largest, most durable, and

Table 6.8   Cozumel Birds: Distribution of Skeletal Elements

SKELETAL ELEMENT	NO. BONES	%
Skull elements[1]	17	4.51
Major limb bones[2]	182	48.27
Vertebrae[3]	59	15.65
Phalanges, carpals, claws (terminal phalanges)	34	9.02
Miscellaneous[4]	76	20.16
Indeterminate	9	2.39
Total	377	100.00

[1]Includes mandibles, premaxillae, skulls, frontals, quadrates, palatines, and nasals.
[2]Includes carpometacarpi, humeri, radii, ulnae, femora, fibulae, tibiotarsi, and tarsometatarsi.
[3]Includes axes, cervicals, thoracics, fused thoracic column, synsacra, and coccygeals.
[4]Includes sterna, furculae, ribs, scapulae, and coracoids.

Table 6.9 Time Periods of Cozumel Birds

TIME PERIOD	NO. BONES	%		MNI	%	
Late Postclassic and historic	155	41.11	} 41.91	45	55.56	} 56.79
Postclassic	3	0.80		1	1.23	
Pre-Postclassic	1	0.26	} 2.65	1	1.23	} 7.41
Pure Florescent	4	1.06		2	2.47	
Terminal Classic	4	1.06		2	2.47	
Early Period (Classic)	1	0.26		1	1.23	
No Date	209	55.44		29	35.80	
Total	377	99.99		81	99.99	

most diagnostic parts of a bird skeleton, factors which may inflate these results. The fact that so few skull elements appear in the sample (less than 5 percent) could be partially due to preservation factors, since bird skulls are usually paper-thin and thus relatively fragile. It may also indicate that many birds were decapitated before being brought back to the sites after capture in the field. All of the other skeletal elements are present in sufficient quantities to suggest that whole birds were used and the carcasses discarded within a relatively small area. Since most of the bird bone is not burned or heat-darkened (90.2 percent), preparation for food purposes probably involved stewing.

Nearly 42 percent of the bones (or almost 57 percent of the MNIs) were excavated from proveniences dated to the Postclassic, Late Postclassic, or historic periods (Table 6.9). Only a very small proportion (less than 3 percent of the bones, or less than 8 percent of the MNIs) came from contexts definitely dated to earlier time periods. There is a significant amount of material from undated proveniences which might modify this picture to some extent. However, it can be concluded that the cultural patterns observed here are primarily Late Postclassic.

7. Dogs

SINCE THE DOG *(Canis familiaris)* is the only mammal domesticated prehistorically by the Maya, it warrants separate discussion. The dog apparently played a unique role in Mayan culture, simultaneously involving religion, diet, and hunting activities. It represents the third most numerically important mammal found in the Cozumel sites. Since coyotes and wolves are not present in this part of Mexico (Leopold 1959; Hall and Kelson 1959), identifying the species of *Canis* found in Cozumel presented little difficulty. The only other canid on the island is the gray fox *(Urocyon cinereoargenteus),* which can be readily distinguished from the dog by skeletal element size and several other distinctive features, particularly the skull.

A total of 645 dog bones was excavated from nine different sites; these represent a minimum of ninety-three individuals (Table 7.1). In order to obtain an approximation of the sizes of these dogs, the height of the mandible was measured at the middle of the first molar (lower carnassial). E. S. Wing (1976a: 2) has established a direct correlation in dogs between body weight (in grams) and this particular jaw measurement (in mm). Her formula, $\log y = 2.1122(\log x) + 1.2722$, was used to calculate body weights from the thirty-one mandibles which were sufficiently complete (Table 7.2). The weights obtained were converted from grams to pounds for ease of reference. The resulting weights ranged from 10.87 to 33.95 pounds; the average Cozumel dog apparently weighed approximately 19.39 pounds (Table 7.2). Some of the lower weights may pertain to young adults, although obviously immature mandibles were not included in these measurements. Figure 7.1 is a scattergram illustrating the distribution of these dogs by weight. An examination of the weights of modern dog breeds (based on American Kennel Club data) leads to the conclusion that the average Cozumel dog was about the size of a small beagle (20–40 pounds), a cocker spaniel (22–28 pounds), or a whippet or miniature poodle (15–25 pounds) (S. J. Olsen, personal communication 1979).

100

Table 7.1   Cozumel Dogs: Totals by Site

SITE	SPECIES	NO. BONES	%	MNI	%
C-2	*Canis familiaris*	3	0.46	2	2.15
C-9	*Canis familiaris*	12	1.86	1	1.07
C-13	*Canis familiaris*	58	8.99	4	4.30
C-15	*Canis familiaris*	19	2.94	2	2.15
C-18	*Canis familiaris*	82	12.71	18	19.35
C-22	*Canis familiaris*	430	66.66	47	50.53
C-22	? *Canis familiaris*	17	2.63	6	6.45
C-25	*Canis familiaris*	17	2.63	9	9.67
C-27	*Canis familiaris*	3	0.46	3	3.22
C-31	*Canis familiaris*	4	0.62	1	1.07
Total		645	99.96	93	99.96

Prehistoric Mexican dogs can generally be divided into two major types: the Mexican Hairless Dog or *Xoloitzcuintli*, and the Small Indian Dog or *Techichi* (Allen 1920; Wright 1970). A third type, the tiny Chihuahua, was probably not present in prehistoric Mexico since there is no reliable evidence for this skeletally, linguistically, or in the Maya Codices. As of 1980, its origin was an enigma (Wright 1970). This particular breed can be excluded from the Cozumel dogs because of its extremely small size: chihuahuas range in weight from 1–6 pounds and are only 4-6 inches high at the shoulder, while the dogs in the Cozumel sample are much larger than this (see Tables 7.2 and 7.5).

The Mexican Hairless dog, or *Xoloitzcuintli* (sometimes abbreviated *Sholo*), is a dog of medium size, rather long-bodied in proportion to its height (exceeding three feet in length) and generally lacking hair. Its skin is usually slatey or reddish gray and is sometimes blotched with white (Allen 1920; Wright 1970). The first European account of this animal appears to be that of Francisco Hernández, who visited Mexico in the sixteenth century (cited in Allen 1920). Not all of the *Sholo* dogs are hairless as this trait is controlled by a dominant gene. All hairless dogs are heterozygous, with one gene for normal coat and one for hairlessness. A mating of two such dogs generally results in 25 percent of the offspring with normal coats (homozygous), 50 percent hairless (heterozygous), and 25 percent stillborn (two genes for hairlessness apparently being lethal) (Wright 1970). This might explain Seler's statement in 1890 that some of these dogs were not naturally hairless but were rubbed with turpentine from early youth, causing the hair to fall out. Of the physical traits Wright (1970: 39) reports as peculiar to the *Xoloitzcuintli*, only one has osteological significance: "an almost invariable absence of teeth between the foremost molars and the incisors." This is puzzling since, as of 1980, no archaeological dog specimens had been reported in the Maya area with all canines and premolars

Table 7.2 **Calculated Weights of Cozumel Dogs**

PROVENIENCE	MANDIBLE HEIGHT*	BODY WEIGHT	LOG Y = 2.1122 (LOG X) + 1.2722
C-22, gr. I, pit 123, bag 943	20 mm.	23.15 lbs.	(10,500 gms.)
C-22, gr. I, pit 123, bag 945	20 mm.	23.15 lbs.	(10,500 gms.)
C-22, gr. I, pit 123, bag 945	19 mm.	20.72 lbs.	(9,400 gms.)
C-22, gr. I, pit 123, burial 26	18 mm.	18.50 lbs.	(8,390 gms.)
C-22, gr. I, pit 123, burial 26	20 mm.	23.15 lbs.	(10,500 gms.)
C-22, gr. I, pit 123, burial 26	22 mm.	28.22 lbs.	(12,800 gms.)
C-22, gr. I, pit 123, burial 26	17 mm.	16.38 lbs.	(7,430 gms.)
C-22, gr. I, pit 123, burial 26	20 mm.	23.15 lbs.	(10,500 gms.)
C-22, gr. I, pit 123, burial 26	15 mm.	12.59 lbs.	(5,710 gms.)
C-22, gr. I, pit 123, bag 973	16 mm.	14.42 lbs.	(6,540 gms.)
C-22, gr. I, pit 124B, bag 984	18 mm.	18.50 lbs.	(8,390 gms.)
C-22, gr. I, pit 124B, bag 985	20 mm.	23.15 lbs.	(10,500 gms.)
C-22, gr. I, pit 124B, burial 24	17 mm.	16.38 lbs.	(7,430 gms.)
C-22, gr. I, pit 124B, burial 24	19 mm.	20.72 lbs.	(9,400 gms.)
C-22, gr. I, pit 124B, burial 24	15 mm.	12.59 lbs.	(5,710 gms.)
C-22, gr. I, pit 124B, burial 24	24 mm.	33.95 lbs.	(15,400 gms.)
C-22, gr. I, pit 124B, burial 24	15 mm.	12.59 lbs.	(5,710 gms.)
C-22, gr. I, pit 124B, burial 24	17 mm.	16.38 lbs.	(7,430 gms.)

C-22, gr. III, pit 143, burial 27	23.15 lbs.	20 mm.	(10,500 gms.)
C-22, gr. III, pit 143, burial 27	23.15 lbs.	20 mm.	(10,500 gms.)
C-22, gr. VI, pit 199, str. 6-C	18.50 lbs.	18 mm.	(8,390 gms.)
C-22, gr. VII, pit 212, bag 1487	10.87 lbs.	14 mm.	(4,930 gms.)
C-9, pit 26, bag 197	18.50 lbs.	18 mm.	(8,390 gms.)
C-9, pit 26, bag 197	18.50 lbs.	18 mm.	(8,390 gms.)
C-18, pit 53, fea. 12, bag 385	18.50 lbs.	18 mm.	(8,390 gms.)
C-18, pit 69, fea. 2, bag 589	18.50 lbs.	18 mm.	(8,390 gms.)
C-18, pit 89B, bag 641	18.50 lbs.	18 mm.	(8,390 gms.)
C-18, pit 101, bag 761	23.15 lbs.	20 mm.	(10,500 gms.)
C-18, pit 101, bag 761	23.15 lbs.	20 mm.	(10,500 gms.)
C-18, pit 100, bag 762	16.38 lbs.	17 mm.	(7,430 gms.)
C-18, pit 96, fea. 7, bag 840	12.59 lbs.	15 mm.	(5,710 gms.)

*Measurement taken on outside surface of jaw at the middle of the first molar (carnassial).

Total: 31 mandibles (601.13 lbs.)
Average weight: *19.39 lbs.*
Mode: *23.15 lbs.* (second mode = *18.5 lbs.*)
Range: *10.87 lbs.-33.95 lbs.*
Median: *18.5 lbs.*

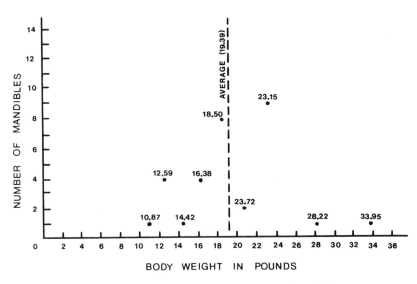

Figure 7.1. Distribution of Cozumel Dogs by Weight.

missing (except as a normal consequence of physical deterioration in the ground). Either this trait has appeared relatively recently as a result of modern selective breeding, or this breed was not used extensively by the prehistoric Maya. The latter explanation is not very likely, since there is abundant evidence that pre-conquest Mexicans used the *Sholo* dog medicinally and for food and assigned it a significant place in their religion (Wright 1970; Tozzer 1941). Spaniards in the Yucatán also observed hairless dogs being used to hunt deer and birds (Roys 1931: 328). Indeed, the Maya language contains a separate word for this particular breed (Allen 1920). Since the lack of skeletal measurements for the hairless dog precludes comparisons with the Cozumel canine material, the possibility that at least some of the Cozumel dogs may be of the *Xoloitzcuintli* variety cannot be ignored.

The other major type of dog present in prehistoric Mexico is the Small Indian Dog or *Techichi* (Allen 1920). According to Allen, this is a small, light-limbed, slenderly proportioned dog with a narrow delicate head, fine muzzle, erect ears, and well-developed tail. Evidence indicates that it was colored black, black and white, or perhaps brown or yellow. The dog appears to have had a widespread distribution extending from central and southwestern North America to parts of northwestern South America. The Museum of Comparative Zoology at Harvard University contains dog bones from the Yucatán, as well as other places, which are thought to belong to this pre-Columbian breed (Allen 1920). Hernández referred to the Techichi as "like our Spaniels, but of sad countenance, though in other respects like ordinary dogs" (cited in Allen 1920). Examination and measurements of Techichi remains from mounds, burials, and refuse deposits in various parts of

Table 7.3 Summary of Dental Measurements of Cozumel Dogs, After Haag (1948)

ALL MEASUREMENTS IN MM.

	I^1-M^2 ALVEOLUS (19)	C-M^2 ALVEOLUS (20)	P^1-M^2 ALVEOLUS (21)	P^2-M^2 ALVEOLUS (22)	M^1-M^2 ALVEOLUS (23)	P^4 CARNASSIAL LENGTH (24)	I_1-M_3 ALVEOLUS (25)	C-M_3 ALVEOLUS (26)	P_1-M_3 ALVEOLUS (27)	P_2-M_3 ALVEOLUS (28)	P_3-M_3 ALVEOLUS (29)	P_4-M_3 ALVEOLUS (30)	M_1-M_3 ALVEOLUS (31)	M_1 CARNASSIAL LENGTH (32)
Sample Size	—	—	—	—	—	17	—	—	3	6	6	9	10	33
Range														
Low	—	—	—	—	—	13.0	—	—	53.0	49.0	42.0	32.0	24.0	16.0
High	—	—	—	—	—	16.5	—	—	60.0	57.0	47.5	38.0	27.0	21.5
Mean ($\overline{X}$)	—	—	—	—	—	15.29	—	—	57.67	53.33	45.33	34.5	25.45	18.25
Standard Deviation (S)	—	—	—	—	—	0.99	—	—	4.04	3.50	2.23	2.03	1.19	1.17
Variance (S^2)	—	—	—	—	—	0.97	—	—	16.34	12.27	4.97	4.125	1.41	1.36

Table 7.4   Summary of Dental Measurements of Small Indian Dogs (Allen 1920:489)

	ALL MEASUREMENTS IN MM.													
	I^1-M^2 ALVEOLUS (19)	C-M^2 ALVEOLUS (20)	P^1-M^2 ALVEOLUS (21)	P^2-M^2 ALVEOLUS (22)	M^1-M^2 ALVEOLUS (23)	P^4 CARNASSIAL LENGTH (24)	I_1-M_3 ALVEOLUS (25)	C-M_3 ALVEOLUS (26)	P_1-M_3 ALVEOLUS (27)	P_2-M_3 ALVEOLUS (28)	P_3-M_3 ALVEOLUS (29)	P_4-M_3 ALVEOLUS (30)	M_1-M_3 ALVEOLUS (31)	M_1 CARNASSIAL LENGTH (32)
Sample Size	8	8	8	8	7	9	2	3	—	3	2	2	2	3
Range Low	74	61	49	42.5	14	14.0	79	74	—	57	48.5	39	30	17.5
Range High	80	67	54	47.0	17	16.6	79	76	—	59	49.0	40	32	18.5
Mean (X)*	—	—	—	—	—	15.36	—	—	—	58.0	48.75	39.5	31.0	18.0
Standard Deviation (S)*	—	—	—	—	—	0.94	—	—	—	1.0	0.35	0.71	1.414	0.5
Variance (S²)*	—	—	—	—	—	0.89	—	—	—	1.0	0.125	0.5	2.0	0.25

*These 3 statistics not calculated for measurements 19-23, 25 and 26 due to lack of these measurements for Cozumel dogs against which comparisons could be made.

Table 7.5 Summary of Postcranial Measurements of Cozumel Dogs, After Haag (1948)

	HUMERUS LENGTH (35)	HEAD DIAMETER HUMERUS (36)	TRAVERSE DIAMETER HUMERUS (37)	LENGTH RADIUS (38)	LENGTH ULNA (39)	ULNA NOTCH LENGTH (40)	FEMUR LENGTH (41)	TIBIA LENGTH (42)
				ALL MEASUREMENTS ARE IN MM.				
Sample Size	2	4	4	—	—	—	—	3
Range								
Low	105.5	27.0	18.0	—	—	—	—	109.0
High	109.0	29.5	20.5	—	—	—	—	135.0
Mean	107.25	28.5	19.375	—	—	—	—	124.17

Table 7.6 Summary of Postcranial Measurements of Allen's (1920) Small Indian Dogs

	HUMERUS LENGTH (35)	HEAD DIAMETER HUMERUS (36)	TRAVERSE DIAMETER HUMERUS (37)	LENGTH RADIUS (38)	LENGTH ULNA (39)	ULNA NOTCH LENGTH (40)	FEMUR LENGTH (41)	TIBIA LENGTH (42)
				ALL MEASUREMENTS ARE IN MM.				
Labna Specimen (Yucatán)	—	—	—	—	—	—	128.0	130.0
Sample Size	—	—	—	—	—	—	1	1
Range	—	—	—	—	—	—	—	—
Mean	—	—	—	—	—	—	—	—

the Americas (see Tables 7.4 and 7.6) indicate, among other things, that all the teeth are relatively small (upper carnassial 14–16.6 millimeters in length) and uncrowded, and the skull is not shortened or broadened in any way. The Cozumel dogs fit this general profile of the breed very well: slender limb bones, narrow head, slender muzzle, relatively small teeth exhibiting no crowding, and a skull of average length (see Tables 7.3 and 7.5). The projected size of the Cozumel dogs makes them roughly comparable to Cocker Spaniels and other small breeds, which concurs with Hernandez' observation of the Techichi. Furthermore, the seventeenth-century writer J. Jonstonus reported that the Indians of Cozumel Island ate these dogs (referring to Techichi) as the Spaniards did rabbits. Those intended for this purpose were castrated in order to be fattened (cited in Allen 1920).

In an attempt to obtain additional evidence that the dogs in the Cozumel sample are the Small Indian Dogs referred to by Allen, measurements were taken of all skulls, mandibles, and certain limb bones, following the standard methods specified by Haag (1948) and Allen (1920) (see Tables 7.3 and 7.5). The mean, standard deviation, and variance were calculated for each dental measurement of both the Cozumel specimens and the Small Indian Dogs listed by Allen (see Tables 7.3 and 7.4). Statistical comparison of the two groups required an F-test for homogeneity of variance. This established that for each separate dental measurement, the variances of the two groups of dogs were not significantly different (Table 7.7), thus satisfying the preliminary requirement for use of the T-test. A T-test was next performed on each measurement the two groups of dogs had in common—numbers 24, 28, 29, 30, 31, and 32. As is apparent in Table 7.8, most of the measurements showed no statistically significant differences between the two groups.

However, measurements 30 and 31 (Alveolus P_4–M_3 and Alveolus M_1–M_3) do show significant differences (Table 7.8). Both of these measurements are taken at the posterior end of the mandibular tooth row. The results indicate that the length of the mandibular molar row varies most significantly between the two groups, with the Cozumel dogs being relatively shorter-jawed, posteriorly. Whereas Allen's dogs average 39.5 millimeters from P_4–M_3, the Cozumel dogs average only 34.5 millimeters. Similarly, Allen's dogs measure on the average 31.0 millimeters from M_1–M_3 while the average of the Cozumel specimens is only 25.45 millimeters. It is difficult to ascertain whether this difference is due to greater crowding of the molar teeth in Cozumel dogs, to smaller overall tooth size, or perhaps to both causes. The two groups of dogs do not differ significantly in the length of M_1 (lower carnassial, measurement 32), which suggests that the degree of tooth crowding is perhaps the most important factor here. This relatively minor difference is entirely consistent with what would be expected of animals from different breeding populations but within the range of a single breed of dog. Dogs in a closed island environment like Cozumel might well

Table 7.7 F-test Values for Cozumel Dogs and Allen's (1920) Small Indian Dogs[1]

MEASUREMENT	CALCULATED F VALUE[2]	DF_1[3]	DF_2[3]	SIGNIFICANT DIFFERENCE
#24- Length P^4 (upper carnassial)	1.0898	16	8	No- variances homogeneous
#28- Alvelous P_2-M_3	12.27	5	2	No- variances homogeneous
#29- Alvelous P_3-M_3	39.76	5	1	No- variances homogeneous
#30- Alvelous P_4-M_3	8.25	8	1	No- variances homogeneous
#31- Alvelous M_1-M_3	1.418	1	9	No- variances homogeneous
#32- Length M_1 (lower carnassial)	5.44	32	2	No- variances homogeneous

[1] These measurements are the only ones in common between the two groups, and thus are the only ones which could be used for comparison.

[2] $F = \dfrac{S_1^2}{S_2^2}$, where S^2 = the variance of each group = $\dfrac{\Sigma x^2 - \dfrac{(\Sigma x)^2}{N}}{N-1}$

[3] df = degrees of freedom. These are calculated from the number of specimens in each group being compared, and are necessary for determining the statistical significance of the calculated F-value.

Table 7.8 T-test Values for Cozumel Dogs and Allen's (1920) Small Indian Dogs[1]

MEASUREMENT	CALCULATED T VALUE[2]	DF[3]	SIGNIFICANT DIFFERENCE	MAXIMUM LEVEL OF SIGNIFICANCE
#24- Length P^4 (upper carnassial)	0.175	24	No	—
#28- Alveolus P_2-M_3	2.192	7	No	—
#29- Alveolus P_3-M_3	2.053	6	No	—
#30- Alveolus P_4-M_3	3.316	9	Yes	.01
#31- Alveolus M_1-M_3	5.911	10	Yes	.001
#32- Length M_1 (lower carnassial)	0.375	34	No	—

[1](See footnote for Table 7.7).

[2]$t = \dfrac{\overline{X}_1 - \overline{X}_2}{\dfrac{S^2}{N_1} + \dfrac{S^2}{N_2}}$, where $S^2 = \dfrac{(N_1 - 1)S_1^2 + (N_2 - 1)S_2^2}{(N_1 - 1)\quad(N_2 - 1)}$

[3]df = degrees of freedom. This is calculated from the sum of the number of specimens in each group: $(N_1 + N_2) - 2$, and is necessary for determining the statistical significance of the calculated t-value.

have become inbred over the centuries and slightly different from other populations of the same type of dog found elsewhere. In contrast, Allen's Small Indian Dogs are from several different widespread localities.

Differences in sample size between the two groups should be mentioned. The statistics on measurement 30 were calculated on the basis of nine Cozumel specimens, while only two of Allen's dogs were complete enough for this measurement. The same is true of 31, where ten Cozumel dogs were used as the basis of computations, again compared to only two of Allen's dogs. These differences in sample sizes might be sufficient to produce spurious T-test results—that is, relatively minor statistical differences between the two groups might be made to appear misleadingly significant.

Whether or not the Cozumel dogs actually differ significantly on a statistical basis from Allen's dogs in length of the posterior mandibular molar row, the similarities between the two groups outweigh their differences. None of the other measurements shows significant differences, particularly in the length of upper and lower carnassials. These teeth seem especially sensitive to size changes caused by selective pressures (Clutton-Brock 1970). A comparison of tibia lengths between the two groups (Tables 7.5 and 7.6) shows the single Allen specimen falling well within the range of the three Cozumel specimens. No other postcranial elements could be compared, since the few limb bones which were available were usually not present in both groups of dogs.

All of the canid elements—teeth as well as limb bones—were aged according to the tables in I. A. Silver (1970) for epiphyseal fusion and dental eruption (see Table 7.9). The ages arrived at should be regarded as minimum ages only, since some permanent teeth (incisors, for example) erupt as early as three months. Nearly 20 percent of the elements are subadult, or less than 21.5 months; this includes the categories of fetal, very immature, immature, 1–5 months, less than 12 months, and less than 21.5 months. This is a conservative estimate, since some of the categories grouped as adult may actually be younger than 21.5 months—for example, those in the greater than 8–9 months or greater than 12 months categories. However, the degree of overlap is probably not very high. Most of these latter categories describe permanent teeth or limb bones from mature animals, but age beyond the date of maturity cannot be determined from the particular tooth or element involved. The adult dogs dominate the sample, representing 66.51 percent of the elements, while the ages of approximately 14 percent could not be determined.

Nearly 14 percent of all dogs fall into the categories of fetal to very immature and 1-5 months (Table 7.10). These represent over 16 percent of the Minimum Numbers of Individuals. This is a significant proportion of the dog population and fits the pattern expected when a domesticated animal is allowed or encouraged to breed and raise young in association with a settled human society. In a wild population of animals being hunted for food and brought back to a site, one might

Table 7.9 Age Distribution of Cozumel Dogs

AGE CATEGORY*	NO. BONES	%
Subadult		
Fetal—very immature	67	10.39
Immature	24	3.72
1-5 months	23	3.56
Less than 12 months	4	0.62
Less than 21.5 months	8	1.24
	126	19.53
Adult		
Adult	161	24.96
Old Adult	2	0.31
Young Adult	1	0.16
More than 5-7 months	172	26.67
More than 8-9 months	27	4.19
More than 10 months	30	4.65
More than 12 months	8	1.24
More than 15-16 months	16	2.48
More than 18 months	12	1.86
	429	66.51
Indeterminate	90	13.95
Total	645	99.99

*Based on tooth eruption and postcranial fusion ages given in Silver 1970.

Table 7.10 Distribution of Cozumel Dogs Aged 5 Months or Less

SITE	NO. BONES	% OF SITES' TOTAL DOG BONES	MNI
C-2	—	—	—
C-9	—	—	—
C-13	51	87.93	1
C-15	—	—	—
C-18	17	20.73	4
C-22	22	4.92	10
C-25	—	—	—
C-27	—	—	—
C-31	—	—	—
Total	90 (= 13.95% of total dog bones)		15 (= 16.13% of all dog MNIs)

expect the percentages of such very young animals to be considerably less (Reed 1970; Perkins 1964). Significant too is the fact that nearly one-third of the bones of these very young puppies are found in human burial contexts; this amounts to 40 percent of the MNIs (Table 7.11).

More than 41 percent of all dog remains are composed of skull elements, mandibles, maxillae, and loose teeth (Table 7.12). This is to be expected, since these elements of the mammalian skeleton are more durable and thus more often preserved archaeologically (Olsen 1971). Noticeable are the relatively high numbers of canines and carnassials among the loose teeth; together, these teeth make up 69.48 percent of the total dog teeth found alone (Table 7.13). Since the normal complement of teeth in an individual dog's dentition is forty-two (based on dental formula 3142/3143 × 2, from Hall and Kelson 1959), the four canines should represent less than 10 percent of the total teeth as should the four carnassial teeth (P^4 and M_1). However, the loose canines represent 37.66 percent of these teeth, while carnassials constitute 31.82 percent (Table 7.12). Both of these categories, then, are overrepresented in the sample by a factor of between three and four times what would normally be expected. This assumes added meaning when one considers that this "loose teeth" category includes only those which could not be matched with or inserted into other mandibles and maxillae excavated from the same proveniences. In many cases the carnassials in particular were found alone and were not associated with any other canid cranial remains. The implication is that these teeth (carnassials and canines) were regarded as somehow special by the Cozumel Maya and were removed for separate use. This cultural pattern apparently characterized the island as a whole and was not specific to any one site (Table 7.14).

The idea that certain dog teeth held special meaning for the Maya is supported by the culturally modified material. Two carnassials were found with holes drilled through their roots as if for stringing for personal adornment. One is an upper right molar, while the other is too fragmentary to allow determination of whether it is an upper or lower Carnassial. (A third tooth, also perforated through the root, is mentioned in Phillips [1979]. Catalogued and removed from the collection in Mexico, it has not been analyzed here.) Two perforated dog canines from two different individuals were also found at Mayapán, two lower canines with drilled or pierced roots were recovered from Altar de Sacrificios, and a lower molar with two drilled holes appeared in the Seibal faunal material (Pollock and Ray 1957; Olsen 1972, 1978).

Positive evidence for cooking practices was limited to thirteen burned or heat-reddened dog bones (one was actually cf. *Canis familiaris*) from only three sites (C-13, C-22, and C-25). These burned bones may represent sacrificial burning of the animals rather than ordinary cooking, since ten of the thirteen bones come from burials or ceremonial structures. This scarcity of burned bone implies not that dogs were not being

Table 7.11 Proveniences of Cozumel Dogs Aged 5 Months or Less*

SITE (A)	PROVENIENCE	AGE	NO. BONES	MNI
C-22	gr. 3, Str. 3-A	1-5 mos.	1	1
C-22	gr. 1, pit 123, Bur. 26	1-5 mos.	4 }	1
C-22	gr. 1, pit 123, Bur. 26	fetal-very imm.	3 }	
C-22	gr. 1, pit 124B, Bur. 24	1-5 mos.	8	3
C-22	gr. 2, pit 128, Str. C	1-5 mos.	1	1
C-22	gr. 3, pit 145	1-5 mos.	1	1
C-22	gr. 3, pit 156, Str. 3-A, HM	fetal-very imm.	1	1
C-22	gr. 7, pit 212, Bur. 37	1-5 mos.	1	1
C-22	gr. 2, pit 129B, Complex 2	fetal-very imm.	2	1
C-18	pit 50	fetal-very imm.	1	1
C-18	pit 82, Str. 2	fetal-very imm.	2	1
C-18	pit 96, Bur. 18	1-5 mos.	7 }	
C-18	pit 96, Bur. 18	fetal-very imm.	6 }	1
C-18	pit 100, midden	fetal-very imm.	1	1
C-13	trench	fetal-very imm.	51	1
Total			90	15

Summary (B)

	No. Bones	%	MNI	%
Burial Contexts	29	32.22	6	40.00
Non-burial Contexts	61	67.78	9	60.00
Total	90	100.0	15	100.00

*Includes the categories fetal to very immature, and 1-5 months.

Table 7.12 Cozumel Dogs: Distribution of Skeletal Elements

SKELETAL ELEMENT	NO. BONES	%	
Skull Elements[1]	37	5.74	
Mandibles and Maxillae	77	11.94	41.55
All Loose Teeth	154	23.87	
Major Limb Bones[2]	89	13.80	
Foot and Toe Bones	100	15.50	
Vertebrae	100	15.50	
Miscellaneous[3]	46	7.13	
Indeterminate	42	6.51	
Total	645	99.99	

[1] Includes premaxillae, skulls, braincases, occipitals, occipital condyles, sphenoids, frontals, parietals, interparietals, temporals, zygomatics, auditory bullae, and periotics.
[2] Includes humeri, radii, ulnae, femora, tibiae, and fibulae.
[3] Includes hyoids, ribs, scapulae, innominates, ilia, ischia, acetabulae, and patellae.

cooked for food, but rather that they were usually not roasted directly over a fire. Stewing might have been employed, leaving no evidence on the bones themselves. No butcher marks were found on any of the dog elements.

Relatively little of the canid material showed evidence of carnivore or rodent gnawing. Only thirty-six elements, or 5.58 percent of all dog bones, had been altered in this way.

Four examples of pathology appeared in this material. One, a nearly complete right tibia (over eighteen months old), showed evidence of bone deformation due to unknown causes. The remaining three were all adult right mandibles exhibiting premortem tooth loss; teeth had been lost and the alveolus completely absorbed.

Burial and ceremonial/administrative contexts account for 69.61 percent of the canid bones (or 47.31 percent of the MNIs—see Table 7.15). Only 4.03 percent of the bones (or 11.83 percent of the MNIs) come from housemound or midden material (Table 7.16). What the remaining proveniences represent is unknown, though it is probable

Table 7.13 Cozumel Dogs: Distribution of Loose Teeth

ELEMENT	NO. TEETH	%	
Indeterminate Teeth	2	1.3	
Incisors	11	7.14	
Canines	58	37.66	
Carnassials ($P^4 + M_1$)	49	31.82	69.48
Other Molars and Premolars	34	22.08	
Total	154	100.00	

Table 7.14 Cozumel Dogs: Distribution of Loose Canines and Carnassials

SITE	NO. OF TEETH	MIN. NO. OF INDIVIDUALS
(A) Distribution of Loose Canine Teeth		
C-9	1	1
C-13	2	2
C-15	2	2
C-18	5	3
C-22	43	15
C-25	4	2
C-31	1	1
Total	58	26
(B) Distribution of Loose Upper Carnassials (P^4)		
C-13	3	2
C-15	1	1
C-18	2	1
C-22	14	9
C-25	1	1
Total	21	14
(C) Distribution of Loose Lower Carnassials (M_1)		
C-15	2	2
C-18	2	2
C-22	20	13
C-25	2	1
C-27	2	1
Total	28	19

that at least some are also housemounds. However, a significant proportion (perhaps the majority) of all canid material was excavated from ceremonial precincts.

The dog is known to have played an important role in Maya religion (Tozzer and Allen 1910; Wright 1970; Pohl 1976; Schellhas 1904; Allen 1920; Tozzer 1941). In particular, the dog was connected with death and destruction. Also regarded as a messenger to prepare the way to the other world, it was often placed in its master's grave to help ferry his soul across a great underworld river. This is consistent with archaeological data from several other Maya sites where dogs have been found in burials. One such burial was the tomb of a high–status male at Kaminaljuyu (J. E. S. Thompson 1966: 218). Zacaleu also contained three dog skeletons (two immature) intentionally interred in two human graves, plus two other fragmentary skulls found in a cache and another burial (Woodbury and Trik 1953). Dog bones occur in at least two different tombs (Lots C-30 and A-125) at Mayapán. In addition, large quantities of the animal were found in debris from the floor of a cenote

**Table 7.15 Dogs in Burials and Ceremonial/
Administrative Contexts***

SITE	PROVENIENCE	DATE	NO. BONES	MNI
C-13	pit 13, Burial #4	DH & LPC	3	1
C-15	pit 179, Burial #31	N.D.	19	2
C-31	pit 250, Burial #39	N.D.	4	1
C-18	pit 69, Tomb	LPC	2	1
C-18	pit 82, Struc. 2	LPC	2	1
C-18	pit 96, Burial #18	PF	13	1
C-25	pit 42, inside Altar	N.D.	1	1
C-22	gr. 1, pit 117, Burials	LPC	4	1
C-22	gr. 1, pit 123, Burial #26	LPC	186	11
C-22	gr. 1, pit 124B, Burial #24	LPC	97	7
C-22	gr. 2, pit 129, Complex 2	LPC	9	3
C-22	gr. 2, pit 131, Struc. 2-B	LPC	1	1
C-22	gr. 3, pit 142, Complex 3	LPC	1	1
C-22	gr. 3, pit 143, Burial #27	LPC	89	2
C-22	gr. 3, pit 144, Complex 3	LPC	2	1
C-22	gr. 3, pit 148, Burial #28	LPC	1	1
C-22	gr. 3, pit 149, Burial #30	LPC	6	1
C-22	gr. 3, struc. 3-A	LPC	2	2
C-22	gr. 6, pit 195B, Struc. 6-A	N.D.	2	1
C-22	gr. 6, pit 199, Burial #36	N.D.	2	1
C-22	gr. 6, pit 216, Tomb	N.D.	1	1
C-22	gr. 7, pit 205, Struc. 7-B	N.D.	1	1
C-22	gr. 7, pit 212, Burial #37	LPC	1	1
Total			449	44

*Includes *Canis familiaris* and ?*Canis familiaris.*

(414 bones) and from building debris between a colonnaded hall and a temple platform (107 bones) at the same site (Pollock and Ray 1957).

Besides its use in burials, the dog has been mentioned numerous times as a sacrificial animal (see especially Landa in Tozzer 1941: 109, 114, 115, 143, 145, 162, 164, 183, 203). Seler (1890) refers to dog sacrifices in the Yucatán, sometimes in place of human beings. The Maya codices show dogs in a variety of attitudes, but nearly always in context with various birds and mammals which are to be sacrificed (Tozzer and Allen 1910). Pohl (1976: 219) refers to Classic period grafitti at Tikal depicting what she believes is a dog in a ceremonial procession which possibly represents the prelude to sacrifice of the animal. This site also contained a multiple burial with dog bones in it. Landa specifically mentions the Ixchel idol on Cozumel where, among other things, dogs were offered as sacrifices (Tozzer 1941: 109). He also describes the sacrifice of a dog "spotted with the color of cacao" on one occasion and states that dogs were the most common objects of sacrifice after

Table 7.16 Cozumel Dogs[1] in Middens and Housemound Contexts[2]

SITE	PROVENIENCE	TIME PERIOD	# BONES	MIN. NO. INDIV.
C-18	pit 81, Housemound	Late Postclassic	1	1
C-18	pit 98, Housemound	Postclassic	1	1
C-18	pit 100, Midden	Late Postclassic	13	3
C-22	pit 157, Housemound	Postclassic	3	2
C-22	pit 163, Housemound	Postclassic	3	2
C-22	pit 164, Housemound	Postclassic	1	1
C-22	gr. 3, pit 156, Str. 3-A, Housemound	Late Postclassic	4	1
Total			26	11

[1]Includes *Canis familiaris* and *?Canis familiaris.*
[2]Includes only those bones in proveniences definitely labeled as middens or housemounds in field notes.

Table 7.17   Dates of Cozumel Dogs*

SITE (A)	TIME PERIOD	NO. BONES	MNI
C-2	LPC	3	2
C-13	DH & LPC	5	2
	No Date	53	2
C-15	No Date	19	2
C-9	No Date	12	1
C-27	No Date	3	3
C-31	No Date	4	1
C-18	No Date	11	5
	LPC	20	8
	PC	38	4
	PF	13	1
C-25	No Date	8	4
	PC	3	1
	LPC	6	4
C-22	LPC	433	43
	No Date	7	5
	PC	7	5
Total		645	93

Summary (B) *Time Period*	*No. Bones*	%		*MNI*	%	
LPC & DH	467	72.40	79.84	59	63.44	74.19
PC	48	7.44		10	10.75	
PF	13	2.01	20.15	1	1.07	25.80
NO DATE	117	18.14		23	24.73	
Total	645	99.99		93	99.99	

*Includes *Canis familiaris* and ?*Canis familiaris.*

human beings. At such times, the heart of the animal was often re-moved and burned, the blood used to anoint the idols, and the animal then cooked and eaten. Early Spanish historians reported that the Indians relished dog flesh as a delicacy, and that hairless dogs in particular were found in the sixteenth-century Mexican marketplace (Wright 1970).

Dogs apparently were also used in hunting. A Classic period poly-chrome vessel shows the use of small dogs in the hunt; in the Yucatán, Spaniards observed hairless dogs being used to hunt deer and birds (Tozzer 1941: 186, 203). Pohl (1976: 218) reports that many scenes on ancient polychrome vessels apparently involve dogs in trading ex-peditions; referring to Landa, she suggests that "the animals may have served as guards against thieves and highwaymen, which apparently were a menace at least in Postclasssic times."

According to Wright (1970: 36–37), dogs may also have been used in medicine. Referring to present-day folk practices in some parts of

Mexico, he suggests that the hairless *Sholo* dog could have been used in place of a hot-water bottle to alleviate such simple ailments as abdominal pains. In some areas, possession of such a dog is still believed to protect people against colds and other illnesses.

The great majority of the Cozumel canids are from Late Postclassic and historic period contexts (72.40 percent of the bones, or 63.44 percent of the MNIs—see Table 7.17). Very few of the dogs are definitely from time periods before the Postclassic—only 2.01 percent of the bones or 1.07 percent of the MNIs. Therefore, cultural patterns discussed here must be characterized primarily as Late Postclassic practices.

8. Other Mammals

MAMMALS OTHER THAN DOGS are second only to fishes in numerical importance on Cozumel, encompassing sixteen different taxa (Table 8.1). These species range from very small animals such as bats and rodents, to large species such as horses, deer and peccaries (see Table 8.2). The major topics addressed with respect to these mammals include habitat requirements, the hunting strategies most likely used to procure them, possible cooking methods, the distribution among different age groups, the percentages of the various skeletal elements, the proveniences and time periods in which they are found, their ceremonial importance, cultural modifications, the possible domestication or taming of certain species, and any pathologies. Species which were available but not used by the Cozumel Maya are also discussed, including the jaguar, armadillo, tapir, monkey, and manatee. Three of the most popular mammals in this sample—peccaries, dogs, and opossums—are relatively fat-rich species, which allows certain deductions to be made concerning the nutrition of Cozumel inhabitants.

Large Mammals

The bones of the collared peccary or javelina (*Tayassu tajacu* = *Pecari* or *Dicotyles tajacu*) represent the most plentiful mammal found in the Cozumel sites. At least 191 individuals are indicated by 1,221 bones (see Tables 8.2, 8.3). Peccaries account for more than 16 percent of the mammal bones, or about 27 percent of the MNI. These percentages should probably be even higher, since many of the unidentifiable large mammal bones (1,623 fragments) are quite likely peccary. The peccary occurs in the Maya codices in a variety of contexts (see Tezzer and Allen 1910). The animal is apparently associated with rain, the sky, constellation bands, and hunting. In the hunting scenes of the Tro-Cortesianus Codex, peccaries are shown being captured alive, either

Table 8.1   Cozumel Mammals: Taxonomic List

Class: Mammalia
  Order Marsupialia
    Family Didelphidae (opossums)
      Didelphis marsupialis (common opossum)
  Order Chiroptera
    Family Phyllostomidae (American leaf-nosed bats)
      ? *Micronycteris megalotis* (Brazilian small-eared bat)
  Order Lagomorpha
    Family Leporidae (hares and rabbits)
      Sylvilagus sp. (cottontail rabbits)
  Order Rodentia
    Family Cricetidae (cricetid rodents)
      Peromyscus cf. P. leucopus (white-footed mouse)
      Peromyscus sp. (white-footed mice)
      Sigmodon hispidus (hispid cotton rat)
    Family Erethizontidae (New World porcupines)
      Coendu mexicanus (Mexican porcupine)
    Family Dasyproctidae (pacas and agoutis)
      Cuniculus (= Agouti) paca
  Order Carnivora
    Family Canidae (coyotes, wolves, dogs, and foxes)
      Canis familiaris (domestic dog)
      Urocyon cinereoargenteus (gray fox)
    Family Procyonidae (raccoons and relatives)
      Procyon cf. P. pygmaeus (Cozumel Island raccoon)
      Nasua cf. N. nelsoni (Cozumel Island coati)
      raccoon/coati
  Order Perissodactyla
    Family Equidae (horses and relatives)
      Equus caballus (domestic horse)
  Order Artiodactyla
    Family Tayassuidae (peccaries)
      Tayassu (= Dicotyles = Pecari) tajacu (collared peccary)
    Family Cervidae (deer and allies)
      Odocoileus virginianus (white-tailed deer)
    Family Bovidae
      Ovis aries (domestic sheep)

in pitfalls or in snares of the "jerk-up" type. The aim of the hunt appears to be to obtain animals for sacrifice (Tozzer and Allen 1910: 293, 352). This animal might be confused osteologically with the white-lipped peccary *(Tayassu pecari)*, which is larger in body size and does not occur on Cozumel or the northern two-thirds of the Yucatán Peninsula (see Hall and Kelson 1959: 996–997). A subspecies of the collared peccary *(T. tajacu nanus)* has been named which is endemic to Cozumel, but some biologists doubt whether it is actually distinct from the adjacent species,

Table 8.2 Cozumel Mammals

TAXON	NO. BONES	%	MNI	%	
Indeterminate	65	0.87	—	—	Indefinite category:
Mammal	437	5.83	—	—	2,707 bones
Large Mammal	1,623	21.64	—	—	36.1%
Medium Mammal	406	5.41	—	—	
Small Mammal	176	2.35	—	—	
? Brazilian Small-eared Bat (Phyllostomidae)	2	0.03	2	0.28	
Cricetid Rodents	1	0.01	1	0.14	
White-footed mice (Peromyscus sp.)	1	0.01	1	0.14	Possible Intrusives:
White-footed mouse (Peromyscus cf. P. leucopus)	2	0.03	1	0.14	74 37
Hispid Cotton Rat (Sigmodon hispidus)	68	0.91	32	4.55	0.99% 5.26%
Opossum	1,110	14.80	90	12.78	

? Opossum	6	0.08	—	—
Cottontail Rabbit	487	6.49	109	15.48
? Cottontail Rabbit	10	0.13	—	—
Coati	608	8.11	88	12.50
Large Procyonid- ?Coati	17	0.23	6	0.85
Raccoon	19	0.25	13	1.85
Raccoon/Coati	22	0.29	12	1.70
Gray Fox	530	7.07	48	6.82
Mexican Porcupine	1	0.01	1	0.14
Paca	1	0.01	1	0.14
Collared Peccary	1,221	16.28	191	27.13
Domestic Dogs + ?Dogs	645	8.60	93	13.21
White-tailed Deer	11	0.15	10	1.42
?White-tailed Deer	3	0.04	—	—
Domestic Sheep	18	0.24	2	0.28
Equus/Bos (Horse/Cow)	4	0.05	1	0.14
Domestic Horse	3	0.04	2	0.28
?Horse	1	0.01	—	—
?Artiodactyl	1	0.01	—	—
Total	7,499	99.98	704	99.93

Small Mammals:
1,613   199
21.51%   28.27%

Medium Mammals:
1,198   169
15.97%   24.0%

Large Mammals:
1,907   299
25.43%   42.47%

Table 8.3   Major Cozumel Mammals in Order of Importance

TAXON	NO. BONES		MNI	
(A) By Bone Count				
Collared Peccary	1,221		191	
Opossum[1]	1,116		90	
All Procyonids[2]	666		119	
Dogs[3]	645		93	
Gray Fox	530		48	
Cottontail Rabbits[4]	497		109	
Total	4,675	(62.34% of all Mammals)	650	(92.33% of all mammal MNIs)
(B) By MNI				
Collared Peccary	1,221		191	
All Procyonids	666		119	
Cottontail Rabbits	497		109	
Dogs	645		93	
Opossum	1,116		90	
Gray Fox	530		48	
Total	4,675		650	

[1]Includes 6 ?opossum bones.
[2]Includes coati, ?coati, raccoon, and raccoon/coati bones.
[3]Includes 17 ?dog bones.
[4]Includes 10 ?cottontail bones.

T.t. yucatanensis (Hall and Kelson 1959: 997; Jones and Lawlor 1965). In any case, no white-lipped peccaries have been reported from the island, and no skeletal evidence indicated that the white-lipped species might also be present. Environmentally, this is logical since the latter "is an animal of the virgin forest and does not frequent cutover or scrub forest as does the javelina" or collared peccary (Leopold 1959: 498). Cozumel would have provided the disturbed rainforest and dense, scrubby ground cover which represent optimal habitat for the collared peccary. Peccaries on the island may have been introduced by man (unlike most of the other animals now living there), but it is not known when this may have occurred (Hall and Kelson 1959; Jones and Lawlor 1965).

The collared peccary is omnivorous, although it derives most of its diet from plants and plant products. It is likely that on Cozumel, as elsewhere, the fruits of tropical trees such as palms, figs, and the *zapote* served as staples. In addition, the animal will occasionally turn to cultivated crops and can cause considerable damage in the *milpas* (Leopold 1959). The compatibility of this species with the island habitat, its attraction to human settlements for food, and the relatively large amount of meat per animal are factors which probably explain its prominence in the Cozumel faunal collection.

The Cozumel peccaries appeared to represent much smaller individuals than their North American counterparts. Since a relatively large comparative collection of Arizona collared peccaries was the only good skeletal series available, measurements were taken for statistical comparison. All measurements were taken following the standard methods indicated in Von Den Driesch (1976). Six different mandibular and maxillary measurements were compared using the T-test (Tables 8.4 & 8.5). As shown in Table 8.6, all of the measurements are significantly different between the two groups of animals. Use of the hypothesis that the Cozumel peccaries would be significantly smaller than the Arizona specimens resulted in positive confirmation at the .0005 level—an extremely high level of significance. However, the calculated F-Test values (Table 8.7) showed the variances of the two groups to be non-homogeneous in several cases: the measurements P_2-P_4, P^2-P^4, M^1-M^3, and total length of upper tooth row. This means that theoretically the T-Test probably should not be performed on those particular measurements. However, recent studies based on thousands of computer-simulated T-Tests indicate that the statistical validity of the results is not altered if homogeneity of variance is violated (R. A. Thompson, personal communication 1979).

Several cranial measurements were also taken on both groups of peccaries (Table 8.8). Unfortunately, very few Cozumel specimens were complete enough for these measurements, so that the use of the T-Test for comparison was not practical. However, with only one exception, the Cozumel peccaries were smaller than even the smallest of the Arizona animals, and they were much smaller than the mean of the Arizona specimens in all cases. This trend follows the same pattern established for the mandibular and maxillary measurements.

The Cozumel peccaries apparently represent a population of animals significantly smaller than those from Arizona. These smaller measurements may confirm the presence of the subspecies said to be peculiar to Cozumel. One cannot be sure, however, since no measurements were available as of 1980 for other Mexican collared peccaries. Preferably, a large sample of peccaries from the adjacent Yucatán peninsula would be examined for comparison with those from Cozumel. Significantly, the range of values for each measurement on the Cozumel specimens is generally much more restricted than the ranges of values for the Arizona peccaries (see Tables 8.4, 8.5 and 8.6). This is what would be expected of a smaller and probably inbred island population of animals. There is nothing to indicate that any of the peccaries excavated from the Cozumel sites were imported from locations outside the island.

A significant proportion (16.05 percent) of the peccaries are subadults (Table 8.9). Most of the mandibles and maxillae were aged using the tooth eruption stages established by Sowls (1961) and Kirkpatrick

Table 8.4 Summary of Cozumel Collared Peccaries
Mandibular and Maxillary Measurements (in mm.)

	LENGTH OF LOWER PRE-MOLAR ROW (P_2-P_4)	LENGTH OF LOWER MOLAR ROW (M_1-P_4)	TOT. LENGTH LOWER TOOTH ROW	LENGTH OF UPPER PRE-MOLAR ROW (P^2-P^4)	LENGTH OF UPPER MOLAR ROW (M^1-M^3)	TOT. LENGTH UPPER TOOTH ROW	CRANIAL WIDTH
Sample Size	28	15	12	15	15	10	
Range							
Low	19.0	32.0	54.0	20.5	28.0	49.5	
High	24.0	37.0	60.0	24.0	31.0	54.0	
Mean ($\overline{X}$)	22.05	33.9	55.87	22.33	29.8	52.0	
Standard Deviation(s)	1.05	1.23	0.62	0.82	0.922	0.40	
Variance (S^2)	1.10	1.51	3.84	0.67	0.85	1.61	

Table 8.5 Summary of Arizona Collared Peccaries
Mandibular and Maxillary Measurements (in mm.)

	LENGTH OF LOWER PRE-MOLAR ROW $(P_2\text{-}P_4)$	LENGTH OF LOWER MOLAR ROW $(M_1\text{-}P_4)$	TOT. LENGTH LOWER TOOTH ROW	LENGTH OF UPPER PRE-MOLAR ROW $(P^2\text{-}P^4)$	LENGTH OF UPPER MOLAR ROW $(M^1\text{-}M^3)$	TOT. LENGTH UPPER TOOTH ROW	CRANIAL WIDTH
Sample Size	43	43	43	38	38	38	
Range							
Low	23.0	39.0	64.0	23.0	31.0	56.0	
High	31.0	46.0	77.0	30.5	39.0	70.0	
Mean $(\overline{X})$	26.15	42.42	68.62	26.95	35.37	62.87	
Standard							
Deviation(s)	1.69	1.74	2.79	1.88	1.88	3.36	
Variance (S^2)	2.86	3.02	7.77	3.54	3.55	11.31	

Table 8.6 T-test Values for Cozumel and Arizona Peccaries

MEASUREMENT	CALCULATED[1] T-VALUE	DF[2]	SIGNIFICANT DIFFERENCE	MAXIMUM LEVEL[4] OF SIGNIFICANCE
Length Lower Premolar Row (P_2-P_4)	11.39	69	Yes[3]	.0005
Length Lower Molar Row	17.42	56	Yes	.005
Total Length Lower Tooth Row	14.83	53	Yes	.005
Length Upper Premolar Row (P^2-P^4)	9.24	51	Yes[3]	.005
Length Upper Molar Row (M^1-M^3)	10.92	51	Yes[3]	.005
Total Length Upper Tooth Row	9.97	46	Yes[3]	.005

$$[1]\,t = \frac{X_1 - X_2}{\sqrt{\dfrac{S^2}{N_1} + \dfrac{S^2}{N_2}}}, \text{ where } S^2 = \frac{(N_1 - 1)S_1^2 + (N_2 - 1)S_2^2}{(N_1 - 1) + (N_2 - 1)}$$

[2]df = degrees of freedom. This is calculated from the sum of the number of specimens in each group: $(N_1 + N_2) - 2$, and is necessary for determining the statistical significance of the calculated t-value.

[3]It should be noted that the F-test for this measurement showed the variances of the two groups to be non-homogeneous.

[4]This level of significance is the result of a *directional* hypothesis (i.e., that the Cozumel peccaries would be significantly smaller than the Arizona peccaries), so that the original probability level found in the t-tables (.001) has been cut in half.

Table 8.7 F-test Values for Cozumel and Arizona Peccaries

MEASUREMENT	CALCULATED[1] F VALUE	$DF_1{}^2$	$DF_2{}^2$	SIGNIFICANT DIFFERENCE
Length Lower Premolar Row (P_2-P_4)	2.6	42	27	Yes, variances not homogeneous
Length Lower Molar Row (M_1-M_3)	2.0	42	14	No, variances are homogeneous
Total Length Lower Tooth Row	2.02	42	11	No, variances are homogeneous
Length Upper Premolar Row (P^2-P^4)	5.28	37	14	Yes, variances not homogeneous
Length Upper Molar Row (M^1-M^3)	4.18	37	14	Yes, variances not homogeneous
Total Length Upper Tooth Row	7.02	37	9	Yes, variances not homogeneous

[1]$F = \dfrac{S_1{}^2}{S_2{}^2}$, where S^2 = the variance of each group = $\dfrac{\Sigma x^2 - \dfrac{(\Sigma x)^2}{N}}{N-1}$. These are calculated from the number of specimens in each group being compared, and are necessary for determining the statistical significance of the calculated F-value.

[2]df = degrees of freedom.

Table 8.8   Cozumel and Arizona Collared Peccaries
Summary of Cranial Measurements (in mm.)

	PROFILE LENGTH (CRANIUM)	EXTENDED PROFILE LENGTH	ZYGOMATIC BREADTH	GREATEST FRONTAL BREADTH
Arizona Specimens				
Sample Size	38	38	38	37
Range				
Low	222	226	96	68
High	252	257	120	86
Mean ($\overline{X}$)	231.33	236.05	104.43	76.35
Cozumel Specimens				
Sample Size	1	—	1	2
Range				
Low	202	—	95	64
High	—	—	—	70
Mean ($\overline{X}$)	—	—	—	97

and Sowls (1962). As with the ages of dogs, these should be regarded only as minimum ages. The adult categories of approximately two years, three years, four years, five years, and more than five years are based on the degree of root closure of the canine tooth (L. K. Sowls, personal communication 1978).

The number of peccaries aged twelve months or less constitutes nearly 14 percent of the bones, or over 24 percent of the MNIs (Table 8.10). This follows the same pattern as the domestic dogs, which is somewhat surprising. Perhaps the Cozumel hunters preferred the tender meat of the younger animals and felt that taking a full quarter of their peccary supplies from this age group was not enough to endanger future population numbers of the animal. However, a relatively high percentage of young animals can indicate human control of the species in question since breeding females and their young would then be present in the site (Reed 1970; Perkins 1964).

The possibility that human intervention occurred on Cozumel with respect to peccaries should be seriously considered. Pohl (1976) discusses in some detail the idea that these animals were kept and tamed by the Maya for eating or ritual purposes, particularly during the Postclassic period at the site of Flores. According to Pohl, native hunters in Central America claim that peccaries are easily fattened and, with special care, lose their gamey taste, acquiring a flavor comparable to pork. Collared peccaries are often kept around houses and used as "watch dogs," and can even be trained to come when called. There is some evidence that these animals thrive in captivity and readily produce young (Crandall 1964: 528–529). However, recent breeding experiments at

Table 8.9   Age Distribution of Cozumel Peccaries

AGE CATEGORY	NO. BONES	%
Subadult		
Fetal—very immature	3	0.25
Immature	144	11.79
1-5 months	2	0.16
Less than 12 months	19	1.56
Less than 21.5 months	28	2.29
	196	16.05
Adult		
Adult	428	35.05
Old Adult	11	0.90
Young Adult	13	1.06
More than 10 months	1	0.08
More than 12 months	12	0.98
More than 18 months	3	0.25
More than 21.5 months	119	9.75
Approximately 2 years	7	0.57
Approximately 3 years	30	2.46
Approximately 4 years	13	1.06
Approximately 5 years	16	1.31
More than 5 years	22	1.80
	675	55.27
Indeterminate	350	28.67
Total	1,221	99.99

a peccary farm in Belize indicate that although the survival rate of off-spring is high (better even than that of domestic pigs), the rate of reproduction may be relatively low (Pohl 1976).

Intriguingly, Bernal Diaz del Castillo mentions corrals on Cozumel containing the "pigs of the land, which have their navels on their backs" (quoted in Edwards 1957: 133). The "navel" apparently refers to the prominent scent gland characteristic of peccaries (see Tozzer 1941: 204). Edwards notes that this reference by Castillo is somewhat tenuous, however, since the latest translation of his manuscript omits completely the section in which corrals are mentioned. Nonetheless, an elderly Maya informant in Belize reported that the ancients had corralled peccaries, preferably near *cohune* palm groves so that food would be available to the animals (Pohl 1976). The stone circles found in several of the Cozumel sites (mentioned in Chapter 6) could easily have been used as peccary pens. This does not necessarily imply that the animals would have been fully domesticated, but could mean that they were merely tamed and kept convenient for human use. This would explain the relatively high numbers of young animals found in the Cozumel sample.

Table 8.10   Distribution of Peccaries Aged 12 Months or Less*

SITE	NO. BONES		% OF SITE'S TOT. PECCARY BONES	MNI	
C-13	2		4.00	1	
C-15	9		56.25	2	
C-18	22		9.78	11	
C-22	41		7.44	16	
C-25	91		26.69	15	
C-27	3		7.89	1	
Total	168	(= 13.76% of total peccary bones)		46	(= 24.08% of all peccary MNIs)

*Includes the categories fetal to very immature, immature, 1-5 months, and less than 12 months.

A predominance of cranial elements (including loose teeth, mandibles, and maxillae) was found. These elements constitute 45.7 percent of all peccary remains (Table 8.11), which is not unexpected given their greater durability in archaeological contexts. There is a relatively high number of loose teeth (204), of which nearly 53 percent are canines (Table 8.12); these represent a minimum of forty-five individuals widely distributed over six different sites on the island (Table 8.13). The four canines in an individual peccary's dentition normally constitute 10.53 percent of its total teeth (based on the dental formula 2133/3133 × 2 = 38, from Hall and Kelson 1959: 994); therefore, loose canines are

Table 8.11   Cozumel Peccaries: Distribution of Skeletal Elements

SKELETAL ELEMENT	NO. OF BONES	%	
Skull Elements[1]	134	10.97	
Mandibles and Maxillae	220	18.02	} 45.70%
Loose Teeth	204	16.71	
Major Limb Bones[2]	187	15.31	
Foot and Toe Bones	271	22.19	
Vertebrae	80	6.55	
Miscellaneous[3]	98	8.03	
Indeterminate	27	2.21	
Total	1,221	99.99	

[1]Includes premaxillae, skulls, braincases, occipital condyles, frontals, parietals, temporals, zygomatics, auditory bullae, periotics, and nasals.
[2]Includes humeri, radii, ulnae, femora, tibiae, and fibulae.
[3]Includes hyoids, sternebrae, ribs, scapulae, innominates, ilia, ischia, pubes, acetabulae, and patellae.

Table 8.12 Cozumel Peccaries: Distribution of Loose Teeth

TOOTH	NUMBER	%
Cheekteeth	1	0.49
Incisors	32	15.69
Canines	108	52.94
Premolars	19	9.31
Molars	44	21.57
Total	204	100.00

overrepresented in the sample by more than five times their expected value. These loose teeth are only those which could not be assigned to other mandibles and maxillae excavated from the same proveniences. As with the dog canines and carnassial teeth, peccary canines apparently had been singled out for preferential treatment.

This conclusion is supported by the culturally modified peccary remains in the sample, which include two canines and a phalanx. One of the canines is a fragmentary lower right immature tooth which had been polished, while the other, catalogued and removed from the collection in Mexico, was reportedly notched near its base. The toe bone was perforated near the lower end. In addition, Phillips (1979) refers to several other probable peccary elements removed in Mexico and not included here: two more teeth (one canine and one cheek tooth), both with holes drilled through their bases, and eight phalanges (seven of the toes are perforated, while one is incised). Five perforated or otherwise modified peccary canines were found at Mayapán (Pollock and Ray 1957), which supports the idea that animal teeth had some special meaning for the Maya. Merwin and Vaillant (1932) also report that perforated jaguar and crocodile canines were recovered from Holmul, Guatemala. They cite numerous examples of carved animal teeth and teeth imitated in jade or pottery from several Latin American sites, concluding that this was probably a widespread cult practice.

Table 8.13 Cozumel Peccaries: Distribution of Loose Canines

SITE	NO. OF TEETH	MIN. NO. INDIVIDUALS
C-13	5	3
C-15	1	1
C-18	34	14
C-22	36	13
C-25	30	12
C-27	2	2
Total	108	45

The intrasite distribution of peccary skull elements versus post-cranial remains produces another significant pattern (Table 8.14). Pohl (1976) found a tendency for skull elements to appear in housemounds and for postcranial remains to be associated with elite contexts at both Seibal and Mayapán. San Gervasio (C-22) was chosen among the Co-zumel sites to test this pattern, since it alone contains a sufficiently large sample of both housemounds and elite proveniences for comparison. The present data strongly support Pohl's correlation. Burials (elite contexts) contained nearly 70 percent of the postcranial peccary re-mains, while over 75 percent of peccaries found in housemounds were skull elements. Pohl suggests that this pattern means the elite preferred the meaty limbs. Put another way, the elite were sufficiently powerful to appropriate for their own use the more desirable cuts of meat. Eth-nographic reports also indicate that eating a baked peccary head may have been practiced in the Yucatán by the Postclassic elite (Roys 1933), although it is not certain whether this custom was of Mexican or Mayan origin. The animal was definitely a common sacrifice in post-Conquest times (see Tozzer 1941: 5, 115). The Cozumel elite apparently followed the same pattern as at Seibal and Mayapán.

The majority of peccaries whose cultural context can be deter-mined come from burials and ceremonial/administrative contexts (Table 8.15). A similar trend was noted at Mayapán, where this species fre-quently occurred in association with dwellings of the aristocracy (Pollock and Ray 1957).

Peccaries are widely distributed among the major sites on the island (Table 8.16), and no unusual patterns are discernible. As expected, the larger sites with generally larger sample sizes of excavated faunal material also produced higher numbers of peccary remains.

Over 50 percent of the peccary bones occur in either Late Postclassic or Postclassic contexts (Table 8.17); this accounts for nearly 61 per-cent of the MNIs. Less than 16 percent of the bones, or fewer than 8 percent of the MNIs, represent the earlier periods. However, approxi-mately 33 percent of the remains (almost 32 percent of the MNIs) were from undated proveniences, and determination of the dates might alter this pattern.

Twenty-five peccary bones from five different sites showed evi-dence of burning or heat-darkening. This implies that at least some of the meat was roasted directly over the fire while still on the bones. How-ever, boiling and stewing were apparently more commonly used to pre-pare the meat.

Only two bones showed evidence of butchering. These were both from La Expedición (C-25); one was the nuchal crest of the skull, while the other was a right mandibular angle. Interestingly, the only butchered peccary bone Pohl (1976) reports from five major Maya sites in the Petén is also a mandible. Perhaps this reflects an attempt to skin the flesh off the skull and jaws, something which might have occurred had the head indeed been an item for consumption.

Table 8.14 Distribution of Peccary Elements at San Gervasio (C-22): Burials Versus Housemounds

CULTURAL CONTEXT	NO. SKULL ELEMENTS	%	NO. POST-CRANIAL ELEMENTS	%	TOTAL	%
Burials	44	30.77	99	69.23	143	100.00
Housemounds	44	75.86	14	24.14	58	100.00

Table 8.15   Distribution of Peccaries by Provenience

PROVENIENCE	NO. BONES	%	MNI	%
Housemounds and middens	136	11.14	30	15.71
Burials and ceremonial/ administrative contexts	600	49.14	53	27.75
Indeterminate	485	39.72	108	56.54
Total	1,221	100.00	191	100.00

A total of fifty-four elements from four sites had been either rodent-gnawed or carnivore-chewed; this represents only 4.42 percent of all peccary bones.

One case of pathology was evident in this material. A lower right canine from an animal approximately three years of age showed evidence of bone deformation. Whether this was due to congenital causes or injury is not known.

WHITE-TAILED DEER

The Cozumel sites represent a striking exception to the usual occurrence of the white-tailed deer, *Odocoileus virginianus,* as the most numerous mammal in Maya sites. Deer were a staple in the Mayan diet, as well as a major tool source. For example, this animal is the predominant species at the sites of Seibal, Zacaleu, Mayapán, Altar de Sacrificios, Dzibilchaltún, and Lubaantún (Olsen 1972 and 1978, Woodbury and Trik 1953, Pollock and Ray 1957, Wing 1975, Wing and Steadman 1980). The Cozumel sites, however, contain a total of fourteen bones (a minimum of ten individuals) (Tables 8.2 and 8.18), making white-tailed deer a relatively insignificant animal in this prehistoric economy. It appears that peccaries displaced deer as the major dietary staple on

Table 8.16   Cozumel Peccaries: Totals by Site

SITE	NO. BONES	%	MNI	%
C-13	50	4.09	6	3.14
C-15	16	1.31	2	1.04
C-18	225	18.42	43	22.51
C-22	551	45.12	76	39.79
C-25	341	27.92	54	28.27
C-27	38	3.11	10	5.23
Total	1,221	99.97	191	99.98

Table 8.17 Cozumel Peccaries: Time Periods

TIME PERIOD	NO. BONES	%		MNI	%	
Late Postclassic and Historic	549	44.96	} 51.27	95	49.73	} 60.73
Postclassic	77	6.31		21	10.99	
Pre-Postclassic	37	3.03	} 15.36	5	2.62	} 7.33
Terminal Classic	5	0.41		2	1.05	
Pure Florescent	142	11.63		5	2.62	
Early Period (Classic)	6	0.49		2	1.05	
No Date	405	33.17		61	31.94	
Total	1,221	100.00		191	100.00	

Table 8.18 Distribution of Minor Mammals by Site

SPECIES	SITE	NO. BONES	%	MNI	%
Paca (*Cuniculus Paca*)	C-22	1	2.32	1	5.88
Mexican Porcupine (*Coendu mexicanus*)	C-25	1	2.32	1	5.88
White-tailed Deer[1] (*Odocoileus virginianus*)	C-13	3	6.98	2	11.76
White-tailed Deer	C-18	1	2.32	1	5.88
White-tailed Deer	C-25	2	4.65	2	11.76
?White-tailed Deer	C-15	1	2.32	—	—
White-tailed Deer	C-27	1	2.32	1	5.88
White-tailed Deer	C-22	6	13.95	4	23.53
Subtotal		14	32.56	10	58.82
Domestic Sheep (*Ovis aries*)	C-27	18	41.86	2	11.76
Domestic Horse[2] (*Equus caballus*)	C-13	2	4.65	1	5.88
?*Equus caballus*	C-31	1	2.32	—	—
Domestic Horse	C-22	1	2.32	1	5.88
Subtotal		4	9.30	2	11.76
Bos/Equus (cow/horse)	C-22	4	9.30	1	5.88
?Artiodactyl	C-22	1	2.32	—	—

[1]Includes 3 ?deer bones.
[2]Includes 1 ?horse bone.

Cozumel. The brown brocket deer, *Mazama gouazoubira,* is present on the adjacent mainland, but no elements of this species appeared in the Cozumel sample. The brocket is much smaller than the white-tailed deer (it weighs approximately half as much as the latter), and thus differentiating osteologically between the two is not difficult (Wright 1970).

Deer probably did not inhabit the island prehistorically. The species was not there as of the early 1980s and is never mentioned as being native to Cozumel (see for example, Hall and Kelson 1959; Jones and Lawlor 1965), even though it is plentiful on the adjacent Yucatán Peninsula. This might explain the paucity of deer remains in the present sample. The few deer which do appear in the Cozumel sites were probably imported from the mainland.

Except for the major meat-bearing lower limbs, most of the major portions of the body are represented—skull, vertebral column, an upper limb bone, sacrum and foot/ankle bones (Table 8.19). The foot and ankle bones constitute almost 43 percent of the sample, while skull elements run second with nearly 36 percent of the deer bone. Since these represent the non-food portions of the body, deer elements were probably imported to Cozumel for other purposes, such as making tools and other artifacts. Landa mentions the use of deer as sacrificial items and specifically refers to the common offering of a haunch of venison (Tozzer 1941: 115, 141, 204). The hunting, trapping, and subsequent sacrificing of deer is also shown in great detail in the Maya codices (Tozzer and Allen 1910: 348). Evidently this custom was not followed on Cozumel. However, choice cuts of boned deer meat (perhaps smoked, dried, or otherwise preserved) might have been brought to the island; these would leave no archaeological evidence. At Seibal, a mainland site where deer remains were considerably more numerous (271 bones), hind leg elements are also limited, even in elite deposits. Pohl cannot explain this and comments, "Many of these elements seem to have [been] destroyed altogether" (Pohl 1976: 163).

The culturally modified deer bone confirms the theory of use for tools or other artifacts. The antler fragments could have been used in

Table 8.19   White-tailed Deer: Skeletal Elements

SKELETAL ELEMENT	NO. BONES	%	
Antler fragments	3	21.43	
Premaxilla, complete	1	7.14	35.71%
Premolar, complete	1	7.14	
Humerus fragment	1	7.14	
Lumbar vertebra process	1	7.14	
Sacrum, complete	1	7.14	
Metatarsal fragments	3	21.43	
Metapodial fragments	2	14.29	42.86%
Astragalus, complete	1	7.14	

making stone tools. One of the three had been burnt, as if fire-hardened for durability. Metapodials (a term which includes both metacarpals and metatarsals, or bones of the fore and hind feet) are also commonly used for such tools as awls and needles. All three of the metatarsal fragments showed evidence of polish, indicating use-wear of some kind, probably as awls. One had been split, and worked between the condyle and the shaft, and exhibited sawmarks lengthwise on its midshaft, in addition to the polish. Another had been smoothed and flattened both laterally and posteriorly, while the third was a fragmentary lateral condyle with polish on it. All five of the metapodials represent only the distal ends of those elements—the end commonly reserved for use as the handle of an awl. Deer toes were supposedly used in shaman divining rituals, and a collection of nineteen, some worked, were found in a burial at Holmul, Guatemala (Merwin and Vaillant 1932). However, no such elements were recovered from the Cozumel sites.

In addition, other culturally modified fragments of bone could not be identified beyond "mammal," "large mammal," or even "indeterminate." Some of these are probably deer, although this cannot be verified. There were five bone beads, three cut or shaped bone fragments, one ornamental carved bone pin, three worked bone awl fragments, one piece of grooved bone, nine fragments with holes drilled in them, sixteen incised or carved fragments, eight fragmentary bone needles, six pieces of painted bone, eight polished fragments, one bone ring, and twenty miscellaneous pieces of worked bone (including six longbone tubes, two large tools with blunt points, and one curved, pointed tool). A more detailed description of these items, including two additional needles, is found in Phillips (1979: 202–216). The large quantity of unmodified indeterminate mammal and large mammal bones (2,060 altogether) probably also includes deer elements.

Besides the one burnt fragment of antler, a burned right premaxilla was also found. Perhaps this latter represents part of a sacrificial offering, since it was found in a burial at San Gervasio (C-22, gr. 7, pit 212, burial 37).

Only one immature deer element occurred in the sample. This was a lower second premolar (found alone) in burial 31, pit 179 at El Cedral (C-15).

Deer elements were distributed at six sites on the island (Table 8.18). Eleven of these (78.57 percent) were dated from Postclassic, Late Postclassic, or historic contexts; two were from undated proveniences, and only one came from a level predating the Postclassic period (C-25, pit 11).

EUROPEAN DOMESTIC ANIMALS

In this category are twenty-six bones of domestic sheep, horse, and cow/horse *(Bos/Equus)* (Table 8.18). Since all are European domesticates, they cannot predate 1519, when Cortez first landed on Cozumel (Sabloff and Rathje 1975: 28). There is no indication that the horse bones precede the modern era. The question is whether these domestic animals represent intrusive material from the modern ranches in the area, or whether they might possibly be the remains of some of the earliest domestic animals brought to the New World by the Spanish explorers. They are probably modern intrusives, although the second explanation cannot be entirely ruled out. All of these bones come from either surface material or the very top levels of the sites in question (see Table 8.20). All of the elements which can be dated are from either the Late Postclassic or historic periods. Curiously, all twenty-six bones were found either in burials or in ceremonial structures (temples and platforms) (see Table 8.20). If these were indeed Spanish animals they might have been accorded special treatment by the natives when they were slaughtered or died naturally. It is also possible that they simply became trapped in the structures and died there, whether they are Spanish or more recent animals.

Sheep *(Ovis aries)* are represented (Table 8.20) by eighteen bones of at least two individuals from one site, Aguada Grande (C-27). The elements present are mainly lower limb bones plus portions of the trunk: a femur, a tibia, an astragalus, a calcaneum, a phalanx, a metatarsal, two thoracic vertebrae, a lumbar vertebra, a sternebra, and eight ribs. Most of these represent major meat-bearing limbs; however, no butcher marks or burning were observed on any of the elements. It is tempting to hypothesize that these were ceremonial offerings, since all of these bones were found in Temple C or on Platform I at C-27. However, their location on the surface at these proveniences may indicate that they are intrusive.

Horses appear at three different sites on the island (Table 8.20), all in burials. At least two individuals are indicated by four bones (the one rib fragment at C-31 can only be identified as ?horse). Again, bones of the lower limbs predominate: besides the rib, there is a metatarsal, a metacarpal, and a patella.

Four vertebrae at San Gervasio (C-22) are so immature (perhaps even fetal) that they could not be identified beyond *Bos/Equus* (cow/horse). Two thoracics and two caudals of a single animal were found in burial 37 at this site.

Medium-Sized Mammals

Procyonids are the third most important of the Cozumel mammals in number of bones (666), and ranks second in MNIs (119) (Table 8.3). The only two members of the procyonid family which appear in the Cozumel sites are the coatimundi and the raccoon; the ring-tailed cat or cacomixtle is absent. Coatimundis (or coatis, as they are usually called) resemble long-tailed, slender raccoons. They are clearly the most significant, constituting 91.29 percent of the procyonids (608 bones) and

Table 8.20 Dates and Proveniences of European Domestic Animals

SPECIES	SITE	PROVENIENCE	# BONES	MNI	DATE
Domestic Sheep	C-27	Pit 14 & Bag 145 Fall in Temple C (above floor) & clearing in front & entrance of temple	16	1	No date
Domestic Sheep	C-27	Fall of Platform I (Surface)	2	1	No date
Horse	C-13	Pit 13, Burial 4, Levels 1 & 2	2	1	Late Postclassic and historic period
?Horse	C-31	Pit 250, Burial 39, Level 1	1	—	No date
Horse	C-22	Group I, Pit 49, Level above floor #1, Burials	1	1	Late Postclassic
Bos/Equus (Cow/Horse)	C-22	Group 7, Pit 212, Level 1, Burial 37	4	1	Late Postclassic
Total			26	5	

73.95 percent of the MNIs (Table 8.21). The Cozumel Island coati is generally accepted as a separate species, *Nasua nelsoni* (Hall and Kelson 1959: 893; Jones and Lawlor 1965: 416). The remains from these sites, while fitting in every way the description of this species (generally smaller size, smaller teeth, and more delicate construction than the mainland species, *Nasua narica*), could not be positively identified as such due to the absence of comparative material. Thus, the designation *Nasua cf. N. nelsoni* has been used here. There were also seventeen large procyonoid bones which could only be identified as ?coati due to their fragmentary or immature condition. Raccoons make up only 2.85 percent of the procyonoids (19 bones), or 10.92 percent of the MNIs (Table 8.21). Again, a separate species has been named from the island—*Procyon pygmaeus* (Hall and Kelson 1959: 889; Jones and Lawlor 1965: 416). As was true for the coatis, the archaeological specimens closely match the descriptions for this species (which is smaller and has smaller teeth than *Procyon lotor*), but the lack of comparative specimens dictated the

Table 8.21   Distribution of Procyonids by Site

SPECIES	SITE	# BONES	%	MNI	%
Cozumel Island Coati	C-2	1	0.15	1	0.84
(Nasua cf. N. nelsoni)	C-13	5	0.75	2	1.68
	C-31	10	1.50	2	1.68
	C-18	36	5.40	18	15.13
	C-25	46	6.91	20	16.81
	C-15	51	7.66	3	2.52
	C-27	6	0.90	2	1.68
	C-22	453	68.02	40	33.61
Subtotal		608	91.29	88	73.95
Large Procyonids ?Coati	C-13	1	0.15	1	0.84
	C-18	12	1.80	1	0.84
	C-22	4	0.60	4	3.36
Subtotal		17	2.55	6	5.04
Raccoon/Coati	C-13	2	0.30	2	1.68
	C-18	11	1.65	3	2.52
	C-25	5	0.75	3	2.52
	C-22	4	0.60	4	3.36
Subtotal		22	3.30	12	10.08
Cozumel Island Raccoon	C-18	4	0.60	4	3.36
(Procyon cf. P. pygmaeus)	C-25	14	2.10	8	6.72
	C-22	1	0.15	1	0.84
Subtotal		19	2.85	13	10.92
Total		666	99.99	119	99.99

use of the designation *Procyon cf. P. pygmaeus*. Finally, twenty-two large procyonid bones were found which could not be differentiated beyond the level raccoon/coati.

Both coatis and raccoons are omnivorous animals, commonly eating fruits, berries, nuts, tender green vegetation, small mammals, birds, insects, rodents, and invertebrates. Raccoons particularly favor crayfish and frogs. In fact, since a large part of a raccoon's diet is obtained in and around water, the only indispensable element in its habitat is a perennial water source. Both procyonids are known to cause considerable damage to orchards and crops, particularly corn fields (Leopold 1959). The corn *milpas* on Cozumel would have attracted these animals. Landa specifically refers to coatis traveling in herds and destroying "to a great extent the fields of maize into which they enter" (Tozzer 1941: 145, 205). Female coatis and their young are highly sociable (groups of fifteen or twenty are common, with aggregations of up to 200 not unknown), while adult raccoons are generally solitary (Leopold 1959). This behavior may explain the high numbers of coatis in the Cozumel sites. Killing one or several of a group of coatis invading one's corn field would be easier than successfully capturing a single elusive raccoon. Moreover, raccoons commonly raid at night, while coatis are most active in the early morning and evening hours, when, presumably, more people would be awake and ready to hunt. Coatis may also simply be much more numerous on Cozumel than raccoons, but no data to confirm this were available in the early 1980s.

Significantly, Bishop Landa does not mention raccoons, even though he describes thoroughly and at length many other animal species used by the sixteenth-century Maya. Either raccoons were much less plentiful than coatis in the Maya area, or the latter species was considered preferable for food. In contrast, Landa states that the Indian women raised coatis and treated them as pets and that the animals were eaten (Tozzer 1941: 204–205). There are Late Classic Period pottery figures from Altar de Sacrificios and Lubaantun representing women holding what Pohl (1976: 150) believes are *pisotes* (coatis). She asserts that the traditional use of this animal as a fertility symbol may explain its association with women. Interestingly, ethnographic evidence from the modern Lacandon Maya indicates that coatis are a food reserved for women (Pohl 1976: 150). The Cozumel sites appear to be unique with respect to the high numbers of coati remains; in fact, none of the faunal reports from major Maya sites surveyed listed any procyonid bones at all (e.g., Seibal, Altar de Sacrificios, Mayapán, Flores, Macanche, Zacaleu, Dzibilchaltun, Lubaantun, and Tikal). The procyonids are also absent from the Maya Codices, which suggests that these animals had no special ceremonial or sacrificial significance.

The use of raccoons and coatis on Cozumel was apparently widespread. Coatis, for example, occur in eight different sites on the island (see Table 8.21). Raccoons were found at only three of the largest and most extensively excavated sites, but the very small sample size of this species could easily account for this relatively limited distribution.

Based on her analysis of Altar de Sacrificios and Seibal, Mary Pohl suggested (1976: 186) that the elites at ceremonial centers did not find coatis to their taste. Archaeological sampling problems at these sites or the generally small size of the faunal collections involved might have resulted in the complete lack of this species. In any case, this pattern does not hold true for the Cozumel elite. Two major elite precincts at one site (San Gervasio—C-22) were selected and the numbers of procyonids contained therein were tabulated. There were 235 such bones (all but one are coati), constituting 8.64 percent of all mammal bones in these elite precincts and 12.73 percent of all mammal MNIs (Table 8.22).

The distribution of skeletal elements for procyonids is shown in Table 8.23. Skull elements, mandibles, maxillae, and loose teeth occur in significant numbers for both raccoons and coatis, as do the major limb bones. (Inferences based on the proportions of elements in the categories raccoon/coati and ?coati cannot be relied upon since these are really "leftovers"; that is, these elements are too fragmentary or insufficiently diagnostic to be definitely identified, and thus the sample is biased.) Coatis, the only group of procyonids with a representative sample size here, show a wide distribution among all parts of the body. This is what would be expected of a medium-sized animal hunted locally, used for food, and discarded at the site where consumption took place.

About two-thirds of the raccoons and coatis represented are adults (Table 8.24). This includes a few bones (approximately 2 percent) which represent old adults. Nearly a third of the sample is comprised of immature or subadult animals, including a few fetal to very immature bones. (1.2 percent). Determining exactly when procyonids become osteologically mature is difficult; no charts appear to be available on the fusion ages of limb bone epiphyses or on dental eruption stages in these animals. Some female raccoons may breed when they are one year old, although males usually do not breed until their second year (Walker 1975). Thus it would seem safe to assume this species could not be considered fully mature before one year of age, and perhaps not before two years. No mention of breeding ages for coatis could be found in

Table 8.22   Distribution of Procyonids in Two Elite Precincts of San Gervasio (C-22)

PROVENIENCE	SPECIES	NO. BONES	MNI
C-22, Group 2	Coati	4	2
C-22, Group 3	Coati	227	15
C-22, Group 3	?Coati	3	3
C-22, Group 3	Raccoon	1	1
Total		235	21
		(8.64% of all mammal bones in groups 2 and 3)	(12.73% of all mammal MNIs in groups 2 and 3)

Table 8.23   Procyonids: Distribution of Skeletal Elements

SKELETAL ELEMENT	NO. BONES	%	
(A) Raccoons			
Skull Elements (zygomatic of malar)	1	5.26	} 52.63%
Mandibles	9	47.37	
Major Limb Bones (humeri, radii, ulnae, femora, tibiae, and fibulae)	8	42.11	
Vertebrae	1	5.26	
Total	19	100.00	
(B) Raccoon/Coati			
Mandibles	4	18.18	
Major Limb Bones	10	45.45	
Foot Bones (metatarsal, calcaneum)	2	9.09	
Vertebrae	3	13.64	
Miscellaneous (ribs, acetabulum)	3	13.64	
Total	22	100.00	
(C) Large Procyonids—?Coati			
Mandibles	1	5.88	
Major Limb Bones	13	76.47	
Vertebrae	1	5.88	
Miscellaneous (rib, scapula)	2	11.76	
Total	17	99.99	
(D) Coati			
Skull Elements (Basisphenoids, periotics, skull, braincases, occipitals, frontals, parietals, zygomatics)	44	7.24	} 27.63%
Mandibles and Maxillae	71	11.68	
Loose Teeth	53	8.72	
Major Limb Bones	153	25.16	
Foot and Toe Bones, Claws	56	9.21	
Vertebrae	171	28.13	
Miscellaneous (Patellae, pelves, innominates, ribs, baculae, scapulae, ilia, ischia)	50	8.22	
Indeterminate	10	1.64	
Total	608	100.00	

the literature. Whatever age is used for maturity, however, the fact remains that a significant proportion of the Cozumel raccoons and coatis were young animals, as determined by incompletely fused limb bones and unerupted teeth. It is probable that these individuals were preferred for their tender meat. Younger animals would also be most easily captured and killed if caught by surprise while raiding cornfields. If *pisotes* (coatis) were commonly raised by the women, as Landa suggests, the inhabitants of Cozumel would have had a convenient nonperisha-

Table 8.24   Age Distribution of Procyonids

AGE CATEGORY	SPECIES	NO. BONES	%	
Fetal to very immature	Coati	8	1.20	
Immature	Coati	177	26.58	
Immature	Raccoon/Coati	8	1.20	31.53%
Immature	Raccoon	5	0.75	Subadults
Immature	?Coati	12	1.80	
Young Adult	Coati	5	0.75	
Adult	Coati	405	60.81	
Adult	Racoon	13	1.95	66.37%
Adult	Raccoon/Coati	14	2.10	
Adult	?Coati	5	0.75	
Old adult	Coati	13	1.95	2.10%
Old adult	Raccoon	1	0.15	
Total		666	99.99	

ble meat supply available from which to choose the tenderest, most flavorful animals.

The majority (approximately 63 percent) of the procyonid material, by MNIs, comes from Postclassic and historic contexts (Table 8.25); less than 8 percent of the MNIs are from earlier periods. Even if the 30 percent remaining could be dated, the Postclassic raccoons and coatis would still clearly dominate the sample.

Only one butcher mark (on the shaft of a coati humerus) was observed. Two male coatis were identified from their baculae (os penis) at San Gervasio (C-22) and Buena Vista (C-18). Stewing may have been the favorite method of preparing raccoons and coatis, since only six burned bones were found (at three different sites). A total of nineteen procyonid bones showed evidence of rodent gnawing or carnivore chewing. Finally, two instances of pathology occurred on coati elements. One was an adult tibia from San Gervasio (C-22) which had been broken and rehealed; the other, an adult humerus from Buena Vista (C-18), showed a deformed distal condyle (possibly congenital).

GRAY FOXES

The gray fox (Urocyon cinereoargenteus) represents the fifth most important mammal in the Cozumel sites by bone count (530) or sixth by MNIs (48) (See Table 8.3). It is the only fox present on either the island or the adjacent Yucatán Peninsula (Hall and Kelson 1959; Leopold 1959). Jones and Lawlor (1965: 416) report that, as was the case with peccaries, coatis, and raccoons, the gray fox found on Cozumel is typically much smaller than the mainland subspecies and smaller than any

Table 8.25 Procyonids: Time Periods

TIME PERIOD	NO. BONES	%		MNI	%	
Late Postclassic and Historic	318	47.75		66	55.46	
Postclassic	12	1.80	49.55	9	7.56	66.03%
Pre-Postclassic	4	0.60		3	2.52	
Pure Florescent	5	0.75	2.10	5	4.20	7.56%
Early Period (Classic)	5	0.75		1	0.84	
No Date	322	48.35		35	29.41	
Total	666	100.00		119	99.99	

other canid in the area. This was true for the specimens examined in this study.

Gray foxes are quite adaptable (see Wright 1970, Leopold 1959): this is one species whose population the presence of man may actually have served to increase, since partially cleared forest regions with brush and other secondary growth provide ideal habitat for this animal. This is the only member of the dog family which is really adept at climbing trees, as it is known to do in escaping packs of hunting hounds. Usually, the gray fox forages at night, obtaining the small mammals which make up the bulk of its diet. However, this species is more omnivorous than most canids and will eat fruits, berries, and insects in addition to reptiles, amphibians, birds, and birds' eggs at certain times of the year. Since they are also active scavengers, these foxes will eat man's garbage as well as carrion (Leopold 1959).

The relatively high numbers of gray foxes appear to be unique to the Cozumel sites. This species is either absent or present in very low numbers at other major Maya sites (see, for example, Pohl 1976; Olsen 1978; or Woodbury and Trik 1953). Although Landa describes the gray fox as being present in the Maya area (Tozzer 1941: 204), he does not comment specifically on what use (if any) was made of the animal. The gray fox, absent from the Maya Codices (Tozzer and Allen 1910), apparently held no special ceremonial or symbolic value for the Maya. However, some of the canids pictured in the Codices may actually represent foxes rather than dogs, as they have so far been interpreted.

Less than 7 percent of the gray fox bones are immature—that is, unfused (Table 8.26); the remaining 93 percent are adult. Such proportions are to be expected of a wild population, especially if the hunters attempted to select mainly adult animals for food purposes, as seems to be the case here.

All portions of the body are represented in the distribution of skeletal elements (Table 8.27). Skull elements, jaws, and loose teeth make up a substantial proportion of the total (nearly 24 percent). The major limb bones are also important, constituting over 21 percent of all gray fox elements. The numbers of vertebrae (almost 35 percent) seem somewhat high when compared to the procyonids, for example (Table 8.23). Differences in the preparation of these animals for eating could account

Table 8.26 Age Distribution of Gray Foxes

AGE CATEGORY	NO. BONES	%
Immature	37	6.98
Young adult	1	0.19
Adult	492	92.83
Total	530	100.00

Table 8.27   **Gray Foxes: Distribution of Skeletal Elements**

SKELETAL ELEMENT	NO. BONES	%	
Skull elements	61	11.51	⎫
Mandibles and maxillae	42	7.92	⎬ 23.96%
Loose teeth	24	4.53	⎭
Major limb bones	114	21.51	
Foot and toe bones	64	12.07	
Vertebrae	184	34.72	
Miscellaneous (ribs, scapulae, ilia, ischia, innominates)	41	7.73	
Total	530	99.99	

for this: whether an animal was halved, quartered, or stewed whole might result in the loss or discard of certain bones.

Gray foxes are widely distributed throughout seven different sites on the island (Table 8.28). The proportions seem to vary directly with the relative sample sizes of mammal bones in each site. However, since over 60 percent of the material by MNIs was excavated from San Gervasio (C-22), or almost 88 percent of the bones, a greater preference for foxes may have applied at this site.

Almost none of these small canids occurs in contexts earlier than the Postclassic period (See Table 8.29). While nearly 78 percent of the gray fox bones have been dated to the Late Postclassic or historic periods, less than 1 percent are pre-Postclassic. Approximately 21 percent are from undated proveniences, but these would not be sufficient to alter the general trend even if they all proved to belong to an early period.

Only four bones (0.75 percent of all gray foxes) from three sites had been either rodent-gnawed or carnivore-chewed. None showed any evidence of butchering, and only one bone had been burned (from

Table 8.28   **Distribution of Gray Foxes by Site**

SITE	NO. BONES	%	MNI	%
C-13	1	0.19	1	2.08
C-31	1	0.19	1	2.08
C-18	9	1.70	6	12.5
C-25	17	3.20	8	16.67
C-15	35	6.60	2	4.17
C-27	1	0.19	1	2.08
C-22	466	87.92	29	60.42
Total	530	99.99	48	100.00

Table 8.29 Time Periods of Gray Foxes

TIME PERIOD	NO. BONES	%	MNI	%
Late Postclassic and Historic	413	77.92	32	66.67
Pre-Postclassic	5	0.94	2	4.17
No Date	112	21.13	14	29.17
Total	530	99.99	48	100.01

C-22, group 2). A single example of pathology was found: an adult tibia which had been broken and rehealed at its distal end.

MEXICAN PORCUPINE

The Mexican porcupine *(Coendu mexicanus)* appears only rarely in Maya sites. Jaw fragments representing a single individual were found at Seibal (Olsen 1978), but no reference to this species could be found at other Maya sites. The only porcupine element which appeared in the Cozumel sample was a single quill excavated from the site of La Expedición (C-25), on the northeast coast of the island (Table 8.18). Found in level 2 of Trench 16-B, it was dated to the Late Postclassic period.

Porcupines have not been specifically mentioned as a species native to Cozumel (Hall and Kelson 1959; Jones and Lawlor 1965). Even in other parts of Mexico, the animal is rarely seen and specimens are few. Leopold (1959) suggests this is probably due to the Mexican porcupine's purely arboreal and nocturnal lifestyle. This species lives in the tall trees of tropical forests and only rarely descends to the ground (Wright 1970; Leopold 1959). The fact that the meat is said to have a very strong and disagreeable taste, coupled with the animal's reclusive lifestyle, makes its occurrence in Maya sites logical. That it appears at all probably reflects uses other than for food; perhaps the quills were employed for decorative or other purposes. Pohl (1976: 181) reports that porcupine quills are used by modern Maya in a manner resembling acupuncture to cure such maladies as headaches. She suggests that the porcupine found at Seibal may have been brought to the site for medicinal or ceremonial purposes. This species is not referred to by Bishop Landa (Tozzer 1941) and does not appear in the Maya Codices in any context (Tozzer and Allen 1910).

PACA

The paca *(Cuniculus paca = Agouti paca)* is a raccoon-sized rodent which, like the porcupine, is rarely visible over most of its range in southern Mexico. An animal with shy, retiring habits, it burrows in the dense, moist undergrowth of the tropical rain forest and emerges at night to feed. In the Yucatán, pacas often live in limestone caves or *cenotes* (Leopold 1959). The paca has been reported on Cozumel, although it may represent an introduced species (Jones and Lawlor 1965). The animal is usually scarce or absent in areas where the dense forest has been cleared (Leopold 1959); in 1980, therefore, Cozumel did not provide the best habitat for pacas. Nevertheless, the meat is said to be quite delicious and is eagerly sought after in tropical Central America today (Wright 1970; Leopold 1959).

A single paca element appears in the Cozumel sites (Table 8.18). This is an adult lower molar which was found in a Late Postclassic context at San Gervasio (C-22) in a housemound. This relative scarcity is also true of other Maya sites; only one paca bone was found at Lubaantun (Wing 1975), the remains of a single individual occurred at Seibal (Olsen 1978), and two elements were excavated at Macanche (Pohl 1976). It seems likely that this animal was used for food whenever possible, but that other species, (easier to procure), were relied upon as staples.

As with the porcupine, pacas are not mentioned in Landa's *Relación*, nor do they occur in any of the Maya Codices.

Small Mammals

The common opossum *(Didelphis marsupialis)* ranks second among the Cozumel mammals in number of bones (1,116) or fifth in MNIs (90)— see Table 8.3. The only other animal in the area which might be confused with the common opossum is the four-eyed opossum *(Philander opossum)*, so named because of the white spot in the fur above each eye. However, the latter is much smaller, about the size of a domestic rat, whereas the common opossum is house-cat-sized (Leopold 1959). The six elements categorized as ?opossum were fragmentary small mammal bones which, owing to their size, may be judged as common opossum.

As with several other mammals in this study, a Cozumel subspecies of opossum, *D. marsupialis cozulmelae*, has been named (Hall and Kelson 1959). However, when Jones and Lawlor (1965) collected ten specimens on the island and compared them with the mainland subspecies, *D. m. yucatanensis*, the two did not differ either in the previously reported cranial features or in body size. Only tail length and color differed somewhat. Although the archaeological bones were often smaller in size, the present study cannot confirm or refute the presence of a separate insular subspecies for opossums.

Opossums are omnivorous animals which consume mostly insects and other invertebrates, although they will readily eat carrion and garbage when available (Leopold 1959). This species is mainly nocturnal, often occupying dens in hollow trees, rock piles, cliffs, or even holes dug in the ground by other animals. Cozumel's many rubble platforms, limestone caves, and cliffs would have provided excellent habitat for opossums. Leopold (1959: 326) refers to the opossum as a "slow-witted, sluggish animal" which can often be seen at night, shuffling slowly along. These characteristics make opossums exceptionally easy to capture; Landa (Tozzer 1941: 204) tells of the Maya catching them by the tail.

Perhaps this ease of capture, together with the fact that it is one of the most common animals in the Americas explains the high frequency of opossums in the Cozumel sites. This species occurs in most other Maya sites, as well (e.g., Altar de Sacrificios, Seibal, Dzibilchaltun, Tikal, Mayapán, Lubaantun), although never in such high numbers as the present sample. Pollock and Ray (1957) note that the presence of at least three individual opossums in a vaulted tomb at Mayapán may be intrusive, since the tomb was not sealed. The burrowing habits of the animal make this a possibility in some cases; however, the more than 1,100 specimens found in the Cozumel sites cannot reasonably be categorized as intrusive.

These animals occur in six sites on the island (Table 8.30) and generally vary in number along with the size of the faunal sample excavated from each site. Almost 59 percent of the opossums (by MNIs) were found at San Gervasio (C-22), or nearly 85 percent of the bones. Perhaps this reflects a particular preference for these fat-rich little animals at San Gervasio in contrast to the inhabitants of other sites.

Vertebrae represent the highest percentage of skeletal elements, as was also true for gray foxes (see Table 8.31). Again, this may represent the conservation of these elements by stewing the animal whole. In contrast, other larger species may show lower proportions of certain elements such as vertebrae which were discarded when the animal was quartered or otherwise cut up for cooking. Skull elements, mandibles, maxillae, and loose teeth together constitute over 32 percent of the elements, which is to be expected of such durable parts of the body. The major meat-bearing limb bones are also well represented (over 17 percent).

Table 8.30   Distribution of Opossums* by Site

SITE	NO. BONES	%	MNI	%
C-13	12	1.07	3	3.33
C-31	1	0.09	1	1.11
C-18	46	4.12	18	20.00
C-25	19	1.70	12	13.33
C-15	92	8.24	3	3.33
C-22	946	84.77	53	58.89
Total	1,116	99.99	90	99.99

*Includes 6 ?opossum bones.

Table 8.31   Opossums:* Distribution of Skeletal Elements

SKELETAL ELEMENT	NO. BONES	%	
Skull elements	106	9.50	⎫
Mandibles and maxillae	129	11.56	⎬ 32.26%
Loose teeth	125	11.20	⎭
Major limb bones	194	17.38	
Foot and toe bones	13	1.16	
Vertebrae	421	37.72	
Miscellaneous (ribs, scapulae, ilia, ischia, innominates, and marsupial bones)	128	11.47	
Total	1,116	99.99	

*Includes six ?opossum bones.

Almost 44 percent of all opossums are immature or fetal to very immature—an extremely high proportion (Table 8.32). However, opossums usually bear litters of ten to twenty, with a gestation period of only thirteen days (Wright 1970). Since the mother carries the young in her pouch for up to three months, the capture of even one or two females with young could greatly inflate the ratio of immature/adult animals found in a given site. The great prevalence of opossums, the short gestation period, and the large litter size would offset the killing and eating of mother opossums with their offspring—a fact which the Maya undoubtedly appreciated. In any case, they certainly did not make any attempt to avoid using the younger animals.

The great majority of opossum remains come from Late Postclassic, Postclassic, and historic period contexts (Table 8.33); almost 72 percent of the bones or nearly 68 percent of the MNIs were excavated from such proveniences. Only 0.63 percent of the bones (or 5.55 percent of the MNIs) are definitely from earlier contexts.

A single element (an adult femur) from La Expedición (C-25) showed evidence of butchering. None of the opossum bones had been burned or heat-darkened, and only twenty-eight (2.51 percent) from four sites

Table 8.32   Age Distribution of Opossums*

AGE CATEGORY	NO. BONES	%	
Fetal to very immature	6	0.54	⎫ 43.73%
Immature	482	43.91	⎭
Young adult	4	0.36	
Adult	618	55.38	
Old adult	6	0.54	
Total	1,116	100.01	

*Includes six ?Opossum bones.

Table 8.33 Time Periods of Opossums*

TIME PERIOD	NO. BONES	%		MNI	%	
Late Postclassic and Historic	786	70.43	} 71.86	55	61.11	} 67.78
Postclassic	16	1.43		6	6.67	
Pre-Postclassic	1	0.09		1	1.11	
Terminal Classic	1	0.09	} 0.63	1	1.11	} 5.55
Pure Florescent	4	0.36		2	2.22	
Early Period (Classic)	1	0.09		1	1.11	
No Date	307	27.51		24	26.67	
Total	1,116	100.00		90	100.00	

*Includes six ?Opossum bones.

had been rodent-gnawed or carnivore-chewed. One instance of pathology occurred; an immature left radius at San Gervasio had been broken and rehealed.

The Maya Codices contain figures which may represent opossums, but the animals portrayed cannot be distinguished with any certainty from dogs or, in one case, from a frog (see Tozzer and Allen 1910: 347). However, the reference in Landa to opossums being captured by the tail implies that they were used, probably for food. This species apparently did not hold any special religious significance for the Maya.

COTTONTAIL RABBIT

Cottontail rabbits *(Sylvilagus sp.)* represent numerically either the sixth most important mammal on Cozumel (497 bones) or the third, if MNIs are counted (109) (see Table 8.3). Although rabbits have not been specifically reported on the island (Jones and Lawlor 1965), two species are known to inhabit the Yucatán Peninsula: the tropical forest rabbit, *Syvilagus brasiliensis*, and the Eastern cottontail, *S. floridanus* (Hall and Kelson 1959; Leopold 1959). These species cannot be satisfactorily differentiated using postcranial elements, especially with fragmentary remains (see Wing 1975); however, body size and habitat requirements might be useful in arriving at distinctions.

Body weights were calculated from the skeletal remains to determine whether Cozumel rabbits were nearer the Eastern cottontail or the tropical forest rabbit in size. First, twenty-two mandibles were measured for the length of the lower cheek tooth row. Calculations were then performed using Wing's (1976b) formula: $\log y = 3.843 (\log x) - 1.452$, where $\log y$ = body weight in grams, $\log x$ is the lower cheek tooth row in mm., and the correlation coefficient is .95 (Wing 1976). The results were

Average body weight	= 1.46 lbs.
Range	= 0.36 to 2.51 lbs.
Modes	= 2.27 and 1.72 lbs.
(most frequent values)	
Median	= 1.72 lbs.

According to Leopold (1959: 353), the Eastern cottontail weighs, on the average, from 1.98 to 2.2 lbs. (900 to 1,000 gms.). No comparable data are supplied for the tropical forest rabbit, but the linear body measurements given in Hall and Kelson (1959) indicate that this species is significantly smaller than the Eastern cottontail. If this smaller body size is reflected in weight (as is logical), then the Cozumel rabbits would appear to match the tropical forest rabbit *(S. brasiliensis)* most closely. The average weight of the cottontails in the present sample (1.46 lbs.) is clearly much lower than even the bottom of the range given for *S. floridanus* (1.98 to 2.2 lbs.). However, the Cozumel rabbits could represent a smaller island subspecies of the Eastern cottontail, although this seems unlikely when environmental factors are considered.

The Eastern cottontail is really a forest species, predominantly of the pine-oak zone, whose range barely extends into the tropics. In contrast, S. brasiliensis thrives in the humid tropical forests of southeastern Mexico (Leopold 1959) and would definitely be more suited to Cozumel. Thus, the rabbits in the present sample are probably representatives of the tropical forest species, even if this cannot be conclusively proven. All of the Cozumel rabbits were left at the generic level of identification (Sylvilagus sp.).

The rabbits are widely distributed throughout six sites on the island (Table 8.34), with the proportions in each site corresponding generally to the sample size of the excavated bone. Pohl (1976: 168–169) found that rabbit bones at Seibal were associated only with elite contexts (as opposed to housemounds) and suggests that this species may have symbolized intelligence and special skills exclusive to the elite. This inference was based on a scene from a Late Classic period polychrome vessel which depicts the rabbit as a scribe, engaged in writing a codex. However, Pohl's sample was very small (two bones), and an examination of the Cozumel rabbits does not support this pattern. Cottontails occur in every kind of provenience on the island—housemounds and non-ceremonial contexts, as well as burials and elite contexts.

Landa (Tozzer 1941: 204) refers to rabbits in the Maya area as good to eat. The species appears in most of the Maya sites surveyed (Seibal, Tikal, Dzibilchaltun, Mayapán. and Zacaleu, for example), which supports the idea that the animal was widely consumed. Rabbits also occur in various of the Maya Codices in connection with serpents, although the meaning of this is not clear (Tozzer and Allen 1910: 354–355).

Almost 26 percent of the skeletal elements are skull elements, mandibles, maxillae, and loose teeth (Table 8.35). The major limb bones constitute the highest proportion (39.03 percent) of the rabbit remains. This might represent differential preservation, although it may also indicate selection of the meatier portions of the body.

The majority of rabbits in the sample were adults (over 75 percent), with less than one-fourth representing immature animals (Table 8.36).

Table 8.34   Distribution of Cottontail Rabbits* by Site

SITE	NO. BONES	%	MNI	%
C-13	28	5.63	5	4.59
C-31	20	4.02	2	1.83
C-18	41	8.25	15	13.76
C-25	76	15.29	26	23.85
C-15	13	2.61	2	1.83
C-22	319	64.18	59	54.13
Total	497	99.98	109	99.99

*Includes 10 ?cottontail rabbit bones.

Table 8.35   Cottontail Rabbits:* Distribution of Skeletal Elements

SKELETAL ELEMENT	NO. BONES	%	
Skull elements	9	1.81	
Mandibles and maxillae	79	15.90	25.96%
Loose teeth	41	8.25	
Major limb bones	194	39.03	
Foot and ankle bones	55	11.07	
Vertebrae	33	6.64	
Miscellaneous (innominates, ilia, ischia, ribs, and scapulae)	69	13.88	
Indeterminate shafts	17	3.42	
Total	497	100.00	

*Includes 10 ?cottontail rabbit bones.

This percentage does not seem excessive, given the relatively high reproductive rates of this mammal. Cottontail rabbits *(Sylvilagus spp.)* have a gestation period of twenty-six to thirty days, and litters generally range from two to eight. The tender meat of the younger animals was undoubtedly desired.

Most of the rabbit material occurs in the Late Postclassic and historic periods (Table 8.37). Bones from contexts dated earlier than the Postclassic constitute only 1.41 percent of the remains, or less than 3 percent of the MNIs, while undated proveniences represent less than 14 percent of the bones (or 18.35 percent of the MNIs).

There were no butcher marks on the rabbit bones, although three were burned. These were from three different housemounds at San Gervasio (C-22), which may indicate domestic cooking practices by roasting the meat directly over a fire. Thirty-one bones from five sites (6.24 percent) showed evidence of rodent-gnawing or carnivore-chewing. A single polished bone bead, made from a longbone shaft, was found in a housemound at Buena Vista (C-18), pit 98. This could be identified only as *cf.* cottontail rabbit due to the absence of diagnostic features on the specimen after cultural modification.

Table 8.36   Age Distribution of Cottontail Rabbits*

AGE CATEGORY	NO. BONES	%
Immature	123	24.75
Adult	374	75.25
Total	497	100.00

*Includes 10 ?cottontail rabbit bones.

Table 8.37 Time Periods of Cottontail Rabbits*

TIME PERIOD	NO. BONES	%		MNI	%	
Late Postclassic and Historic	403	81.09 }	84.91	79	72.48 }	78.90
Postclassic	19	3.82 }		7	6.42 }	
Pre-Postclassic	2	0.40 }	1.41	2	1.83 }	2.75
Pure Florescent	5	1.01 }		1	0.92 }	
No Date	68	3.68		20	18.35	
Total	497	100.00		109	100.00	

*Includes 10 ?cottontail rabbit bones.

Probable Intrusives

At least two genera of cricetid rodents appear in the Cozumel sites—white-footed mice *(Peromyscus sp.)* and hispid cotton rats *(Sigmodon hispidus)*. These rodents are numerically insignificant, constituting less than 1 percent of all mammal bones and less than 5 percent of the MNIs (Table 8.2). They are most likely intrusive species in the sites where they occur; their burrowing habits and small size would easily allow them to invade tiny crevices in burials, temple platforms, and housemounds (see Hall and Kelson 1959).

The three specimens of white-footed mice *(Peromyscus sp.)* are probably all *P. leucopus cozumelae,* since this is the insular subspecies which has been reported on Cozumel (Jones and Lawlor 1965; Hall and Kelson 1959). All of these bones occurred at San Gervasio (C-22) (see Table 8.38) in burial contexts (gr. 7, burial 35, and gr. 3, burial 27). This was also true of the single fragmentary element identified only to the family level (Cricetidae), which was found in gr. 3, burial 27.

The remains of hispid cotton rats *(Sigmodon hispidus)* were much more numerous and widespread (Table 8.38). They occurred in six different sites and in a variety of cultural contexts, totaling sixty-eight bones and thirty-two individuals. This seems to be a relatively high frequency for an intrusive species, but as Hall and Kelson (1959: 671) have commented (referring to the natural environment), "wherever cotton rats occur they usually are the most numerous mammals and are active both day and night." Since they can be serious pests in agricultural areas, these little rodents would logically have occurred in great numbers in the Cozumel sites.

BATS

Two bat skulls were excavated from San Gervasio (C-22, gr. 3, pit 149, burial 30) (Table 8.38). This order of mammals (Chiroptera), like rodents, is one of the most numerous and variable of all animals. These two specimens could not be definitely identified further than the tropically distributed family Phyllostomidae (American leaf-nosed bats). The Brazilian small-eared bat *(Micronycteris megalotis)* resembles the present material most closely, and this species does occur on the island (Jones and Lawlor 1965). These remains probably represent intrusive animals at San Gervasio. This species in particular is known to roost singly or in small colonies in crevices and hollow trees (Hall and Kelson 1959). Leaf-nosed bats were also present at Mayapán; Pollock and Ray (1957) concluded these were intrusive as well.

The leaf-nosed bat, another species, had a place in the Maya pantheon. It appears several times in the Maya Codices, with the nose leaf depicted prominently in these artistic representations (Tozzer and Allen 1910). Bats could easily have become endowed with religious significance, since they no doubt frequented the temples and other buildings by day, as they do now.

Table 8.38 Distribution of Probable Intrusive Mammal Species by Site

SPECIES	SITE	NO. BONES	%	MNI	%
Phyllostomidae-?Micronycteris Megalotis (Brazilian small-eared bat)	C-22	2	2.70	2	5.40
Crocetid rodents	C-22	1	1.35	1	2.70
Peromyscus sp. (White-footed mice)	C-22	1	1.35	1	2.70
Peromyscus cf. P. leucopus (White-footed mouse)	C-22	2	2.70	1	2.70
Sigmodon hispidus (Hispid cotton rat)	C-13	4	5.40	3	8.10
Sigmodon hispidus	C-31	4	5.40	1	2.70
Sigmodon hispidus	C-18	3	4.05	3	8.10
Sigmodon hispidus	C-25	2	2.70	2	5.40
Sigmodon hispidus	C-15	1	1.35	1	2.70
Sigmodon hispidus	C-22	54	72.97	22	59.46
Total		74	99.97	37	99.96

Missing Mammals, Hunting Techniques, and Nutritional Implications

Some of the animals one might reasonably expect to find in Maya sites were missing altogether. For example, no jaguars or other cats appeared in the Cozumel sites, although this animal is known to have been of very special importance to the Maya and has occurred in other archaeological sites. Jaguars were an essential part of Maya religion. Their beautiful skins were in great demand for ceremonial purposes, they were used as sacrifices, they occur in religious contexts in the Maya Codices, and they appear repeatedly in ceremonial architecture at various sites (see Pohl 1976: 177–179; Wright 1970: 26–28; Tozzer and Allen 1910: 355–358; Tozzer 1941: 11, 122, 163, 183, 202). Jaguars apparently are not native to Cozumel (Hall and Kelson 1959; Jones and Lawlor 1965), but one might expect the skins to have been imported for use in the island's religious ceremonies. No phalanges, claws, teeth or skull fragments were found which would indicate this practice. Undoubtedly, by late Postclassic times much of the grandeur of the classic Mayan ceremonies had faded. Perhaps, too, the elite of Cozumel were overshadowed by the priests and rulers of cities like Tikal, and could not compete successfully for these rare, valuable animal skins.

Armadillos, tapirs, monkeys, and manatees are other species which are known to have been eaten by the Maya and have appeared in prehistoric sites (Tozzer 1941; Pohl 1976; Wing 1974), but do not occur in the Cozumel sites. Of these, at least two (the manatee and the armadillo) would have been readily accessible to the islanders. An animal very similar to the seacow, the manatee inhabits the waters along the west coast of Cozumel as well as the adjacent coast of the nearby peninsula and Manatee Island to the south (Jones and Lawlor 1965). Landa describes in great detail the method used for harpooning these animals (Tozzer 1941: 191), whose meat the Maya reportedly enjoyed very much. That such an easily obtained source of meat was ignored by the Cozumeleños seems strange. Armadillos were plentiful on the island in the early 1980s and were said to be a favorite wild food of the native villagers. In 1978, the author saw several piles each containing the discarded remains of up to seven armadillos. Evidently the prehistoric villagers preferred other species. In contrast, armadillo remains were relatively abundant at the Late Postclassic site of Macanche (Pohl 1976: 186).

Although no tangible evidence of hunting activities is preserved in the Cozumel sites, some of the methods which were likely employed should be mentioned. Pohl's (1976: 258–263) thorough discussion of Maya food procurement methods need not be repeated in detail here. Documentation exists for the use of dogs in a stalking-and-ambush technique (for obtaining deer, birds, and small game); the use of blowguns, spears, atlatls, and possibly bows and arrows; the use of "jerk-up" snares, baited cage traps, and deadfall or pitfall traps; the use of torches at night to dazzle game feeding or drinking at water sources; and the use of various calls, whistles, and other noisemakers to imitate animal sounds (Pohl 1976; Landa in Tozzer 1941: 203; Tozzer and Allen 1910: 293).

One characteristic of the Cozumel mammal assemblage is the predominance of fat-rich species. As Pohl (1976: 227–231) has pointed out, such animals provide extra calories per gram of protein, which may have been at a premium among the prehistoric Maya. The fats also aid in the absorption of vitamin A, which is known to be deficient in modern Maya diets. Overconsumption of fat (especially saturated fats from meat and other animal products) is a relatively recent phenomenon. Prehistorically, as well as in present-day less-developed nations, fats have been associated with "good" diets. Therefore, it may be significant nutritionally that four of the five fat-rich mammals specifically mentioned by Pohl occur in the Cozumel sites—peccary, dog, opossum, and paca—and that the first three are so numerous. These species together account for 62.25 percent of the identifiable mammal bone, or 53.27 percent of all MNIs. The percentage would likely be higher if the fat content of some of the other species—i.e., procyonids and gray foxes—were known, and if at least some of the 1,623 unidentifiable large mammal bones were ascertained to be peccary. These results confirm a trend towards increased reliance on fat-rich animals observed by Pohl (1976) at some late sites.

9. Patterns of Animal Use on Cozumel

IN ORDER TO ANALYZE and apply the information obtained on animal use by the Maya of Cozumel, the relative numerical importance of each category of fauna excavated from the ten sites on the island was calculated and compared (Table 9.1).

Intersite Comparisons

Table 9.2 shows the ranges and average percentages the Cozumel animals represented in each site. Since the relatively small sample sizes in most of the sites could skew these results, a "selected average" was also calculated on the basis of bone counts and MNIs from the three largest and most important sites on the island—Buena Vista (C-18), San Gervasio (C-22), and La Expedición (C-25)—each of which had sample sizes of more than 3,000 bones. This selected average thus acts as a control or a basis of comparison for the averages obtained from all ten sites.

An evaluation of these figures (Table 9.2) results in the following order for the Cozumel fauna, in descending order of statistical importance:

1. Fishes and crabs
2. Mammals
3. Reptiles
4. Birds
5. Amphibians

This order applies whether one uses selected average percentages of bones or MNIs, or total average percent of MNIs. If the total average

Table 9.1 Distribution of Cozumel Fauna by Site

SITE	CATEGORY OF FAUNA	NO. BONES	%	MNI	%
C-2	Reef fishes	1	5.88	—	—
	Amphibians	1	5.88	1	11.11
	Dogs	3	17.65	2	22.22
	Other mammals	3	17.65	1	11.11
	Turtles	3	17.65	1	11.11
	Iguanids	6	35.29	4	44.44
Subtotal		**17**	**100.00**	**9**	**99.99**
C-9	Dogs	12	85.71	1	100.00
	Other mammals	2	14.29	—	—
Subtotal		**14**	**100.00**	**1**	**100.00**
C-12	Iguanids	11	100.00	4	100.00
C-13	Crabs	3	0.26	1	0.78
	Sharks	7	0.62	4	3.12
	Reef fishes	765	67.28	70	54.69
	Amphibians	1	0.09	1	0.78
	Dogs	58	5.10	4	3.12
	Peccaries	50	4.40	6	4.69
	Other mammals	149	13.10	20	15.63
	Turtles	64	5.63	14	10.94
	Iguanids	5	0.44	3	2.34
	Crocodiles	3	0.26	1	0.78
	Birds	32	2.81	4	3.12
Subtotal		**1,137**	**99.99**	**128**	**99.99**
C-15	Sharks	2	0.30	2	4.88
	Stingrays	5	0.74	1	2.44
	Reef fishes	31	4.59	1	2.44
	Amphibians	1	0.15	1	2.44
	Dogs	19	2.81	2	4.88
	Peccaries	16	2.37	2	4.88
	Other mammals	280	41.48	11	26.83
	Turtles	38	5.63	3	7.32
	Iguanids	150	22.22	7	17.07
	Birds	133	19.70	11	26.83
Subtotal		**675**	**99.99**	**41**	**100.01**
C-18	Crabs	21	0.68	14	2.92
	Sharks	19	0.61	11	2.30
	Reef fishes	1,210	38.97	178	37.16
	Amphibians	7	0.23	5	1.04
	Dogs	82	2.64	18	3.76
	Peccaries	225	7.25	43	8.98
	Other mammals	439	14.14	69	14.41
	Turtles	421	13.56	82	17.12
	Iguanids	281	9.05	52	10.86
	Crocodiles	14	0.45	3	0.63
	Indeterminate reptiles	375	12.08	—	—
	Birds	11	0.35	4	0.84
Subtotal		**3,105**	**100.01**	**479**	**100.02**

Table 9.1   Distribution of Cozumel Fauna by Site (continued)

SITE	CATEGORY OF FAUNA	NO. BONES	%	MNI	%
C-22	Crabs	103	0.92	49	4.57
	Sharks	31	0.27	24	2.24
	Stingrays	21	0.19	9	0.84
	Reef fishes	4,268	37.97	315	29.36
	Amphibians	271	2.41	28	2.61
	Dogs	447	3.98	53	4.94
	Peccaries	551	4.90	76	7.08
	Other mammals	3,626	32.26	224	20.88
	Turtles	862	7.67	150	13.98
	Iguanids	934	8.31	103	9.60
	Crocodiles	11	0.10	7	0.65
	Indeterminate reptiles	5	0.04	—	—
	Birds	111	0.99	35	3.26
Subtotal		**11,241**	**100.01**	**1,073**	**100.01**
C-25	Crabs	42	1.33	20	4.18
	Sharks	10	0.32	8	1.67
	Reef fishes	1,426	45.31	160	33.47
	Amphibians	1	0.03	1	0.21
	Dogs	17	0.54	9	1.88
	Peccaries	341	10.84	54	11.30
	Other mammals	703	22.34	82	17.15
	Turtles	388	12.33	69	14.44
	Iguanids	127	4.04	46	9.62
	Crocodiles	6	0.19	2	0.42
	Indeterminate reptiles	1	0.03	—	—
	Birds	85	2.70	27	5.65
Subtotal		**3,147**	**100.00**	**478**	**99.99**
C-27	Crabs	3	0.59	3	5.08
	Reef fishes	53	10.45	13	22.03
	Dogs	3	0.59	3	5.08
	Peccaries	38	7.50	10	16.95
	Other mammals	356	70.22	6	10.17
	Turtles	40	7.89	17	28.81
	Iguanids	13	2.56	6	10.17
	Crocodiles	1	0.20	1	1.69
Subtotal		**507**	**100.00**	**59**	**99.98**
C-31	Crabs	11	1.38	5	5.56
	Sharks	6	0.75	4	4.44
	Reef fishes	617	77.61	62	68.89
	Amphibians	1	0.13	1	1.11
	Dogs	4	0.50	1	1.11
	Other mammals	75	9.43	7	7.78
	Turtles	26	3.27	4	4.44
	Iguanids	50	6.29	6	6.67
	Birds	5	0.63	—	—
Subtotal		**795**	**99.99**	**90**	**100.00**
Total		20,649		2,362	

Table 9.2 Importance of Cozumel Fauna by Site

CATEGORY OF FAUNA	% OF ALL BONES IN EACH SITE (RANGE)	TOTAL AVERAGE % OF ALL BONES	SELECTED AVERAGE* % OF BONES	% OF ALL MNIS IN EACH SITE (RANGE)	TOTAL AVERAGE % OF ALL MNIS	SELECTED AVERAGE % OF MNIS
Reef fishes	4.59- 77.61	36.01	40.75	2.44- 68.69	33.43	33.33
Crabs	0.26- 1.38	0.86	0.98	0.78- 5.56	3.85	3.89
Sharks	0.27- 0.75	0.48	0.40	1.67- 4.88	3.11	2.07
Stingrays	0.19- 0.74	0.47	0.19	0.84- 2.44	1.64	0.84
Amphibians	0.03- 5.88	1.27	0.89	0.21- 11.11	2.76	1.29
Turtles	3.27- 17.65	9.20	11.19	7.32- 28.81	13.52	15.18
Iguanids	0.44-100.0	20.91	7.13	2.34-100.0	23.42	10.03
Crocodiles	0.10- 0.45	0.24	0.25	0.42- 1.69	0.83	0.57
Indet. reptiles	0.03- 12.08	4.05	4.05	—	—	—
Birds	0.35- 19.70	6.20	4.68	0.84- 26.83	7.94	3.25
Dogs	0.50- 85.71	13.28	2.39	1.11-100.0	16.33	3.53
Peccaries	2.37- 10.84	6.21	7.66	4.69- 16.95	8.98	9.12
Other mammals	9.43- 70.22	26.10	22.91	7.78- 26.83	15.50	17.48

Grouped subtotals (braces):

TOTAL AVERAGE % OF ALL BONES: Reef fishes–Stingrays = 37.82; Turtles–Crocodiles = 34.40; Dogs–Other mammals = 45.59

SELECTED AVERAGE % OF BONES: Reef fishes–Stingrays = 42.32; Turtles–Crocodiles = 22.62; Dogs–Other mammals = 32.96

TOTAL AVERAGE % OF ALL MNIS: Reef fishes–Stingrays = 44.03; Turtles–Crocodiles = 37.77; Dogs–Other mammals = 40.81

SELECTED AVERAGE % OF MNIS: Reef fishes–Stingrays = 40.13; Turtles–Crocodiles = 25.87; Dogs–Other mammals = 30.13

*Selected averages are based only on sites with sample sizes over 3,000 bones (C-18, C-22, and C-25).

169

percent of bones were to be used, mammals and fishes would be reversed in importance. However, bone counts are probably less reliable than MNIs, since they do not reflect the number of animals represented but merely the number of bone fragments recovered at a site. In addition, the total average percentage of bones includes sites with statistically small sample sizes. For these reasons, the order listed above is preferable to the latter average.

Table 9.3 illustrates the results of comparing the three major sites on the island (C-18, C-22, and C-25). San Gervasio (C-22), the largest, most complex and farthest inland of all the Cozumel sites, contained fishes and crabs in proportions nearly equal to mammals. Reptiles were secondary in importance, and birds and amphibians were last with very low percentages. Of all three sites, C-22 has proportionately the most mammals and, correspondingly, the fewest fishes and crabs. This may be due to its location in the north-central heartland of Cozumel, which is farther inland than either C-18 or C-25. It may also reflect a greater dietary preference for land fauna, or the possession of enough social and economic power to obtain these culturally preferred species. Dogs in particular represent higher proportions at San Gervasio than elsewhere.

This site also contains the highest percentages of amphibians. The probable use of dogs and marine toads for ceremonial purposes (see Chapters 4 and 7) suggests that the San Gervasio elite may have been more involved than other elites in such activities. Of the three sites, San Gervasio was the only source of stingray spines and vertebrae, again perhaps indicating greater ceremonial use of certain fauna than elsewhere. However, the sample size of stingrays is so small—twenty-six in all—that this distribution may be somewhat misleading. Five elements of these fish also occurred at C-15, El Cedral.

Buena Vista (C-18) differs from San Gervasio in being a tightly nucleated center in the southern portion of the island, containing huge rubble platforms of unknown function, and lying much closer to the seacoast. Here, fishes and crabs are clearly the predominant group of animals, followed fairly closely by reptiles, with mammals third. Birds and amphibians again played a relatively minor role (Table 9.3). The emphasis on marine fauna with respect to land animals can be partly explained by the site's proximity to the sea. The fact that reptiles constitute a greater proportion of the sample than mammals is initially surprising. However, the author discovered in 1978 that reptiles, especially iguanids, are very plentiful in the environs of Buena Vista. This site exhibits the highest percentages of reptiles in general (Table 9.3), with turtles and iguanids in particular outnumbering those at C-22 and C-25.

La Expedición (C-25), a coastal site located near the northeastern tip of the island, appears to have been a ceremonial center with very close ties to San Gervasio. Fishes and crabs again were the most important fauna used at the site. As with Buena Vista, this may be due to the site's location near the sea. Marine fauna are followed by mammals

Table 9.3 Comparison of Fauna in Three Major Cozumel Sites

CATEGORY OF FAUNA	BUENA VISTA C-18		SAN GERVASIO C-22		LA EXPEDICIÓN C-25	
	% TOTAL BONES	% MNI	% TOTAL BONES	% MNI	% TOTAL BONES	% MNI
Reef fishes	38.97	37.16	37.97	29.36	45.31	33.47
Crabs	0.68	2.92	0.92	4.57	1.33	4.18
Sharks	0.61	2.30	0.27	2.24	0.32	1.67
Stingrays	—	—	0.19	0.84	—	—
	40.49	43.42	39.35	37.01	46.96	39.32
Amphibians	0.23	1.04	2.41	2.61	0.03	0.21
Turtles	13.56	17.12	7.67	13.98	12.33	14.44
Iguanids	9.05	10.86	8.31	9.60	4.04	9.62
Crocodiles	0.45	0.63	0.10	0.65	0.19	0.42
Indet. reptiles	12.08	—	0.04	—	0.03	—
	35.14	28.61	16.12	24.23	16.59	24.48
Birds	0.35	0.84	0.99	3.26	2.70	5.65
Dogs	2.64	3.76	3.98	4.94	0.54	1.88
Peccaries	7.25	8.98	4.90	7.08	10.84	11.30
Other mammals	14.14	14.41	32.26	20.88	22.34	17.15
	24.03	27.15	41.14	32.90	33.72	30.33

and then by reptiles, which were definitely third in importance. Birds, followed by amphibians, again represent relatively low percentages of the site's total fauna (Table 9.3). La Expedición, however, contains a significantly greater proportion of birds than either C-22 or C-18. Many of these avian species most likely represent non-food uses, particularly ceremonial functions, and the great variety of birds here matches the many species at San Gervasio. As discussed in Chapter 6, this diversity of avifauna probably reflects the fact that C-22 and C-25 are the two most important sites on the island for elite ceremonial and civil administrative functions. That birds make up a greater proportion of the total fauna at La Expedición than elsewhere may indicate that this site specialized in the use of avifauna for non-food purposes. This site also has the highest percentage of peccaries relative to C-18 and C-22, and the lowest proportion of dogs. Peccaries may have been the mammal of choice for the elite at La Expedición, either as a sacrificial item or a fat-rich addition to their diet.

A summary of these comparisons appears below, showing the order of importance of the fauna in each of the three sites:

Buena Vista (C-18)	*San Gervsio (C-22)*	*La Expedición (C-25)*
1. Fishes and crabs	1. Fishes, crabs and mammals	1. Fishes and crabs
2. Reptiles	2. Reptiles	2. Mammals
3. Mammals	3. Birds and amphibians	3. Reptiles
4. Birds and amphibians		4. Birds
		5. Amphibians

Faunal use in these sites can also be compared by calculating species diversity and equitability indices (MacArthur and MacArthur 1961; Sheldon 1969). These statistics have been used to evaluate the degree of selection which was exercised at specific sites relative to the available fauna (see, for example, Wing 1977). Calculating these indices involves the percentage of individuals (MNIs) of each identified taxon. The underlying assumption is that the number of identified taxa and their percentages accurately represent faunal use at the site; that is, bias due to variable preservation of the remains or excavation sampling procedures is presumably absent. The number of identified taxa present in the Cozumel sites varies considerably, from one at C-9 to eighty-five at C-22. This suggests that the diversity of animal species exploited at these sites differed significantly. However, Don Grayson (personal communication) asserts that the number of taxa present in a site is often directly related to the number of bones—in other words, species diversity and equitability are directly dependent on the excavated sample size. To test this hypothesis with the present data, the number of excavated bones from Cozumel has been plotted on a graph against the number of identified taxa for each site (Fig. 9.1). If the correlation between these two variables was statistically perfect, a straight line at a 45-degree angle would result. As Figure 9.1 illustrates, the

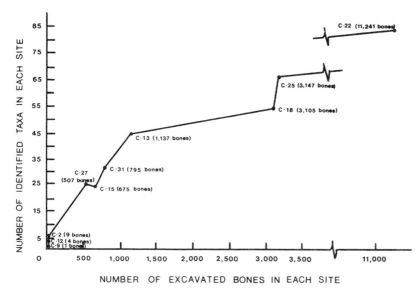

Figure 9.1. Number of Excavated Bones and Identified Taxa in Each Site.

Cozumel sites show an undeniably strong trend toward this direct correlation. Thus, the larger the excavated bone sample at any given site on the island, the greater the likelihood that more species will be identified from that site. Therefore, calculating species diversity and equitability indices would be meaningless here. However, if additional excavations were to be carried out at some of these sites, the likely result would be a greater similarity of species use on the island as a whole (or at least a greater uniformity in the numbers of different species used by the inhabitants of the various sites).

Comparison by Provenience

One aim of this project was delineation of elite and non-elite patterns of faunal use. Field notes from the 1972–73 excavations were used to separate the faunal material in housemound refuse from burials and ceremonial/administrative precincts. The cultural significance of a substantial proportion of the sample could not be determined, although much of this probably represents domestic refuse (Table 9.4). The working assumption is that either these two kinds of proveniences represent different socio-economic classes, or different sets of activities occurring in the two areas have resulted in the deposition of varying proportions of animal remains.

Distinct differences do appear when the fauna from these proveniences are compared (Table 9.5). Housemounds are characterized by

Table 9.4   Distribution of Cozumel Fauna by Provenience

PROVENIENCE	NO. BONES	%	MNI	%
Burials and Ceremonial/ Administrative contexts	9,485	45.93	909	38.48
Housemounds	1,907	9.24	360	15.24
Indeterminate	9,257	44.83	1,093	46.27
Total	20,649	100.00	2,362	99.99

a relatively high dependence on fishes and crabs, followed by reptiles and then mammals, with very few birds or amphibians. Turtles in particular appear to have been a major resource. Mammals in general were used much less frequently than in the ceremonial/administrative proveniences, although peccaries were present in somewhat greater proportions. In contrast, burials and ceremonial/administrative contexts contain a very high percentage of mammals, followed by reptiles, fishes, and crabs, and, last, by birds and amphibians. More iguanids occur proportionately in these precincts, although exploitation of reptiles in general was much less common than in the housemounds. Dogs, birds, and amphibians are found in somewhat greater percentages here than in housemounds, a finding consistent with the postulated ritual uses of these animals. To summarize these differences, here is the relative order of importance of the fauna excavated from these proveniences:

Burials and Ceremonial/
Administrative Contexts
1. Mammals
2. Reptiles, fishes,
    and crabs
3. Birds and amphibians

Housemounds
1. Fishes and crabs
2. Reptiles
3. Mammals
4. Birds
5. Amphibians

Apparently, then, marine animals represented the basic food resource of the Cozumel Maya, while mammals were used most often in ceremonial occasions, perhaps being reserved primarily for consumption by the elite. A word of caution should be inserted here, however. Unlike other Maya sites, such as Tikal or Seibal, no clear-cut spatial or architectural division between elite and non-elite precincts is evident on Cozumel. Indeed, the presence of more than one social class at these sites has not been clearly established. And even if two or more classes did exist, Rathje and Sabloff (1975: 20) have suggested that the leveling effects of long-distance trade would have caused a general homogeneity of cultural remains from all classes. Researchers might logically expect this even distribution of material goods throughout all social classes to be reflected in the animal remains, with no discernible differences in faunal use.

Table 9.5 Comparison of Cozumel Fauna by Provenience

CATEGORY OF FAUNA	BURIALS AND CEREMONIAL/ADMINISTRATIVE CONTEXTS			HOUSMOUNDS		
	% TOTAL BONES	% MNIS		% TOTAL BONES	% MNIS	
Fishes and Crabs	18.34	33.33		43.73	41.67	
Amphibians	2.83	3.19		0.10	0.56	
Turtles	7.93	12.54	⎫ 23.95 bones	25.80	22.78	⎫ 30.78 bones
Iguanids	12.03	9.79	⎬ 22.55 MNIs	3.83	8.06	⎬ 32.23 MNIs
Crocodiles	0.04	0.22	⎭	0.94	1.39	⎭
Indet. reptiles	3.95	—		0.21	—	
Birds	2.60	5.50		0.63	1.39	
Dogs	4.73	4.84	⎫ 52.27 bones	1.36	3.06	⎫ 24.75 bones
Peccaries	6.33	5.83	⎬ 35.42 MNIs	7.13	8.33	⎬ 24.17 MNIs
Other mammals	41.21	24.75	⎭	16.26	12.78	⎭
Total	99.99	99.99		99.99	100.02	

However, two distinct patterns do emerge from this analysis of cultural proveniences. A conservative interpreter would attribute these differences to a variation in the activities occurring in these locations. Regardless of the social classes involved, trash resulting from domestic activities and deposited in housemounds should differ from the remains left after formal ceremonial or administrative functions. But the possibility that these two precincts of the Cozumel sites may indeed represent distinct social classes should also be considered.

Changes through Time

At least two-thirds of the Cozumel faunal sample has been dated to the Postclassic, Late Postclassic, and Historic periods (Table 9.6). Less than 6 percent of the bone (or fewer than 7 percent of the MNIs) is from earlier time periods. Even the material from mixed or undated contexts would not significantly affect this overall pattern, since it represents only about 27 percent of the total bones or MNIs. The marked scarcity of fauna from pre-Postclassic contexts would render detailed comparisons by period statistically tenuous. Therefore, all material dated to time periods before the Postclassic has been combined for comparison with the later periods. Tables 9.7, 9.8 and 9.9 illustrate the distribution of all categories of fauna broken down into three major subdivisions, respectively: pre-Postclassic fauna, all Postclassic fauna, and Late Postclassic/Historic fauna.

When the faunal remains from the earlier time periods (Table 9.7) are compared to those from all Postclassic periods (Table 9.8), several trends can be discerned. Dogs, gray foxes, opossums, rabbits, and amphibians all increase slightly in importance through time, while the percentage of peccaries declines. Reptiles (especially iguanids) are very significant in the pre-Postclassic periods, while mammals play a comparatively lesser role. By Postclassic times, this pattern is reversed. Crocodiles, horses, porcupine, paca, and bats occur only in the Postclassic, although this could easily owe to the very small sample sizes of these particular fauna. The remaining taxa show little consistent variation through time if both bone counts and MNIs are examined.

When the pre-Postclassic fauna is compared with remains from Late Postclassic/Historic contexts only (Table 9.9), the same trends are noticeable. That is, the amphibians and mammals mentioned above have increased through time, while peccaries are relatively less significant. As before, the reptiles (especially iguanids) have become less important than the mammals by Late Postclassic times, again reversing the pattern which applied prior to the Postclassic.

Figure 9.2 illustrates this major change in faunal exploitation. Including MNIs in this pattern makes it somewhat less dramatic than when only bone counts are used, but the trend is still unmistakable. Perhaps the social leveling effects of the thriving Late Postclassic trade

Table 9.6 Time Periods of Cozumel Fauna

TIME PERIOD	NO. BONES	%		MNI	%	
Late Postclassic and Historic	13,094	63.41	13,950 ⎱	1,397	59.14	1,554 ⎱
Postclassic	856	4.15	67.56% ⎰	157	6.65	65.79% ⎰
Pre-Postclassic	418	2.02		41	1.74	
Pure Florescent	563	2.73		73	3.09	
Terminal Classic	15	0.07	1,142	6	0.25	164
Early Period (Classic)	14	0.07	5.53%	6	0.25	6.94%
Early₁ (Mixed Preclassic, Classic, Terminal Classic)	59	0.29		18	0.76	
Early₂ (all Pre- Late Postclassic periods)	73	0.35		20	0.85	
Mixed and No Date	5,557	26.91		644	27.27	
Total	20,649	100.00		2,362	100.00	

Table 9.7 Relative Importance of Cozumel Fauna Prior to Postclassic

CATEGORY OF FAUNA	NO. BONES	%		MNI	%	
Fishes and Crabs	324	28.37		73	44.51	
Amphibians	5	0.44		3	1.83	
Turtles	317	27.76	⎫	24	14.63	⎫
Iguanids	135	11.82	⎬ 39.58%	19	11.59	⎬ 26.22%
Birds	10	0.86	⎭	6	3.66	⎭
Peccaries	190	16.64	⎫	14	8.54	⎫
Dogs	13	1.14		1	0.61	
Deer	1	0.09		1	0.61	
?Artiodactyl	1	0.09		—	—	
Procyonids	14	1.23	⎬ 30.75%	9	5.49	⎬ 23.79%
Gray Foxes	5	0.44		2	1.22	
Opossums	7	0.61		5	3.05	
Rabbits	7	0.61		3	1.83	
Rodents	6	0.53		4	2.44	⎭
Indet. Mammals (Large, medium, small)	107	9.37	⎭	—	—	
Total	1,142	100.00		164	100.01	

*Includes all bones from Pre-Postclassic, Pre-Late Postclassic, Pure Florescent, Terminal Classic, and Mixed Preclassic contexts.

Table 9.8   Relative Importance of Cozumel Fauna in All Postclassic Periods

CATEGORY OF FAUNA	NO. BONES	%		MNI	%	
Fishes and Crabs	6,182	44.32		602	38.99	
Amphibians	272	1.95		29	1.88	
Turtles	1,261	9.04	⎫	228	14.77	⎫
Iguanids	1,018	7.30	⎬ 19.28%	159	10.30	⎬ 25.85%
Crocodiles	31	0.22		12	0.78	⎭
Indet. reptiles	380	2.72	⎭	—	—	
Birds	158	1.13		46	2.98	
Peccaries	626	4.49	⎫	116	7.51	⎫
Dogs	515	3.69		69	4.47	
Deer	11	0.08		8	0.52	
Horses	3	0.02		2	0.13	
Cow/Horse (*Bos/Equus*)	4	0.03	⎬ 33.32%	1	0.06	⎬ 30.95%
Procyonids	330	2.37		75	4.86	
Gray Foxes	413	2.96		32	2.07	
Opossums	802	5.75		61	3.95	
Rabbits	422	3.03		86	5.57	
Porcupine and Paca	2	0.01		2	0.13	
Bats	2	0.01		2	0.13	
Rodents	47	0.34	⎭	24	1.55	⎭
Indet. mammals	1,471	10.54		—	—	
Total	13,950	100.00		1,544	100.65	

*Includes all bones from Late Postclassic, Postclassic, and Historic contexts.

Table 9.9 Relative Importance of Cozumel Fauna in the Late Postclassic and Historic Periods

CATEGORY OF FAUNA	NO. BONES	%	MNI	%
Fishes and Crabs	5,847	44.65	543	38.87
Amphibians	272	2.08	29	2.08
Turtles	1,105	8.44 ⎤	202	14.46 ⎤
Iguanids	980	7.48 ⎥ 19.0%	145	10.38 ⎥ 25.48%
Crocodiles	27	0.21 ⎥	9	0.64 ⎦
Indet. reptiles	376	2.87 ⎦	—	—
Birds	155	1.18	45	3.22
Peccaries	549	4.19 ⎤	95	6.80 ⎤
Dogs	467	3.57 ⎥	59	4.22 ⎥
Deer	10	0.08 ⎥	8	0.57 ⎥
Horses	3	0.02 ⎥	2	0.14 ⎥
Cow/Horse (Bos/Equus)	4	0.03 ⎥ 33.09%	1	0.07 ⎥ 30.33%
Procyonids	318	2.43 ⎥	66	4.72 ⎥
Gray Foxes	413	3.15 ⎥	32	2.29 ⎥
Opossums	786	6.00 ⎥	55	3.94 ⎥
Rabbits	403	3.08 ⎥	79	5.65 ⎥
Porcupine and Paca	2	0.02 ⎥	2	0.14 ⎥
Bats	2	0.02 ⎥	2	0.14 ⎥
Rodents	46	0.35 ⎦	23	1.65 ⎦
Indet. Mammals	1,329	10.15	—	—
Total	13,094	100.00	1,397	99.98

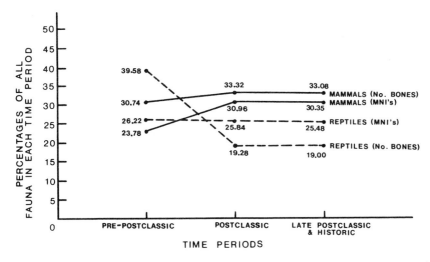

Figure 9.2. Fluctuation of Mammals and Reptiles through Time.

networks resulted in greater access for all socioeconomic classes to the more highly valued mammal foods. However, increased competition for the peccaries on the island may have significantly lowered their population levels, so that most people had to content themselves with the smaller game species (such as dogs, gray foxes, opossums, and rabbits) by Late Postclassic times.

The degree of dependence on marine fauna can also be examined within the context of temporal change. The majority of all reef fishes, sharks, stingrays, crabs, and sea turtles appeared in Late Postclassic and historic contexts (Table 9.10), as is predictable, since the majority of all excavated fauna came from these time periods. Calculating the relative importance by percent of all species within each period (Table 9.11) is more meaningful. Results based on relative percentages indicate that people in the Postclassic and later periods exploited marine animals to a slightly greater degree than those in pre-Postclassic times (especially when bone counts are employed). The implication is that the heavy dependence on such fauna (relative to land animals) remains fairly consistent through time.

Environmental Implications

Some animals, particularly amphibians, birds and reptiles, have relatively narrow environmental requirements. Therefore, these fauna can often be used to make deductions concerning past environmental changes, as well as to determine human exploitation of ecological zones.

Table 9.10 Distribution of Cozumel Marine Fauna* through Time*

TIME PERIOD	No. BONES	%		MNI	%	
Late Postclassic/historic	5,862	67.58	} 71.45%	551	57.10	} 63.32%
Postclassic	336	3.87		60	6.22	
Pre-Late Postclassic	73	0.84		20	2.07	
Pre-Postclassic	2	0.02		1	0.10	
Pure Florescent	192	2.21	} 2.89%	35	3.63	} 5.50%
Mixed Preclassic, Classic, and Terminal Classic	59	0.68		18	1.87	
Mixed and No Date	2,150	24.79		280	29.02	
Total	8,674	99.99		965	100.01	

*Includes all reef fishes, sharks, stingrays, crabs, and sea turtles.

Table 9.11 **Relative Importance of Marine Fauna through Time**

TIME PERIOD	NO. BONES	%[1]	MNI	%[2]
All Pre-Postclassic[3] periods	253	23.67	54	37.50
Postclassic	6,198	44.43	611	39.57
Late Postclassic and historic	5,862	44.77	551	39.44

[1]Represents percentage of all bones at this time period.
[2]Represents percentage of all MNIs at this time period.
[3]Does not include any pre-Late Postclassic bones.

Nothing discovered regarding the reptiles or amphibians indicated that the climate or hydrology had changed appreciably (see Chapters 4 and 5). The birds, however, included three species which require old rainforest conditions that no longer exist on Cozumel. Thus, Maya agricultural practices may have resulted in gradual habitat modification over a long period of time.

Uses of Fauna for Tools and Religious/Ceremonial Purposes

A notable characteristic of the Cozumel fauna is the relative scarcity of bone tools or artifacts of any kind. Only 141 culturally modified elements were included in this study, making up less than 1 percent of the total faunal sample (Table 9.12). (Phillips [1979] reports twenty additional animal bone artifacts, catalogued and removed from the

Table 9.12 **Distribution of Culturally Modified Bone Elements**

CATEGORY OF FAUNA	NO. BONES	% OF THIS CLASS OF FAUNA
Peccary	3	0.25
Deer	3	21.43
?Rabbit	1	0.20
Turtle	36	1.95
Dogs	2	0.31
Birds	3	0.80
Crabs	1	0.55
Sharks	11	14.66
Indeterminate mammals	81	2.99
Total	141	(represents 0.68% of all Cozumel bones)

collection in Mexico, which were not analyzed in the present study, although they have been listed when appropriate.) A few of the 141 artifacts in this sample were recognizable as definite tools such as awls or needles, but most items were merely cut, shaped, or polished in some way (especially the mammal longbones), or had holes drilled in them as if used for ornamentation (e.g., the shark vertebrae and teeth). One explanation for this scarcity may be that the large numbers of shell scoops, hammers, and gougers represent substitutions for tools usually made of bone. Even the shell artifacts, however, included no awls and very few fine-working tools (Vokes 1978). The need for these functions was evidently fulfilled by stone tools (Phillips 1979).

Despite the lack of concrete archaeological evidence, many animals present in these sites were probably used for purposes other than food. Evidence from the Maya Codices, ethnohistoric documents, and modern ethnographic data suggests that some of the birds, the marine toads, dogs, peccaries, stingrays, and sharks very likely had ceremonial or decorative functions.

Food Preparation Practices

Clues to prehistoric food preparation can often be obtained from a study of butchered and burned bone, as well as from the presence or absence of various skeletal elements. The Cozumel material, however, yielded only fifteen bones with discernible butcher marks (Table 9.13), and most were fragmentary mammal longbones. Although this sample size is too small to allow many conclusions, the fact that the marks were usually small and light may indicate attempts to separate muscle masses from the bone, rather than chopping actions designed to cut the limbs apart at the joint. The paucity of such marks on the bones may mean that the butchers were fairly expert at their craft; a practiced slaughterer can separate joints and bone cuts of meat without leaving any tangible evidence.

Table 9.13   Distribution of Butchered Fauna

CATEGORY OF FAUNA	NO. BONES	% OF THIS CLASS OF FAUNA
Peccary	2	0.16
Coati	1	0.16
Opossum	1	0.09
Indeterminate mammals	10	0.37
Bird	1	0.27
Total	15	(represents 0.07% of all Cozumel bones).

The burned and heat-affected elements represent slightly more than 15 percent of all Cozumel fauna (Table 9.14). The Cozumel inhabitants evidently preferred to stew or boil most of their game and fish; only turtles, iguanids, and crabs include a majority of elements which are burned or heat-darkened. These particular animals were probably roasted directly over a fire or hot coals. Some of the burned bones might be the result of sacrificial practices, although the reptiles and crabs, at least, held no known religious significance among the Maya.

As far as skeletal elements are concerned, skull bones were generally predominant. This is to be expected on the basis of differential preservation, as well as the relative ease of identifying cranial elements, since other parts of the body are much less diagnostic. Some species, particularly such smaller mammals as gray foxes and opossums, exhibited a more even distribution in the percentages of all skeletal elements. Perhaps these animals were cooked whole and disposed of nearby. Larger species may have been butchered beforehand and dismembered prior to consumption and disposal.

Animal Modification and Pathologies

One measure of how much a faunal sample has been disturbed and possibly removed from its original depositional context is the percentage of elements which have been rodent-gnawed or carnivore-chewed. Less than 2 percent of the Cozumel fauna were so affected (Table 9.15).

Table 9.14   Distribution of Burned or Heat-darkened Fauna

CATEGORY OF FAUNA	NO. BONES	% OF THIS CLASS OF FAUNA
Peccary	25	2.05
Deer	2	14.29
Coatis	6	0.97
Gray Foxes	1	0.19
Rabbits	3	0.60
Dogs	13	2.02
?Artiodactyl	1	100.00
Indeterminate mammals	38	1.40
Turtles	1,764	95.77
Iguanids	1,100	69.75
Birds	37	9.80
Crabs	137	74.86
Reef fishes	32	0.38
Amphibians	3	1.06
Total	3,162	(represents 15.31% of all Cozumel bones)

Table 9.15   **Distribution of Fauna Modified by Rodents and Carnivores**

CATEGORY OF FAUNA	NO. BONES	% OF THIS CLASS OF FAUNA
Coatis	19	3.13
Gray Foxes	4	0.75
Peccaries	54	4.42
Opossums	28	2.51
Rabbits	31	6.24
Dogs	36	5.58
?Artiodactyl	1	100.00
Indeterminate mammals	27	1.00
Turtles	20	1.09
Iguanids	91	5.77
Birds	75	19.89
Amphibians	4	1.41
Fishes and Crabs	14	0.16
Total	404	(represents 1.96% of all Cozumel bones)

The distribution is somewhat uneven, showing that rodents and other scavengers (probably primarily dogs) seem to have preferred to gnaw on birds and certain mammals. Still, the relatively low overall incidence of this activity may indicate that the majority of faunal refuse was covered soon after deposition and was not radically disturbed thereafter.

Also significant, though mainly from a biological viewpoint, is the number of pathological elements present. Twenty-three such elements—mostly broken limb bones which had rehealed, along with a few bone deformations—occurred in the Cozumel material (Table 9.16). More than half are iguanid elements which had been broken and rehealed.

Table 9.16   **Distribution of Pathological Fauna**

CATEGORY OF FAUNA	NO. BONES	% OF THIS CLASS OF FAUNA
Peccaries	1	0.08
Coatis	2	0.33
Gray Foxes	1	0.19
Opossums	1	0.09
Dogs	4	0.62
Indeterminate mammals	1	0.04
Turtles	1	0.05
Iguanids	12	0.76
Total	23	(represents 0.11% of all Cozumel bones)

The overall pattern of faunal use in the ten Cozumel sites can be described as one which greatly emphasized marine resources and in which reptiles played a very significant role—factors which make Cozumel fairly unique. Other sites such as Cancún and Lubaantún are known to have used quantities of marine resources, but these findings have been based on very small sample sizes from much earlier time periods (especally the Formative). As of 1983, the present faunal sample of over 20,000 bones was the largest such data base analyzed and reported for the Maya area. The great quantity of these remains increases the statistical value of these conclusions. Beyond the discovery of certain specific kinds of information, there has been a more important goal underlying this entire work. I believe that this study will serve as an example of how faunal analysis can be used to make deductions or to evaluate previous inferences concerning different aspects of a prehistoric culture and its lifeways.

Acknowledgments

THE SCIENTIFIC ANALYSIS of a body of data as large and diverse as the Cozumel fauna necessarily involved a lengthy learning process on my part. This would not have been possible without the information, advice, and encouragement so generously supplied by many individuals.

Dr. Bruce D. Smith of the Smithsonian Institution, then an archaeology graduate student at the University of Michigan in Ann Arbor, was responsible for giving me a taste of faunal analysis and encouraged me to pursue it. I especially wish to thank all the members of my dissertation committee: Professor Stanley J. Olsen, my chairman, Dr. William L. Rathje, and Dr. R. Gwinn Vivian. Each of these men provided invaluable guidance, support, and constructive criticism during the course of this study as well as on the thesis which was the basis of this book. Professor Olsen first introduced me to the formal study of zooarchaeology. In addition, he kindly lent me several of his comparative specimens, suggested pertinent references, provided laboratory space, and generally offered his assistance in many ways. I am indebted to Dr. Rathje and Dr. Jeremy A. Sabloff, co-directors of the Cozumel Archaeological Project, for making the Cozumel faunal material available to me. Bill Rathje provided constant and unfailing support in a variety of ways during this project, for which I am very grateful. He consistently gave me useful advice on reference materials and other practical matters, granted access to the archaeological field notes, provided funds for the analysis of soil samples, was instrumental in obtaining financial support from the National Geographic Society for this work, and was of inestimable help when I needed personal encouragement. Gwinn Vivian did an especially fine job of editing the rough draft of this manuscript and offered his cheerful support and encouragement along the way.

I would also like to thank the many people who aided in the identification and preliminary analysis of the faunal materials. Dr. Elizabeth

S. Wing allowed me to use the comparative fish collections at the Florida State Museum in Gainesville, patiently helped me learn how to identify the thousands of fish bones in this sample, and generously provided the hospitality of her home during this time. Dr. Amadeo M. Rea aided immeasurably in identifying the bird remains. He not only used his personal comparative collection and that of the University of Arizona Department of Ecology and Evolutionary Biology, but also borrowed material from the U.S. National Museum (Smithsonian Institution) in Washington D.C. and obtained permission from Lyndon L. Hargrave for us to use his bird collection in Prescott, Arizona. Dr. Pierce Brodkorb (University of Florida, Gainesville) also helped identify some of the bird bones. The reptile and amphibian remains were identified with the generous aid of Dr. Thomas R. VanDevender (then of the University of Arizona, Department of Geosciences) who lent me specimens from his personal collection and offered many constructive suggestions. Kevin Moody, of the same department, was also helpful in identifying the turtle specimens. Although all of these individuals provided invaluable aid, the author was always present when identifications were made and accepts sole responsibility for the results. In addition, I am grateful to Dr. Donald A. Thomson (Curator of Fishes, University of Arizona, Department of Ecology and Evolutionary Biology) who supplied information on the ecology and habits of reef fishes as well as fishing techniques; to Dr. Lyle K. Sowls (Head of the Arizona Cooperative Wildlife Research Unit, University of Arizona) who helped determine the ages of the Cozumel peccary remains and provided modern peccary skulls for comparative measurements; and to John B. Sparling (then of the University of Arizona Department of Anthropology) who obtained comparative crab specimens for me and helped in the preliminary sorting and identification of the faunal sample. Thanks are also due John Carpenter (then an undergraduate student, University of Arizona, Department of Anthropology) for measuring all of the dog, peccary, and rabbit specimens used in this study.

Several individuals in other specialized fields provided valuable assistance as well. Ted McCreary, head of the University of Arizona Soils, Water, and Plant Tissue Testing Laboratory, analyzed the Cozumel soil samples and kindly interpreted them for me. Dr. Richard A. Thompson (University of Arizona, Department of Anthropology) gave helpful advice concerning the use and interpretation of statistical techniques for this project. I am grateful to Susan Ciolek-Torrello and Carol Margolis (University of Arizona Computer Center, Research Support Section) for their help in the computer analysis phase of this research. Similarly, I wish to thank my husband, John P. Green (then in the City of Tucson Computer Services Divison) for his advice and support in computerizing these data.

The fieldwork aspect of this project was greatly facilitated by Luis Rojas, resident of Cozumel, who served as translator and guide to the archaeological sites on the island, supplied pertinent information on local animals and plants, and was generally helpful in many ways.

Dr. Mary Pohl (Florida State University, Department of Anthropology, Tallahassee) generously provided faunal data from her work in the Petén and offered many good suggestions, particularly on the analysis of the Cozumel birds. David A. Phillips (University of Arizona, Department of Anthropology) acted as consultant on Mayan archaeology, especially with reference to Cozumel. Using ceramics, he dated the excavated proveniences on the island as closely as possible, so that temporal comparisons could be made here. Anthony P. Andrews (then at the University of Arizona, Department of Anthropology) provided constructive criticism of the bird chapter. Barbara McClatchie Andrews was responsible for photographing and preparing several of the illustrations. I would also like to thank my sister, Linda Hamblin Jones, for typing portions of the rough draft, drafting several of the illustrations, and for her continual support. Hazel Gillie typed the final version and was most helpful in taking care of many last-minute details.

The necessary financial support for fieldwork, travel expenses, and computer analysis was provided by a grant from the National Geographic Society, a United States Steel Foundation Fellowship, and a Sigma XI Grant-in-aid-of-Research.

I also wish to express my deep appreciation to Mrs. Dorothy Caranchini, then graduate secretary of the Department of Anthropology, University of Arizona. She went far beyond the call of duty in providing advice, encouragement, and even a shoulder to cry on, whenever necessary during my graduate career.

It is appropriate here to thank the Peabody Museum of Archaeology and Ethnology at Harvard University for its kind permission to reprint three figures from *Changing Pre-Columbian Commercial Systems: The 1972–1973 Seasons at Cozumel, Mexico* by Jeremy A. Sabloff and William L. Rathje, copyright 1975.

References

Allen, Glover M.
  1920 *Dogs of the American Aborigines.* Bulletin of the Museum of Comparative Zoology, Harvard University, vol. 63, no. 9. Cambridge, Mass.

Ball, Joseph W., and Jack D. Eaton
  1972 Marine resources and the prehistoric lowland Maya: A comment. *American Anthropologist* 74 (no. 3): 772–76.

Bean, Tarleton, H.
  1890 Notes on fishes collected at Cozumel, Yucatán, by the U.S. Fish Commission, with descriptions of new species. Bulletin of the U.S. Fish Commission 8 (1888, no. 4): 193–206.

Blake, Emmet R.
  1953 *Birds of Mexico: Guide for field identification.* Chicago: University of Chicago Press.

Bokonyi, S.
  1970 A new method for the determination of the number of individuals in animal bone material. *American Journal of Archaeology* 74: 291–92.

Borhegyi, Stephan F. De
  1961 Shark teeth, stingray spines, and shark fishing in ancient Mexico and Central America. *Southwestern Journal of Anthropology* 17 (no. 3): 273–96.

Carr, Archie F.
  1952 *Handbook of turtles.* Ithaca, N.Y.: Cornell University Press, Comstock Publishing Company.

Carter, George F.
  1971 Pre-Columbian chickens in America. In *Man Across the Sea,* ed. Carroll L. Riley, J. Charles Kelley, Campbell W. Pennington and Robert Rands, 178–218. Austin: University of Texas Press.

Casteel, Richard W.
  1972 Some archaeological uses of fish remains. *American Antiquity* 37 (no. 3): 404–19.

Casteel, Richard W., *cont'd.*

1974   A method for estimation of live weight of fish from the size of skeletal elements. *American Antiquity* 39 (no. 1): 94–98.

1976   *Fish remains in archaeology and paleo-environmental studies.* New York: Academic Press, Inc.

Cleland, Charles E.

1966   *The prehistoric animal ecology and ethnozoology of the upper Great Lakes region.* University of Michigan Museum of Anthropology Papers, no. 29. Ann Arbor, Mich.

Clutton-Brock, Juliet

1970   The origins of the dog. In *Science in archaeology,* ed. Don Brothwell and Eric Higgs, 303–9. New York: Praeger Publishers.

Coe, Michael D.

1971   The shadow of the Olmecs. *Horizon* 13 (no. 4): 67–74.

Coe, Michael D., and Kent V. Flannery

1967   *Early cultures and human ecology in s. coastal Guatemala.* Smithsonian Contribution to Anthropology, vol. 3. Washington, D.C.: Smithsonian Press.

Coe, William R.

1959   *Piedras Negras archaeology: Artifacts, caches and burials.* Museum Monographs. Philadelphia: The University Museum, University of Pennsylvania.

Collier, Albert

1964   The American Mediterranean. In *Handbook of Middle American Indians,* ed. Robert Wauchope, 1: 122–42. Austin: University of Texas Press.

Connor, Judith G.

1975   Ceramics and artifacts. In *Changing pre-Columbian commercial systems,* ed. Jeremy A. Sabloff and William L. Rathje, 114–35. Peabody Museum Monograph no. 3. Cambridge: Harvard University.

Crandall, L. S.

1964   The management of wild animals in captivity. Chicago: University of Chicago Press.

Cutting, C. L.

1962   The influence of drying, salting, and smoking on the nutritive value of fish. In *Fish in nutrition,* ed. Eirik Heen and Rudolf Kreuzer, 161–79. Food and Agriculture Organization of the U.N., Technology Branch, Fisheries Division. London: Fishing News, Ltd.

Daly, Patricia

1969   Approaches to faunal analysis in archaeology. *American Antiquity* 34 (no. 2): 146–53.

Davidson, William V.

1975   The geographical setting. In *Changing pre-Columbian commercial systems,* ed. Jeremy A. Sabloff and William L. Rathje, 47–59. Peabody Museum Monograph no. 3. Cambridge: Harvard University.

Delacour, Jean T., and Dean Amadon

1973   *Curassows and related birds.* New York: American Museum of Natural History.

Dobkin de Rios, Marlene
1974   The influence of psychotropic flora and fauna on Maya relgion. *Current Anthropology* 15 (no. 2): 147–52.

Driesch, Angela Von Den
1976   *A guide to the measurement of animal bones from archaeological sites.* Peabody Museum of Archaeology and Ethnology Bulletin no. 1. Cambridge: Harvard University.

Driver, H.
1961   *Indians of North America.* Chicago: University of Chicago Press.

Duellman, William H.
1970   *The hylid frogs of Middle America.* Museum of Natural History Monograph, no. 1, vols. 1–2. Lawrence: University of Kansas.

Edwards, C. R.
1957   Quintana Roo: Mexico's empty quarter. Technical Report. Berkeley: Department of Geography, University of California.

Edwards, Ernest P.
1972   *A field guide to the birds of Mexico.* Ernest P. Edwards: Sweet Briar, Va.

Efremov, J. A.
1940   Taphonomy: A new branch of paleontology. *Pan-American Geology* 74: 81–93.

Fabing, H. D., and J. R. Hawkins
1956   Intravenous injection of bufotenine in the human being. *Science* 123: 886–87.

Fagan, Brian
1966   Two soli smelting furnaces from Lusaka, Northern Rhodesia. *South African Archaeological Bulletin,* no. 17, pp. 27–28.

Flannery, Kent V.
1968   The vertebrate fauna and hunting patterns. In *The Prehistory of the Tehuacan Valley,* ed. Douglas Byers, 1: 132–78. Austin: University of Texas Press.

Follett, W. I.
1963   *Fish remains from Deer Creek Cave, Elko County, Nevada.* Nevada State Museum of Anthropology Paper 11.

Forshaw, Joseh M.
1973   *Parrots of the world.* Melbourne, Australia: Landsdowne Press.

Freidel, David A.
1976   Late Postclassic settlement patterns on Cozumel Island, Quintana Roo, Mexico. Ph.D. diss., Harvard University.

Freidel, David A., and Richard M. Leventhal
1975   The settlement survey. In *Changing pre-Columbian commercial systems,* ed. Jeremy A. Sabloff and William L. Rathje, 60–76. Peabody Museum Monograph no. 3, Cambridge: Harvard University.

Furst, Peter T.
1974   Comment on "The influence of psychotropic flora and fauna on Maya religion," by Marlene Dobkin de Rios. *Current Anthropology* 15 (no. 2): 154.

Gaige, Helen T.
1936   Some reptiles and amphibians from Yucatan and Campeche, Mexico. In Arthur S. Pearse et al., eds., *The Cenotes of Yucatan*, 289–304. Carnegie Institution of Washington Publication no. 457. Washington, D.C.: Carnegie Institution.

Gans, Carl
1975   *Reptiles of the world*. New York: Ridge Press, Inc.

Gifford, Diane P., and Diana C. Crader
1977   A computer coding system for archaeological faunal remains. *American Antiquity* 42 (no. 2): 225–38.

Grayson, Donald K.
1973   On the methodology of faunal analysis. *American Antiquity* 38: 432–39.
1974   The Riverhaven No. 2 vertebrate fauna: Some comments on methods in faunal analysis and on aspects of the subsistence potential of prehistoric New York. *Man in the Northeast* 2: 23–39.
1978   Minimum numbers and sample size in vertebrate faunal analysis. *American Antiquity* 43 (no. 1): 53–65.
1979   Archaeological vertebrates and paleoenvironmental reconstruction. Paper presented at annual meeting of the Society for American Archaeology, Vancouver.

Greene, Merle
1967   *Ancient Maya relief sculpture*. Greenwich, Conn.: New York Graphic Society.

Gregory, David A.
1975   San Gervasio. In *Changing pre-Columbian commercial systems,* ed. Jeremy A. Sabloff and William L. Rathje, 88–106. Peabody Museum Monograph no. 3, Cambridge: Harvard University.

Guha, B. C.
        The role of fish in human nutrition. In *Fish in nutrition,* ed., Eirik Heen and Rudolf Kreuzer, 39–42. Food and Agriculture Organization of the U.N., Technology Branch, Fisheries Division. London: Fishing News, Ltd.

Guilday, John
1970   *Animal remains from archaeological excavations at Ft. Ligonier*. Annals of the Carnegie Museum 42: 177–86.

Haag, William G.
1948   *An osteometric analysis of some aboriginal dogs*. University of Kentucky Reports in Anthropology, vol. 7, no. 3. Lexington: University of Kentucky Publication.

Hale, H. Stephen
1977   Quarterly report on the development of a key for the identification of shark species on the basis of variation in vertebral morphology. Florida State Museum, Gainesville.

Hall, E. Raymond, and Keith R. Kelson
1959   *The mammals of North America*, vols. 1–2. New York: The Ronald Press Co.

Hamblin, Nancy L.
1975   Use of animals by the inhabitants of Cozumel, Mexico. Department of Anthropology, University of Arizona, Arizona State Museum Library, Tucson.

Hamblin, Nancy L., Victoria Dirst, and John B. Sparling
1978   An analysis of the Antelope House faunal collection, Canyon de Chelly National Monument, Arizona. *The Kiva* 43 (nos. 3–4): 201–30.

Hamblin, Nancy L., and Amadeo M. Rea
1979   La avifauna arqueologica de Cozumel. *Boletín de la Escuela de Ciencias Antropológicas de la Universidad de Yucatán* no. 37, pp. 21–49.

Hoese, H. Dickson, and Richard H. Moore
1977   *Fishes of the Gulf of Mexico, Texas, Louisiana, and adjacent waters.* College Station: Texas A&M University Press.

Johannes, Robert E.
1976   Life and death of the reef. *Review,* December 1976.

Jones, J. Knox, and Timothy E. Lawlor
1965   *Mammals from Isla Cozumel, Mexico with description of a new species of harvest mouse.* University of Kansas Publications, Museum of Natural History 16 (no. 3): 400–19.

Jones, Rhys
1978   Why did the Tasmanians stop eating fish? In *Explorations in ethnoarchaeology,* ed. Richard A. Gould, 11–47. Albuquerque: University of New Mexico Press.

Kidder, Alfred V., Jesse D. Jennings, and Edwin H. Shook
1946   *Excavations at Kaminaljuyu, Guatemala.* Carnegie Institution of Washington Publication no. 561. Washington, D.C.

Kirkpatrick, Ralph D., and Lyle K. Sowls
1962   Age determination of the collared peccary by the tooth-replacement pattern. *Journal of Wildlife Management* 26 (no. 2): 214–17.

Kuhnau, Joachim
1962   Importance of minor elements in food, especially in fish. In *Fish in nutrition,* ed. Eirik Heen and Rudolf Kreuzer, 298–300. Food and Agriculture Organization of the U.N., Technology Branch, Fisheries Division. London: Fishing News, Ltd.

LaBarre, Weston
1970   *The Ghost Dance: Origins of religion.* Garden City, N.Y.: Doubleday and Co.

Lange, Frederick W.
1971   Marine resources: A viable subsistence alternative for the prehistoric lowland Maya. *American Anthropologist* 73 (no. 3): 619–39.

Leopold, A. Starker
1959   *Wildlife of Mexico: The game birds and mammals.* Berkeley and Los Angeles: University of California Press.

Lowe-McConnell, R. H.
1977   *Ecology of fishes in tropical waters.* The Institute of Biology's Studies in Biology no. 76. London: Edward Arnold, Ltd.

MacArthur, R. H., and J. W. MacArthur
1961   On bird species diversity. *Ecology* 42: 595–98.

Martin, Paul S.
1958   *A biogeography of reptiles and amphibians in the Gomez Farias region, Tamaulipas, Mexico.* Miscellaneous Publications, Museum of Zoology, no. 101. Ann Arbor: University of Michigan.

Mayer, Jean
1962   Fish proteins in nutrition and their importance in the prevention of protein malnutrition. In *Fish in nutrition,* ed., Eirik Heen and Rudolf Kreuzer, 248–56. Food and Agriculture Organization of the U.N., Technology Branch, Fisheries Division. London: Fishing News, Ltd.

McBryde, Felix W.
1947   *Cultural and historical geography of southwestern Guatemala.* Institute of Social Anthropology Publication no. 4, Smithsonian Institution. Westport, Conn.: Greenwood Press.

McCormick, Harold W., and Tom Allen, with Captain William E. Young
1963   *Shadows in the sea, the sharks, skates, and rays.* Radnor, Pa.: Chilton Co.

Merwin, Raymond E., and George C. Vaillant
1932   *The ruins of Holmul, Guatemala.* Memoirs of the Peabody Museum of American Archaeology and Ethnology, vol. 3, no. 2. Cambridge: Harvard University.

Michelsen, Ralph C.
1967   Pecked metates of Baja California. *The Masterkey* 42 (no. 2): 73–77.

Miller, Arthur G.
1977   The Maya and the sea: Trade and cult at Tancah and Tulum, Quintana Roo, Mexico. In *The Sea in the pre-Columbian World,* ed. Elizabeth P. Benson, 97–138. Washington: Dumbarton Oaks Research Library and Collections.

Minton, Sherman A., Jr., and Madge R. Minton
1973   *Giant reptiles.* New York: Charles Scribner's Sons.

Moholy-Nagy, Hattula
1963   Shells and other marine material from Tikal. *Studios de Cultura Maya* 3: 65–85.

Olsen, Stanley J.
1971   *Zooarchaeology: Animal bones in archaeology and their interpretation.* Reading, Mass.: Addison-Wesley Publishing Co.
1972   Animal remains from Altar de Sacrificios. In *The artifacts of Altar de Sacrificios,* ed. Gordon R. Willey, 243–46. Papers of the Peabody Museum of Archaeology and Ethnology, vol. 64, no. 1 Cambridge: Harvard University.
1978   Vertebrate faunal remains. In *Excavations at Seibal,* ed. Gordon R. Willey, no. 1, pp. 172–76. Memoirs of the Peabody Museum of Archaeology and Ethnology, vol. 14, nos. 1–3. Cambridge: Harvard University.

Payne, S.
1972   On the interpretation of bone samples from archaeological sites. In *Papers in economic prehistory,* ed. Eric S. Higgs, 65–82. Cambridge: Cambridge University Press.

Paynter, Raymond A., Jr.
1955   The Ornithogeography of the Yucatán Peninsula. Peabody Museum of Natural History Bulletin 9. New Haven: Yale University.

Perkins, Dexter, Jr.
1964   The prehistoric fauna from Shanidar, Iraq. *Science*, no. 3626, pp. 1565–66.

Perkins, Dexter, Jr., and Patricia Daly
1968   The potential of faunal analysis: An investigation of the faunal remains from Suberde, Turkey. *Scientific American* 219 (no. 5): 96–106.

Peterson, Roger T., and Edward L. Chalif
1973   *A field guide to Mexican birds*. Boston: Houghton-Mifflin Co.

Phillips, David A.
1979   Material culture and trade of the Postclassic Maya. Ph.D. diss., University of Arizona, Tucson.

Pohl, Mary E. D.
1976   Ethnozoology of the Maya: An analysis of fauna from five sites in the Peten, Guatemala. Ph.D. diss., Harvard University, Cambridge.

Pollock, H. E. D., and Clayton E. Ray
1957   *Notes on vertebrate animal remains from Mayapan*. Carnegie Institution Report no. 41. Department of Archaeology, Carnegie Institution, Washington, D.C.

Pope, Clifford H.
1964   *The Reptile world*. New York: Alfred A. Knopf, Inc.

Pritchard, Peter C. H.
1967   *Living turtles of the world*. Neptune City, N.J.: TFH Publications, Inc.

Randall, John E.
1968   *Caribbean reef fishes*. Jersey City, N.J.: TFH Publications, Inc., Ltd.

Rathje, William L., and David A. Phillips
1975   The ruins of Buena Vista. In *Changing pre-Columbian commercial systems*, ed. Jeremy A. Sabloff and William L. Rathje, 77–87. Peabody Museum Monograph no. 3. Cambridge: Harvard University.

Rathje, William L., and Jeremy A. Sabloff
1975   Theoretical background: General models and questions. In *Changing pre-Columbian commercial systems*, ed. Jeremy A. Sabloff and William L. Rathje, 6–20. Peabody Museum Monograph no. 3. Cambridge: Harvard University.

Rathje, William L., Jeremy A. Sabloff, and David A. Phillips
1974   The 1973 Cozumel Archaeological Project: Buena Vista. Paper presented at the 1974 International Congress of Americanists in Mexico City.

Rech, Richard H., and Kenneth E. Moore
1971   *An Introduction to psychopharmacology*. New York: Raven Press.

Reed, Charles A.
1970   Osteoarchaeology. In *Science in archaeology*, ed. Don Brothwell and Eric Higgs, 204–16. New York: Praeger Publishers.

Reed, Charles A., and Robert Braidwood
1960   The environmental sequence in northeastern Iraq. In *Explorations in Iraqi Kurdistan,* ed. Robert J. Braidwood and B. Howe. Chicago: Oriental Institute of the University of Chicago.

Roys, R. L.
1931   *The Ethnobotany of the Maya.* Middle American Research Institute Publication no. 2. New Orleans: Tulane University.
1933   *The Book of Chilam Balam of Chumayel.* Carnegie Institution Publication no. 438, Washington, D.C.
1943   *The Indian background of colonial Yucatan.* Carnegie Institution Publication no. 548, Washington, D.C.

Ryder, M. L.
1970   Remains of fishes and other aquatic animals. In *Science in archaeology,* ed. Don Brothwell and Eric Higgs, 376–94. New York: Praeger Publishers

Sabloff, Jeremy A.
1977   Old myths, new myths: The role of sea traders in the development of ancient Maya civilization. In *The Sea in the pre-Columbian world,* ed. Elizabeth P. Benson, 67–88. Washington, D.C.: Dumbarton Oaks Research Library and Collections.

Sabloff, Jeremy A., and William L. Rathje
1973   A study of pre-Columbian commercial patterns on the island of Cozumel, Mexico. In *Atti del XL Congresso Internazionale degli Americanisti,* 1: 455–63. Roma and Genoa.
1975a   Introduction: History of the project. In *Changing pre-Columbian commercial systems,* ed. Jeremy A. Sabloff and William L. Rathje, 1–5. Peabody Museum Monograph no. 3. Cambridge: Harvard University.
1975b   Cozumel's place in Yucatecan culture history. In *Changing pre-Columbian commercial systems,* ed. Jeremy A. Sabloff and William L. Rathje, 21–28. Peabody Museum Monograph no. 3. Cambridge: Harvard University.

Sabloff, Jeremy A., and William L. Rathje, eds.
1975   *Changing pre-Columbian commercial systems.* Peabody Museum Monograph no. 3. Cambridge: Harvard University.

Sabloff, Jeremy A., William L. Rathje, D. A. Friedel, J. G. Connor and P. L. W. Sabloff
1974   Trade and power in postclassic Yucatán: Initial observations. In *Mesoamerican archaeology: New approaches,* ed. Norman Hammond. Austin: University of Texas Press.

Schellhas, Paul
1904   *Representations of deities of the Maya Manuscripts.* Papers of the Peabody Museum of American Archaeology and Ethnology, vol. 4, no. 1. Cambridge: Harvard University.

Schmitt, Waldo L.
1965   *Crustaceans.* Ann Arbor: University of Michigan Press.

Scholes, F. V., and R. L. Roys
1948   *The Maya Chontal Indians of Atalan-Tixchel.* Carnegie Institution Publication no. 560, Washington, D.C.

Schorger, A. W.
1966   *The Wild Turkey.* Norman: University of Oklahoma Press.

Schultes, Richard Evans, and Albert Hofmann
1973   *The Botany and chemistry of hallucinogens.* Springfield, Ill.: Charles C. Thomas, Publisher.

Seler, E.
1890   The Dog in ancient Mexico. Congress des Américanistes, Berlin, 1888, session 7, pp. 321–24.

Sever, Lowell E.
1975   Zinc and human development: A review. *Human ecology* 3 (no. 1): 43–57.

Sheldon, Andrew L.
1969   Equitability indices: Dependence on the species count. *Ecology* 50: 466–67.

Shook, E. M., and A. V. Kidder
1952   *Mound E-III-3, Kaminaljuyu, Guatemala.* Carnegie Institution Publication 596, Washington, D.C.

Shotwell, J. Arnold
1955   An approach to the paleoecology of mammals. *Ecology* 36: 327–37.

Silver, I. A.
1970   The Ageing of domestic animals. In *Science in archaeology,* ed. Don Brothwell and Eric Higgs, 283–302. New York: Praeger Publishers.

Smith, Hobart M.
1946   *Handbook of lizards.* Ithaca, N.Y.: Cornell University Press, Comstock Publishing Company.

Sowls, Lyle K.
1961   Hunter-checking stations for collecting data on the collared peccary *(Pecari tajacu). Transactions of the North American Wildlife and Natural Resources Conference* no. 26: 496–505. Washington, D.C.: Wildlife Management Institute.

Stansby, Maurice E.
1962   Proximate composition of fish. In *Fish in nutrition,* ed. Eirik Heen and Rudolf Kreuzer, 55–60. Food and Agriculture Organization of the U.N., Technology Branch, Fisheries Division. London: Fishing News, Ltd.

Stebbins, Robert C.
1962   *Amphibians of western North America.* Berkeley and Los Angeles: University of California Press.
1966   *A field guide to western reptiles and amphibians.* Boston: Houghton-Mifflin Co.

Stephens, John Lloyd
1841   *Incidents of travel in Central America, Chiapas, and Yucatan,* vol. 2. New York: Harper and Brothers.

Street, Philip
1966   *The crab and its relatives.* London: Faber and Faber, Ltd.

Stuart, L. C.
1963   *A checklist of the herpetofauna of Guatemala.* Miscellaneous Publications, Museum of Zoology, no. 122. Ann Arbor: University of Michigan.
1964   Fauna of Middle America. In *Handbook of Middle American Indians,* ed. Robert Wauchope, 1: 316–62. Austin: University of Texas Press.

Szara, Stephen
1970   DMT (N,N-Dimethyltryptamine) and homologues: Clinical and pharmacological considerations. In *Psychotomimetic drugs,* ed. Daniel H. Efron, 275–84. New York: Raven Press.

Thomas, David H.
1969   Great basin hunting patterns: A quantitative method for treating faunal remains. *American Antiquity* 34 (no. 4): 392–401.
1971   On distinguishing natural from cultural bone in archaeological sites. *American Antiquity* 36 (no. 3): 366–71.

Thompson, Edward H.
1932   *People of the serpent: Life and adventure among the Mayas.* Boston and New York: Houghton-Mifflin Co.

Thompson, J. Eric S.
1932   *The Civilization of the Mayas.* Chicago: Field Museum of Natural History.
1944   *The Fish as a Maya symbol for counting and further discussion of directional glyphs.* Cambridge, Mass.: Carnegie Institution of Washington, Division of Historical Research.
1954   *The Rise and fall of Maya civilization.* Norman: University of Oklahoma Press.
1958   *Thomas Gage's travels in the New World.* Norman: University of Oklahoma Press.
1966   *The Rise and fall of Maya civilization.* Rev. ed. Norman: University of Oklahoma Press.
1970   *Maya history and religion.* Norman: University of Oklahoma Press.
1974   Comment on "The influence of psychotropic flora and fauna on Maya religion," by Marlene Dobkin de Rios. *Current Anthropology* 15 (no. 2): 160.

Tinker, Spencer W., and Charles J. DeLuca
1973   *Sharks and rays.* Tokyo: Charles E. Tuttle Co., Inc.

Tozzer, Alfred M.
1941   *Landa's Relación de las cosas de Yucatán.* Papers of the Peabody Museum of American Archaeology and Ethnology vol. 18. Cambridge: Harvard University.

Tozzer, Alfred M., and Glover M. Allen
1910   *Animal figures in the Maya Codices.* Papers of the Peabody Museum of American Archaeology and Ethnology vol. 4, no. 3. Cambridge: Harvard University.

Trewartha, Glenn T.
1954   *An Introduction to climates.* New York: McGraw-Hill, Inc.

Vokes, Arthur W.
1978   They don't make them like they used to. Paper presented at the 43rd annual meeting of the Society for American Archaeology, Tucson.

Walker, Ernest P.
1975   *Mammals of the world*, vols. 1–2. Baltimore: Johns Hopkins University Press.

Wallace, Henry
1978   The Strange case of the Panucho plugs: Evidence of pre-Columbian apiculture on Cozumel. Department of Anthropology, University of Arizona.

Wasson, V. P., and R. Gordon Wasson
1957   *Mushrooms, Russia, and history*, vols. 1–2. New York: Pantheon Books.

Weaver, Muriel Porter
1972   *The Aztecs, Maya, and their predecessors.* New York: Seminar Press.

West, Robert C.
1964a   Surface configuration and associated geology of Middle America. *In Handbook of Middle American Indians*, ed. Robert Wauchope, 1: 33–83. Austin: University of Texas Press.
1964b   The Natural regions of Middle America. In *Handbook of Middle American Indians*, ed. Robert Wauchope, 1: 363–83. Austin: University of Texas Press.

White, Theodore E.
1953   A Method of calculating the dietary percentage of various food animals utilized by aboriginal peoples. *American Antiquity* 18 (no. 4): 396–98.
1956   The Study of osteological materials in the plains. *American Antiquity* 21 (no. 4): 401–4.

Wing, Elizabeth S.
1974   Vertebrate faunal remains. In *Excavation of an early shell midden on Isla Cancun, Quintana Roo, Mexico*, by E. Wyllys Andrews IV et al., 186–88. Middle American Research Institute Publication no. 21. New Orleans: Tulane University.
1975   Animal remains from Lubaantun. In *Lubaantun, a classic Maya realm*, ed. Norman Hammond, 379–83. Peabody Museum Monograph no. 2. Cambridge: Harvard University.
1976a   Uses of dogs for food as an adaptation to the coastal environment. Paper presented at annual meeting of the Society for American Archaeology, St. Louis.
1976b   Ways of going from a sliver of bone to a calorie. Paper presented at annual meetings of the Society for American Archaeology, St. Louis.
1977   Subsistence systems in the Southeast. *The Florida Anthropologist* 30 (no. 2): 81–87.

Wing, Elizabeth S., and Norman Hammond
1974   Fish remains in archaeology: A comment on Casteel. *American Antiquity* 39 (no. 1): 133–34.

Wing, Elizabeth S., and D. Steadman
1980   Vertebrate faunal remains from Dzibilchaltun. In *Excavations at Dzibilchaltun, Yucatan, Mexico*, by E. W. Andrews IV and E. W. Andrews V, 326–31. Middle American Research Institute Publication no. 48. New Orleans: Tulane University.

Woodbury, Richard B., and Aubrey S. Trik
  1953   *The Ruins of Zacaleu, Guatemala,* vols. 1–2. Richmond, Va.: The William
          Byrd Press, Inc.

Wright, Albert H. and Anna Allen Wright
  1949   *Handbook of frogs and toads of the U.S. and Canada.* Ithaca, N.Y.: Com-
          stock Publishing Co.

Wright, N. Pelham
  1970   *A Guide to Mexican mammals and reptiles.* Mexico City: Minutiae Mexicana.

Index